LUCKY DOGS

LUCKY DOGS

Enjoy
Coca-Cola
Menu
LUCKY DOG: 5.75
PEGULAR HOT DOG: 4.75
SMOKED SAUSAGE: 6.25
SOFT DRINKS: 2.75
Coca-Cola
New Orleans Tradition
SINCE 1946
LUCKY DOGS

From Bourbon Street to Beijing and Beyond

JERRY E. STRAHAN

University Press of Mississippi / *Jackson*

The University Press of Mississippi is a member
of the Association of American University Presses.

Manufactured in the United States of America

First printing 2016

∞

Library of Congress Cataloging-in-Publication Data

Names: Strahan, Jerry E., 1951– author.
Title: Lucky Dogs : from Bourbon Street to Beijing and beyond / Jerry Strahan.
Description: Jackson : University Press of Mississippi, [2016]
Identifiers: LCCN 2016005801 (print) | LCCN 2016008369 (ebook) | ISBN
9781496808325 (hardback : alk. paper) | ISBN 9781496808332 (ebook)
Subjects: LCSH: Lucky Dogs, Inc. | Hot dog stands. | Hot dog
stands—Louisiana—New Orleans.
Classification: LCC TX945.5.L845 S73 2016 (print) | LCC TX945.5.L845 (ebook)
| DDC 641.6/60976335—dc23
LC record available at http://lccn.loc.gov/2016005801

British Library Cataloging-in-Publication Data available

For
Jack and Matthew

CONTENTS

ACKNOWLEDGMENTS

It is not easy to write about a topic in which one is so personally involved. I have tried to remain objective, but frankly I'm not certain that I have always succeeded. If I didn't, hopefully the end result is that the reader ends up with an even better insight into the company.

As in any book, there are numerous people who have helped turn the rough draft into a published work. I needed them all. My grammatical faults are many. I have never seen a comma that I didn't like or a semi-colon that I couldn't use. Bless those who have corrected my mistakes as I transferred verbal stories to the printed page.

First, I owe a tremendous debt of gratitude to Robert Coram. Coram read an early draft of the manuscript and gave me not only encouragement, but suggestions on ways to improve the work. He is one of the most talented writers I have ever read. His book *Boyd: The Fighter Pilot Who Changed the Art of Warfare* is one of only a handful of works where I have finished the last line, and immediately started rereading from page 1. It is that phenomenally well written and that enjoyable.

Along with Coram, reading an early version and offering valuable suggestions and corrections were Ingrid and Alana Garvey. I truly appreciate the time and effort that they dedicated to the project. Additionally, I asked my wife, Jane, if she would point out my mistakes. I should have been a tad more specific and said, "Please restrict all remarks to the manuscript." I do appreciate Jane's critical insight, at least as it relates to the book.

I next asked a friend and very talented professional copy editor, Paula Devlin, to go over the work. Paula had recently retired after spending over twenty-five years as a copy editor for the *New Orleans Times-Picayune*. I am not certain but strongly suspect that Microsoft Word created the ability to "track changes" in documents because the ink industry couldn't supply Paula with a sufficient amount of red pens. As she delved into the manuscript, I became concerned that by the time she finished, I might end up with a short story. Truthfully, she did a marvelous job and I thank her.

Also, I owe a special debt of gratitude to the University Press of Mississippi and especially to Craig Gill for believing in the manuscript. In addition, I would like to thank Will Rigby, the copy editor assigned to my book by the UPM. Will did a marvelous job.

Lastly, but most importantly, I am deeply indebted to all of the Lucky Dog vendors mentioned in the book: James Hudson, Rick Puggini, Tim Danner, Roy Gant, Charles Pruett, Harold Vincent, Jason Pierce, George Overton, Conrad Wyman, Choya Smith, Steve Capps, Darryl Lindsey, Thomas (Snake) Bickle, Tammy Whited, Thomas Porter, Joe Bellomy, and John Burris. I thank you all for allowing me to use your names and especially for the time we spent together reliving and laughing about the past. Becky, Susan, Karl, Nick, Todd, and Gene: for a variety of reasons I have chosen not to use your true identities. I know this will disappoint some of you, but I firmly believe that children and relatives should not have to be haunted by your past, especially when there is an alternative. In the case of Matt and Daniel, I was uncertain as to how the China experiment might affect your present positions, so I chose to be cautious.

Once again, I thank you all.

LUCKY DOGS

INTRODUCTION

Smitty walked into my office sporting a tight-fitting black leather miniskirt, a frilly white blouse, and spiked heels. Without so much as a "hello," he got right to the point. "The other vendors said you're not gonna let me work in this 'cause I'm a guy. That's not fair. Admit it, I look good."

"Honestly, you don't. Now, the yellow sundress you wore last spring; that was becoming, but this is definitely not your style. Frankly, you don't have the legs."

"Don't have the legs? *Don't have the legs?* Oh, you're wrong. I . . . I got great legs!"

Smitty was stunned. He couldn't believe what he had just heard. His face reddened; his forehead tensed. "You gonna lemme wear it or not?"

"That depends. You know we follow the Catholic school dress code: if you kneel down and the dress touches the floor, you can wear it. If it doesn't, you have to change."

He knelt down and the skirt was about an inch too short. "Damn," he muttered. Then, without saying another word, he rose and walked out. An hour later he returned, wearing a pair of traditional men's blue jeans, his heels replaced by a pair of worn brown cowboy boots.

Lucky Dogs is not your typical American corporation, and our employees are certainly not cut from the classic corporate cloth. For almost forty years, I have been general manager of this transient labor–filled, highly dysfunctional, family-owned, almost three-quarters-of-a-century old, U.S. Supreme Court–protected (*City of New Orleans v. Nancy Dukes*), Bourbon Street mobile hot dog vending business.

Some of our customers are third-generation patrons. We have served their fathers and their fathers' fathers. We were there when they came to the Quarter with their parents. We were there when they came back as hell-raising college students, and we are still there as they come back with their children and grandchildren.

Many of the other old-time local favorites exist no more. K&B Drug Stores are gone. Maison Blanche and D.H. Holmes retail stores are gone. McKenzie Bakery closed its doors for good. Dixie Beer is but a memory. The electric buses on Canal Street have long since vanished. Sugar Bowl Stadium—the site of early Super Bowls and the New Orleans Saints' first home—was reduced to rubble and trucked off to some landfill, and Pontchartrain Beach Amusement Park was demolished and replaced by the University of New Orleans Research and Technology Park. Much of what many New Orleanians grew up with has disappeared, but Lucky Dogs' hot dog–shaped wagons still roll out of the company's commissary each afternoon just as they have since the late 1940s.

Admittedly, I never aspired to run a company that sells weenies out of ten-foot-long hot dog–shaped carts. My academic training was as a historian. I studied under Stephen Ambrose (of *Band of Brothers, D-Day*, and *Undaunted Courage* fame) at the University of New Orleans and T. Harry Williams (Ambrose's mentor and author of the Pulitzer Prize–winning *Huey Long*) at Louisiana State University. I was fortunate to have been taken under the wings of two of the nation's preeminent historians, and my hope was to follow in their footsteps.

I was sixteen in 1967 when Doug Talbot, the future owner of Lucky Dogs, hired me to work in his Orange Julius fast food kiosk in a suburban New Orleans mall. At seventeen, I was transferred to the new Orange Julius location he was opening on Bourbon Street. There, on weekends, New Year's Eves, and Mardi Gras I worked until 2 or 3 in the morning selling steamed hot dogs, grilled hamburgers, buttered corn-on-the-cob, and keg after keg of ice-cold draft beer. My customers were jazz musicians, strippers, panhandlers, ladies of the evening, artists, con artists, bartenders, street thugs, returning Vietnam veterans, hippies, college kids, tourists, and the occasional religious group that made a pilgrimage to the Quarter to save the souls of the downtrodden. It was a seventeen-year-old's dream job. Oddly enough, my parents never seemed to share that opinion.

I managed to graduate from high school. I was an average student. I accepted that fact. Let's face it, selling beer to strippers like Linda Brigette (the Cupid Doll), Rita Alexander (the Champagne Girl), or Allouette (billed as the world's greatest tassel dancer) was a lot more invigorating than studying chemistry and math.

In the fall, I chose to attend the University of New Orleans. The tuition was cheap and I could cut additional costs by living at home. It was during my undergraduate years that I took my first course under Ambrose. He was a phenomenal lecturer. I, like hundreds of other students, sat mesmerized in his classes. He never looked at notes. Yet, at the beginning of the next class he picked up exactly where he had previously ended. Students didn't cut his classes; they cut other professors' classes so they could sit in on his.

Later, Ambrose suggested that I attend LSU and do graduate work in history under Williams. It was great advice. T. Harry, as he was affectionately called on campus, was every bit as extraordinary in the classroom as Ambrose. There were times at the end of his lectures when the three-hundred-plus students in the large auditorium would give him a standing ovation. I understood why Ambrose wanted me to study under his mentor.

I returned to UNO so Ambrose could direct my master's thesis. World War II was his area of expertise and my thesis was on Andrew Jackson Higgins, designer and manufacturer of many of the landing craft and PT boats used in the Allied invasions.

After completing my master's program, Tulane University awarded me a fellowship and I began working on a doctorate in history, but I didn't remain long. I lost interest, burned out, and withdrew from school. In a matter of days, I moved from doctorate to dogs, from the hallowed halls of academia back to the bawdy streets of the French Quarter, where the bars never close and the gorgeous women might not be women at all. I was back with Lucky Dogs, Inc., where I had worked as a part-time manager during my undergraduate days.

In *Managing Ignatius,* I detailed Doug Talbot's purchasing of Lucky Dogs and my first twenty-five years managing the company. It was the wildest of times; the 1970s were the days of hippies, free love, tie-died jeans, bell bottoms, the Vietnam War, and a Lucky Dog crew comprised of misfits. Vendors constantly came and left. Some worked one night, others lasted weeks, a few stayed for years. In the end, the street wore them all down. Drunken customers, long hours, working in the cold, heat, and rain made life hard. Frustrations mounted and vendors often disappeared without a word.

But I knew they would return. The swallows return to Capistrano and vendors always return to Lucky Dogs. Time would erase the negatives. The excitement of the street, the freedom the job offered, and the bonds they had with others who worked on Bourbon Street eventually drew them back. Life anywhere else seemed dull. As Jim Campbell, a longtime vendor, put it: "Working in the Quarter was like going to Woodstock every day." The street became their life, fellow vendors their family. Sooner or later they all came home.

This dysfunctional family achieved worldwide fame in a prize-winning novel set in New Orleans, and there was at least one instance when that fame had surprising results. A high-ranking U.S. State Department official during the Reagan administration came to New Orleans to lecture on foreign policy, and at the end of the evening, he left the conference and strolled through the Quarter. To his amazement, on almost every corner of Bourbon Street there was a hot-dog-shaped cart. Each unit was identical to the one that Ignatius had pushed through the streets of New Orleans in John Kennedy Toole's Pulitzer Prize–winning novel *A Confederacy of Dunces.*

Our carts are eye-catching, but to the State Department official they were far more than that. His entire office had read Toole's work, and lengthy discussions had ensued about the outrageous Ignatius. For this man, discovering the existence of such carts was tantamount to finding the Holy Grail. He was certain that his discovery would astound his co-workers. But instead of expressing astonishment, they scoffed in disbelief. They even went so far as to suggest that he had succumbed to the liquid sins of the French Quarter and imagined the carts. (This was, after all, before smart phones, which would have enabled the man to snap a picture as proof.)

Out of desperation, the official called my office and asked for a photograph of the carts so he could prove to his skeptical staff that the wagons were real. To me, the call smacked of a hoax, and I never followed up on his request. A week later, I received a second telephone call from the same gentleman, who claimed that he was being subjected to unmerciful teasing. He had promised the skeptics that evidence proving the existence of the hot dog–shaped carts would soon arrive, but he had received nothing.

I still wasn't convinced that this wasn't some kind of practical joke, so I asked for a telephone number where he could be reached in a few minutes. He complied. I was sure that when I called, I would hear an "out of order" recording. Instead, a pleasant voice answered, "Office of the Secretary."

"Excuse me, but secretary of what?"

"Secretary of State." After a short pause, the pleasant voice said, "Sir, are you certain you have dialed the correct exchange? This is a private line."

"Truthfully, I'm not sure," I answered. "I'm with Lucky Dogs, Incorporated, of New Orleans, and I am trying to reach Mr. X."

"My God!" she exclaimed. "He's been telling the truth."

I had bypassed all switchboards and was on a direct line into the Secretary of State's office. The country was in the midst of the Cold War. President Reagan was battling the "Evil Empire's" attempt at world domination. He was demanding that Soviet Union leader Mikhail Gorbachev "tear down this wall!" And meanwhile, his Secretary of State's staff was reading *A Confederacy of Dunces* and pondering the existence of Lucky Dogs.

It all worked out in the end. Mr. X got his photos of the cart and the Berlin Wall eventually came down.

The 1970s, '80s, and early '90s were filled with humorous events, although I can't say I found them amusing at the time. Like the night I came to our old shop at 211 Decatur, and discovered what appeared to be a hookers' convention taking place in our kitchen. The police were doing a sweep of the Quarter in an attempt to eliminate all "undesirables." The night manager figured the police couldn't be referring to these lovely ladies, because they certainly looked desirable to him. Thus, our shop had been turned into a temporary safe house.

Other nights were just plain amusing, like the evening a vendor and his fiancée got married while working a cart at the corner of Bourbon and Toulouse streets.

I had been out of graduate school for fifteen years. I was entrenched at Lucky Dogs. I had risen to the top of the company's short corporate stepladder. The idea of doing historical research was no longer a part of my life, or so I thought.

On New Year's Eve 1991, the shop (now at 517 Gravier Street) was packed with vendors eager to hit the street, each wanting his supplies immediately. A few were furious because their helpers had partied too much the night before and failed to show for work. Big Alice, a long-time vendor, was screaming about needing onions, and Smitty kept mumbling something about hot dog tongs. Another vendor accidentally dropped his full pan of chili and the mess spread across the floor. Five or six vendors were complaining that their carts had not yet been cleaned. The cleanup man was shouting that he was cleaning them as fast as he damn well could.

In the midst of this mayhem, the phone rang. It was my old mentor, Stephen Ambrose. He said something about wanting me to speak about Andrew Higgins at UNO. I agreed, assuming I was to give a short lecture to his undergraduate modern military history class. I was grossly mistaken.

A month later, I received a program from UNO's Eisenhower Center for Leadership Studies detailing its upcoming War in the Pacific Conference. Listed as speakers were Maj. Gen. David M. Jones, whose topic was "The Doolittle Tokyo Raid: A Personal Memoir"; George Gay, the lone survivor of Torpedo Squadron 8, speaking on "Witnessing the Battle of Midway"; historians from the U.S. Naval Academy and several other prestigious universities—and me.

I telephoned my old professor, thanked him for his confidence, offered to serve Lucky Dogs free of charge at the event, and politely declined his invitation to speak. He responded that the programs had already been printed and I was listed as delivering a thirty-minute lecture on Higgins and the evolution of amphibious landing craft.

In the end, all went well. A few minutes after my speech, I changed from a suit back into jeans and headed for the shop. It was again time to focus my attention on the present, not the past.

A few weeks after the War in the Pacific Conference, Ambrose invited me to lunch. During my college career, I had taken five of his courses, served as his graduate assistant, and worked closely with him as he directed my thesis. Now, as he sat across the table from me, he suddenly demanded: "Do you want to finish your doctorate, or write a book?" I immediately reverted to the student/teacher relationship and chose the second option, to write a book on Andrew Higgins. As I walked away, I wondered whatever happened to the choice, "C, none of the above."

From early 1991 until mid-January 1993, my days were at Lucky Dogs but my nights and weekends were devoted to research and writing. In May 1993, LSU Press accepted my manuscript. The book came off the press and hit the shelves in May 1994, just before the 50th anniversary of D-Day.

On Sunday, May 8, at 6:30 a.m., the phone rang, jolting me out of a sound sleep. In the few seconds that it took me to reach the receiver, I was thinking something must be wrong at the shop. But it wasn't the shop calling. It was Ambrose.

"Have you seen the morning's newspaper?"

"Not yet."

"I'll hold while you get it."

When I returned to the phone, he instructed me: "Look on page 13 of *Parade*."

I found the magazine and there, under "What's Up This Week" was the heading, "The best books about the most crucial hours of World War II." The first of the nine short book reviews was on Cornelius Ryan's classic *The Longest Day*. Next I saw Ambrose's recent bestseller, *D-Day, June 6, 1944: The Climactic Battle of World War II*. And the third one to catch my eye was *Andrew Jackson Higgins and the Boats that Won World War II*—my book. I was stunned. And then I felt an incredible wave of personal satisfaction. Ambrose told me that he had published thirteen books before he got his first one in *Parade*. He said, "Damn, you got in on your first try."

Of course, the higher one's ego soars, the further one has to fall. A few hours later, as I stood in the kitchen at Lucky Dogs, I noticed that one of the vendors had a copy of the morning paper. I showed him the review and expected a "Wow!" Instead, I got, "Yeah, nice. Now slap a piece of dry ice on the page and wrap it up so I can put it in my ice chest and push outta here."

The Higgins book led to appearances in documentaries for the History Channel, the Discovery Channel, ABC, NBC, and CBS. I made a
brief appearance on the *CBS Evening News with Dan Rather* on the 50th
anniversary of D-Day. The Marine Corps Historical Center and the
Naval Historical Center asked me to appear during its World War II in
the Pacific Conference in Washington, D.C., on a panel with Lt. Gen.
Victor "Brute" Krulak. Krulak is honored in the military's amphibious
Hall of Fame. I understood his selection. I was shocked by mine.

Krulak and I were the entire amphibious warfare panel. As I stood
at the podium in a room filled with generals and admirals, a thought
entered my mind: "If the military needs the Lucky Dog guy to lecture
on the evolution of amphibious warfare, just how defenseless are we?"

I later wrote a second book, *Managing Ignatius*, about the general
craziness of working at Lucky Dogs. *Parade* never reviewed this work,
but Uncle Frank of the Hot Dog Hall of Fame did. He awarded me the
"Frankie" for "Outstanding Contribution to Hot Dog History." The
statue is an upright, five-inch gold wiener supported by two human-
looking legs, sitting atop a granite base. It's nice to be honored by one's
peers, even if the statue is often mistaken for something that it is not.

The future at Lucky Dogs would hold experiences I could never have
imagined: in Beijing, in Katrina-devastated New Orleans, and on the
streets of the French Quarter. *Lucky Dogs* is part business history, part
autobiography, a story of survival, and an insider's look at the bizarre
lives of some of Bourbon Street's most peculiar characters—our vendors. It is both humorous and tragic, and though it may read like fiction, it is all fact.

The quirkiness of the Quarter and the eccentricity of our vendors
have kept life interesting for the past four decades. I've probably stayed
at the company because, like the vendors, I too simply do not fit into
mainstream America. Robert Frost wrote in his poem "The Road Not
Taken": "Two roads diverged in a wood, and I— / I took the one less
traveled by / And that has made all the difference."

Frost understood the attraction of a non-mainstream lifestyle. I bet
he would've made a heck of a vendor.

BEIJING BOUND

Lucky Dogs first rolled its wagons onto the narrow, balcony-lined streets of New Orleans' French Quarter in 1947. By 1949 the company's unique hot dog–shaped carts had attracted so much attention that its founders, Stephen and Erasmus Loyacano, decided to create a network of distributors and market their invention.

Interest came from as far away as Uruguay, Hong Kong, Guam, Britain, Venezuela, and Spain. However, the Loyacanos soon found that creating distributorships proved far more challenging than they had anticipated. Additionally, the cost of manufacturing the specialized carts was higher than projected. And suddenly, their French Quarter operation began requiring more attention because of labor problems. By mid-1952 the brothers gave up their expansionist dreams and refocused their efforts entirely on their New Orleans operation.

Thirty-six years later, the company's new owner, Doug Talbot, and I started receiving letters from distant lands. Unfamiliar names in faraway places wanted to purchase or lease the unique hot dog–shaped carts. To quote that great American philosopher Yogi Berra, it was "like déjà vu all over again." We were familiar with the Loyacanos' failed expansion attempts, but we were hoping for a more positive outcome.

Our first out-of-the-country opportunity presented itself north of the American border. In 1985 a major shopping center developer contacted us about acquiring the exclusive Lucky Dog rights for Canada. We were ecstatic. Within weeks, we shipped a cart to Toronto for a trial run.

The test sales proved promising. However, the mall's fast food retailers revolted when they discovered that they were now in direct competition with their landlord, and they were joined by other mall tenants. If their landlord got away with selling hot dogs today, what would prevent him from selling clothing, shoes, or home furnishings tomorrow? In response to the pressure, the developer dropped the idea, and the next morning, I was on a plane heading south.

Several years later, another opportunity for expansion came up, this time in Fort-de-France, Martinique. Once again, we were enthusiastic. A cart was shipped to the French island in the Caribbean and I flew down to train personnel and do a boots-on-the-ground assessment. Everything looked promising. By day four, our newly hired crew was soloing, and I was on board an Air France flight heading home.

The trial was to continue for thirty days, but suddenly we lost contact with our partner. His telephone in Martinique was out of service. His stores in Guadeloupe and the Dominican Republic had not heard from him, and his freight-forwarder in Miami was baffled by his disappearance. To this day, we have no idea what happened to him—or to our wagon.

Next came interest from Mexico, Honduras, and Russia. The devaluation of the peso halted any expansion into Mexico. In Honduras we quickly realized that operating a street vending business might be more of a challenge than we wished to undertake; every establishment I visited was guarded by an *hombre* carrying a shotgun or an Uzi. Where there was cash, there were guns.

The decision to pass on Moscow was even easier when it appeared that our potential partners might be members of the Russian mob. I had no proof, but I got the feeling that they wanted to operate street carts as a front for laundering money. And so died the intriguing idea of operating Lucky Dog carts in Red Square.

After all, there was no reason to take unnecessary risks. Our main base, the French Quarter street operation, was profitable, and in addition, we had six other Lucky Dog kiosks: two in the New Orleans International Airport, and four at local casinos. We had a successful record in the United States. And although testing foreign markets had so far proved unsuccessful, we were still open to expansion opportunities.

In 1996 the chance of a lifetime presented itself in the form of a young man named Matt Webster, who had grown up in New Orleans, where he was introduced to the Chinese language during high school. He continued his study of the Mandarin dialect in college. But Matt did not stop there. Between his junior and senior years, he spent the summer in Beijing, China's capital city, immersing himself in the culture and honing his language skills under the direction of a local tutor. After graduation, he packed his bags and, in a bold move, headed back to the land of the Great Wall.

Matt was under the impression that a job would be awaiting him at the U.S. Embassy. But the man who had extended the offer had been reassigned to Washington, and according to his replacement, no jobs were available.

Matt found work as a translator for an American who told Matt he was working in the Communist capital as an urban planning specialist. At best, the position was temporary, and to lawfully remain in the country, he had to be permanently employed. Thus, as strange as it sounds, the idea of bringing Lucky Dogs to the Far East entered his thoughts.

Matt approached us in October 1996 while home for a visit. At the time, Kentucky Fried Chicken, McDonald's, Pizza Hut, Dunkin' Donuts, Kenny Rogers Roasters, Hard Rock Café, A&W, and Dairy Queen were all successfully operating in China and beginning to dominate Beijing's American-style fast food market. Both A&W and Dairy Queen featured hot dogs on their menus, but no one was selling them from carts. Matt asked us: Why not introduce Lucky Dogs to the streets of Beijing?

He figured if A&W could generate a profit after investing millions in walk-in restaurants, surely Lucky Dogs could be profitable using less expensive carts and kiosks. That made sense to us.

But deciding to test the market was just the first step. The second step of actually becoming permitted in the People's Republic of China and shipping a cart to the distant land proved far more complicated than any of us imagined. In order to receive a license, a physical stamp of approval from twenty-eight different agencies was required on the business application. Negotiating the bureaucratic maze would take, at a minimum, several months. For some companies, the process took years. If a single bureau withheld its approval, the license would be denied.

Companies often never received an outright rejection. Instead, a much less obvious—but just as effective—technique was employed: Paperwork seemed to simply disappear in the bowels of China's gigantic bureaucracy. The company then had to resubmit its application and, in some cases, spend months or years repeatedly going through reams of red tape. Many would simply give up. Thus, the government accomplished its goal without ever having to officially explain why the permit was not issued.

To help avoid this situation, Matt recommended that we find a legitimate, trustworthy, and well-connected Chinese partner. It would be this local partner's responsibility to handle the monumental licensing process. He or she would also be in charge of the entire Chinese side of the operation: employees, importing the carts, and all other aspects that only a local resident could perform. Additionally, this partner would be responsible for securing all locations, especially the two that Matt deemed top priority: the Beijing airport and the Xidan Shopping Mall, both with enormous pedestrian traffic.

Once this partner was in place, Matt would move forward with the process of establishing Lucky Dogs as a legal entity in the People's Republic of China. He projected this would take several months and very little capital, and if at any time the endeavor appeared too risky, the plug could be pulled without a major financial loss. The new entity was to be registered as "Beijing Lucky Dogs Fast Food Co., Ltd." As for where the carts would operate, it was Matt's understanding that that we would have access to parks, subway stations, and major shopping malls.

However, until we were in operation, he had to rely on his other part-time jobs to pay his bills. The most unusual (and perhaps impressive) was his role in a televised Chinese soap opera, where he portrayed a debonair Australian entrepreneur in love with a beautiful Chinese woman. Unfortunately, after the first few episodes, he was written out of the script.

In early 1997, the expansion process began picking up speed. One of Matt's Beijing friends recommended that we consider a Madame Lin as our local partner. According to the friend, Lin represented "the new breed of Chinese entrepreneur." Additionally, one of her childhood friends was now a high-ranking Communist Party official who

Official "Beijing Lucky Dogs Fast Food Co. Ltd." stamp.

might prove helpful in securing locations and licenses, and handling a variety of potential problems. Suddenly, China didn't seem so foreign. In fact, its "good old boy network" reminded me of Louisiana.

Matt now had a local associate to help him cut through red tape and negotiate bureaucratic mine fields. Her first recommendation was to register the company in Liaoning Providence, Beijing. By doing so, the business would avoid all domestic taxes for six years. It was great advice.

The next move was to form a Sino-American joint-venture company. Our Letter of Intent stated that both sides would "invest together to establish 'Beijing Lucky Dogs Fast Food Co., Ltd.,'" and in accordance with Chinese regulations, $100,000 of "registered capital" would be deposited in the Bank of China. The Chinese partner would put up $15,000 and the U.S. partners would deposit $85,000.

Lucky Dogs owner Doug Talbot believed that it was now time for me to visit Beijing so I could meet our new partner, visit potential suppliers, and help evaluate the market.

My bags were packed, my visa acquired, and on March 16, the Boeing Triple Seven that I was aboard touched down on Communist soil. As I exited the aircraft, there was no doubt this wasn't Kansas. The airport was a large, no-frills, cinder-block building. Security officers were dressed in People's Liberation Army drab green fatigues. I was excited, apprehensive, tired, and hungry.

After having my passport stamped, retrieving my luggage, and clearing customs, I exited the secured area and stepped into the airport's main lobby. Suddenly, I was besieged by a sea of people who were waving, shouting, and grabbing at my bags.

"Mister! Mister! Taxi for you! Cheapa for you! Cheapa for you!" Everyone was trying to hustle the new money in town. Luckily, Matt was there, and within minutes we were in a cab heading toward the Great Wall Sheraton, which was next door to the Hard Rock Café. Maybe we *were* in Kansas.

When I awoke the next morning and looked out of my hotel window, the sight below was unbelievable. The past and present were intertwined right before my eyes. Tractor-trailer trucks traveled the same roadway with bicycles, automobiles, and wooden ox-drawn carts, all weaving in and out and around one another. The right-of-way went to the person with the most guts, be it an ox-cart driver, a bicyclist, or the driver of an eighteen-wheeler.

At 8:30 a.m., Matt and Lin arrived. She was extremely personable, but she did not speak English and I do not speak Chinese, so Matt served as translator. From body language and facial expressions, I could see that they worked well together. To have attempted such a venture without an excellent relationship would have been unthinkable.

A *New York Times* article of the period stated that foreign businesses in China often complained of "an unpredictable legal system" and frequent instances of "corruption and bribery." Lin was local. Her true value would be her ability to guide us through the lengthy permitting maze while protecting us from unscrupulous officials.

In China, it is common knowledge that one's success is often determined by one's connections, and our situation would be no exception. On one of my flights to Beijing, an American businessman who had been operating in China for several years told me that a company is only as strong as its minority partner. If that partner is not well-connected, he said, the company will never be successful. Thus, Lin's importance would be her contacts. Matt's importance, on the other hand, would be his ability to bridge the two cultures and to oversee the operation once it was up and running.

That morning, Lin drove us to a meat factory in her shiny new black BMW sedan—an obvious symbol of her success. We traveled about eighty-five miles in distance, but it seemed like centuries back in time. As we made our way down the narrow tree-lined roads, farmers were working the fields using wooden hand rakes and ox-drawn plows.

In some fields, men and women were pulling large carts with wooden wagon wheels. Stacked atop them as high as possible were branches that would later be used as firewood. Other workers were pulling carts loaded with freshly cut crops. As the field hands laboriously pulled their medieval-style wagons, we cruised down the highway in an air-conditioned vehicle, looking through the window at people working the land as if the Industrial Revolution had never occurred.

After two hours of driving, we left the thoroughfare, turned onto a gravel road, and a few hundred yards later, pulled into a parking lot next to a factory. Its outer walls were constructed of cinder blocks, its windows metal-framed and outward-tilting. They were the kind of windows used in U.S. warehouses back in the 1930s. From its appearance, the meat-packing plant looked to have been around for decades, but in reality, it was less than five years old.

We were escorted to the main office where pleasantries were exchanged and samples of both their pork and chicken hot dogs were served. The sampling and lengthy discussions were actually a delaying tactic to allow time to halt production and clean equipment before our tour began. I understood. They wanted to put their best foot forward. At the conclusion of our tour, the plant manager invited us to lunch in the company's cafeteria.

The dining room was large enough to seat at least three hundred people, and ceiling fans kept the air circulating. In short, it was a bland, no-frills cafeteria like an old U.S. military mess hall.

Most employees ate lunch at the plant. Later in the day, many took advantage of the on-premises showers; the company's facilities had hot water, and most of the workers' homes did not. Several employees actually chose to live on-site.

We were led through the main dining hall to a smaller twenty-by-twenty-foot room, fitted with a large round table that could accommodate about fifteen people. I was seated facing the door, which, according to Lin, was the position of honor. I had no idea. All I knew was that the table was round, and that I was going to follow her and Matt's lead.

Joining us were the plant manager, a few top-level company administrators, the production supervisor, the local Communist Party representative, a farmer from Northern China who supplied the meat packing facility with pork, a young plant officer, and an elderly Chinese gentleman with an extremely weathered face and long white beard, later introduced as the local historian. The gathering had been assembled in an attempt to impress us, their American guests.

Lunch seemed to be a never-ending meal. In the center of the table was a lazy Susan piled high with food, and according to custom, we were expected to sample each product. To do less would have been considered an insult. I never asked what we were eating; considering that I was expected to taste everything, I thought it was better that I not know.

Along with our meal, we were served warm beer, and the young plant officer took it upon himself to offer several toasts. After each, he would raise his glass and say "Gan Bei," which literally means "clear the glass" or "bottoms up." This happened four or five times and then he followed with even more toasts. However, now instead of beer, we were downing shots of a warm, strong, and smelly rice whiskey called Baijiu.

As a server filled my glass with whiskey, Matt leaned over and warned me not to look at it, smell it, or attempt to drink it slowly—it was strong. After returning to the States, I ran across a definition of Baijiu that described it as "pure distilled evil in liquid form," and "Chinese firewater that could be used to put a man on the moon of a planet in a faraway galaxy." This definition also suggested that the whiskey could be used as an "engine degreaser, curry stain remover, or glass etcher." I don't recall how many toasts of Baijiu we downed that day but I do know that Matt and I gulped as much liquid fire and ate as many pickled pigs' feet as did our hosts. It was a matter of national pride.

I believe the young officer kept making toasts in an effort to find our limit. He failed, and after a few stern looks from his boss, happy hour came to a close. At that point, the local historian began to speak. For thirty minutes the gentleman lectured us on his country's four-thousand-year history. From the look of his aged wrinkled face, I figured he probably had witnessed most of it firsthand. Matt translated, and I listened. When the old man finished, he looked at me and said, "Now tell us about your country's history."

I immediately understood his point. I responded, "Our nation is just a little more than 200 years old. We don't really have a history. What we have is more a record of current events." Our hosts nodded and smiled, happy with my answer.

Once the lunch and lecture were over, we were invited back to the main office for tea. Such lengthy protocol often discouraged Westerners. What took us three-and-a-half hours at the factory would have been accomplished in less than fifteen minutes in the States. Nevertheless, if you want to do business in the People's Republic of China, you have to accept that you have no control over when something happens, or over any of the details of an event. Lunch was a good example of that; every time a toast was made, we were obligated by Chinese custom to honor our host by participating. During that one meal, I consumed more alcohol than I had in the previous five years.

I later asked Matt how a contract could possibly be negotiated when both parties were three sheets to the wind. He informed me that Chinese custom actually allows one to bring a "designated drinker." In such scenarios, the surrogate consumes the toasts on the negotiator's behalf.

"My God," I thought. "If the guys at the shop ever find out about this, they'll all be stowing away on China-bound freighters." Drink for free and get paid for it! I didn't have the heart to tell them.

The good news was we had discovered an acceptable hot dog. It wasn't perfect, but it was acceptable. The plant's manager assured us that he could produce it in any size required. After a few cups of customary green tea, Matt, Lin, and I took our leave and headed back to Beijing.

Traffic was heavy, so the trip was slower than expected, allowing me plenty of time to sightsee out the window. We passed roadside barbers who set up shop under the shade of trees next to the street, offering haircuts with old hand-powered clippers in exchange for a few renminbi, "the people's currency" in Communist Party terminology. Strolling past them on the sidewalks were people with birdcages in hand. Apparently, it's common for the Chinese to take their feathered friends for a walk early in the morning and late in the evening. In the parks along the roadside, others were practicing the art of Tai Chi. On the road itself, we passed hordes of delivery bikes with flat rear platforms stacked three and four feet high with various items. This was, indeed, a distant and different land.

By the time we arrived back in Beijing, we had been on the go for ten hours, and although it was now only 6:30 p.m., my biological clock was insisting that it was much closer to 6:30 a.m. Lin chose to stop for the day, and neither Matt nor I objected.

The next morning, we hit the streets again, this time devoting the day to evaluating potential vending sites. We discovered that shopping malls were overly demanding, and the manner in which they operated was unfavorable to our product. Under their system, we would have to ring up the sale, then give the customer a receipt without accepting payment. The customer would then take that receipt to the main register, which was operated by the mall, where the mall's cashier would again ring up the sale, collect the money, and stamp the customer's original receipt. The customer would bring that stamped receipt back to our kiosk and pick up his or her purchase. It was a time-consuming and cumbersome procedure. The process completely eliminated impulse buys, which would be extremely detrimental to our operation, considering the fact that a hot dog is, without question, an impulse item.

Additionally, in most Chinese malls, food courts generally do not take prominence. In the malls we visited, the food courts were usually in the back corner of some upper floor, which, as one might suspect, also was not very conducive to impulse sales. Suddenly, malls were looking less attractive.

Pricing also posed a major problem, as China was split into two distinct markets: Western tourists and upper-middle-class Chinese consumers who could afford our product, and families with extremely limited incomes—the considerably larger market.

Unfortunately, we were having no luck acquiring locations most frequented by our desired customer base. On the contrary, the areas accessible to us seemed to be almost entirely inhabited by those who were not affluent enough to purchase our products. The exchange rate at the time was eight-to-one in the U.S. dollar's favor. We were hoping to sell a hot dog for at least eight yuan. We viewed the price of the dog as a dollar; the Chinese viewed the price as eight dollars. Thus, I could not see our product being competitive and profitable in a purely local market.

Lin's husband oversaw several grocery and retail stores. Around noon one day, Lin accidentally-on-purpose drove by one of his markets, and suggested we stop in for lunch and a tour.

The grocery had a little of everything: raw vegetables still in their wooden-slat shipping crates, unwrapped breads stuffed into baskets, canned goods, and rack after rack crammed with clothing, household goods, and hardware. There were tanks filled with fish, eels, and a slew of other strange aquatic creatures. The deli section was simply a wooden stall where food was cooked in large iron pots over open freestanding burners. The finished product was then sold across unpainted plywood counters to the public, who would take their purchases outside, sit at a wooden picnic table, and eat.

The store reminded me of what an old frontier trading post might have looked like. It was nowhere near modern Western standards. The merchandise was inexpensive and the cooking stalls would never pass U.S. health regulations, but the locals flocked there in droves. The registers all had long lines. Overall, it was doing a marvelous job of capturing the local clientele.

As we made our way down one of the aisles, the store's manager walked up and greeted Lin. He informed us that his store could furnish whatever condiments we might require. He also guaranteed that his bakery could produce whatever bun we needed and that no one in Beijing could match his price. This guarantee and treatment, of course, was because of our relationship with Lin. He introduced us to his master baker, who explained to Matt that he would personally bake all of our buns. I asked (through Matt) who would bake them when he was off; he said that he was never off. I asked who would bake them if he was out sick.

"I never miss work," he responded. "I will always bake your bread." The Party apparently had bun-baking under control.

After leaving the market, we devoted our time to visiting potential warehouse and office sites. One seemed workable, but the lessor wanted additional rent because the office came with a Western-style bathroom. The other choices shared a community toilet, which was simply an enclosed half-walled stall with an open hole in the concrete floor.

Lin took over the negotiations, and it was agreed that Matt would get the office with the bathroom at no extra charge. However, in return, we had to accept the stipulation that no Westerners would ever be allowed to sleep on the premises. Chinese employees could live there, but Matt would have to reside elsewhere. We certainly didn't consider that to be a deal-breaker.

We decided to pass on the deal, but at least we knew that we had an office if we couldn't find anything more appropriate. Once again, we had been on the go for more than twelve hours, and Matt was mentally exhausted from translating. We decided to call it a day.

The following morning, we had an early meeting with Gregory Wong, commercial attaché for the U.S. embassy in Beijing. We were hoping that Wong could shed some light on the confusing Chinese tax situation and perhaps even suggest potential cart sites.

Wong recommended that we be patient in our business negotiations. "The Chinese," he said, "are distrustful of those who are in a hurry."

"What types of businesses have the most problems?" I asked.

"Joint ventures," he responded.

The reason for this, I learned, is that Western partners generally want to reinvest the profits in the company so that it grows; Chinese partners, on the other hand, most often want to withdraw their portions.

Wong believed that American fast food was doing quite well. According to him, A&W in particular was posting good numbers in all of their Beijing locations. Matt and I already had A&W on our list of places to visit. We wanted to taste their product, discover who baked their buns, and find out what condiments they offered. We also wanted to see the language used to describe their hot dog—did they call it a hot dog, a sausage, a frank, or a pig-in-a-blanket?

Tiananmen Square at 5 p.m. on a work day.

After the meeting, Matt had other obligations, so I hailed a taxi and headed for Tiananmen Square and the Forbidden City. As the cab took off, the driver switched radio stations, and out of the speakers came a most unexpected Louis Armstrong singing "When the Saints Go Marching In." Had I been Russian, he probably had another channel where the Red Army Choir was singing "The Cossacks Song." The man might have been a Communist, but he was a master of the capitalistic art of hustling a tip.

For the next four hours, I scouted the Square and the Forbidden City. For more than five hundred years, the Forbidden City had served as the Imperial Palace of Chinese emperors. Had one lived there today, he could have eaten at any of the numerous mobile food kiosks located throughout the grounds, or perhaps at one of the five larger, permanent concession stands set up within the walls of the ancient city. Food prices were extremely low. One vendor was selling meat sticks— pieces of spiced mutton on a wooden skewer—for the equivalent of ten cents, but even his business was slow.

Just outside the Palace's massive high walls, a teenage boy was embracing capitalism by selling copies of *Quotations from Chairman*

Just me and the panda at the Beijing Zoo.

Mao Tse-tung. It was so paradoxical that I felt obligated to buy a few for souvenirs.

The next morning, we continued searching for potential locations. At lunchtime, we headed to A&W for a dog and a bit of corporate espionage. Our goal was not only to sample their product, but, more importantly, to discover who produced their buns.

The place was packed. As I stood in line waiting to order, a teenager cut in line directly in front of me. I had grown up watching *The Three Stooges* on television. I knew exactly what to do. I reached forward and tapped him on his right shoulder, and when he turned to see who wanted him, I maneuvered around his left side. Before he realized what had happened, I was back in front of him. His friends burst out laughing, and began explaining my maneuver to him with arm and hand gestures. Even the line breaker had to smile.

A&W's dog was tough, yet obviously to the local clientele's liking. But the bun was good. Unfortunately, the bread wrappers had no markings, and the assistant manager professed to have no idea who baked or delivered the buns. We purchased a few extra plain dogs, tossed the wieners in the trash, and gave the buns to Lin so that she could show them to her husband's baker.

The Great Wall at Badaling.

After leaving A&W, Matt again had other non–Lucky Dog business requiring his attention. So I jumped in a taxi and headed for the zoo. When I arrived, it was mostly deserted, except for a young boy, perhaps five years old, walking hand-in-hand with what appeared to be his grandfather. What caught my attention was the boy's baseball cap. Across the front panel were the words "Duty, Honor, Country—West Point." A few years earlier, one would have been arrested for wearing such a hat. Today, no one seemed to notice but me.

Moments later, I came upon the panda cages. In the States, I had seen people stand in line for hours hoping to catch a glimpse of one of the black and white bears. Here, it was simply the pandas and me. I watched them and they watched me until we both got bored.

The following day, I scouted the last potential location of the trip; on Lin's suggestion, I visited the Great Wall at Badaling. She assured me that we would be able to place a cart there.

The Wall is a major tourist attraction. However, it is seventy-five kilometers outside of Beijing. Distance could potentially be a problem, but it was worth a look. I booked a seat on a tour bus and headed out. Once at the Wall, I had two hours of free time before having to rejoin my tour for lunch.

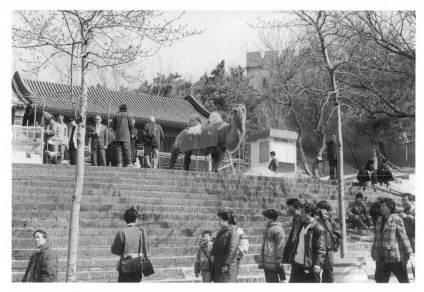

The camel patiently waiting for a customer.

I visited the small stalls selling drinks and snacks to assess our potential competition. Then, after surveying the surrounding area, I started hiking the Wall. Several hundred yards into the trek, I came across an elderly Chinese man with a camera and tripod. For a fee, you could have your picture taken sitting atop his camel. Thousands of people walked by, but he had no takers.

As I hiked, I stopped every few hundred yards to view the historic surroundings. It was an awesome sight. At one point, as I stood gazing out into the distance, a handsome young man, probably in his late twenties, walked up with a camera. I thought he wanted me to take a photo of him and his wife, but I was wrong. He wanted to take a picture of *me* with *my* arm around his wife. Then, he wanted her to take a picture of him shaking hands with me. By the time she had taken the photo, there were about fifteen other people crowding around, waiting to have their pictures taken with me.

Two Australian tourists just to my left broke out laughing. "What's so funny?" I asked.

"Everyone wants their picture taken with you, mate."

The author on the Great Wall just minutes before the line started forming.

"Mate," I responded, "you might want to turn around. Both of you also have lines."

We "Westerners" had a crowd while the poor guy and his camel stood all alone. It wasn't that the people thought we were celebrities; they simply wanted their pictures taken with a Westerner. We were more of a novelty than the camel.

One important outcome of the trip to the Great Wall was I discovered that lunch is included in most tour packages. Thus, while there were thousands upon thousands of people at the Wall every day, very few would be potential customers. And as we drove back to town amid massive traffic jams, I realized it would be virtually impossible to move carts around daily via truck or trailer. We had to find fixed locations where the wagons could be left and the product replenished each day.

During my last day in Beijing, Doug Talbot's oldest son, Mark, now involved in the business, emailed wanting to know if we had any locations under contract. I responded, "Unfortunately, no. We are still in the 'getting to know you' stage." As the locals say, "You must build a shelter before it rains."

Matt and Lin assured me that after I left, they would continue pursuing amusement parks, the zoo, bowling alleys, historical parks, the train station, and the airport. They figured the airport and train station would be long-term projects, but valuable locations nonetheless. I stressed that before we could start shipping carts, we had to have locations under contract.

China was intriguing. The country was starting to develop a middle class and looked as though it was on the verge of bursting into a consumer-based economy. I wrote to Doug: "I think we can do well here, but some experimenting and creativity will be required. Finding our niche will not be quick, nor will it be easy." It was a given that it almost certainly would not be cheap.

I had eaten all of the pigs' feet, Mongolian hot pot, and dumplings that I could stand. The following morning, I boarded a flight back to the States. As we crossed the various time zones, I tried to catch up on sleep. Matt sent an email to Mark: "Jerry left Beijing at 9:30 a.m. on Sunday morning. He should land in Detroit at 9:30 a.m. Sunday morning. Ask him if he liked eating the stirred rat soup."

2

SAVING FACE

I had been back in town for less than a week when the night manager called my office in a panic. One of our vendors was out on Bourbon Street, flashing her breasts for Mardi Gras beads. A crowd was forming around her cart, but as of yet, the police had not arrived.

Obviously, the young woman had gotten caught up in the excitement of the street. Add to that several cold alcoholic beverages, and the result was our present predicament.

In spite of the crowd's loud vocal objections, I shut down both the wagon and the show. As I was pushing the cart back to the shop, I thought that nothing I saw in Beijing could top what nightly takes place on Bourbon Street. As strange as it sounds, I felt great. It was good to be back in my element.

The next day, I got an email from Matt. "Congratulations to us all," he wrote. "We have received our license. This document gives western companies the right to operate in China. It is the most difficult of all to come by. We still have several more to go."

Though we were moving forward in obtaining our licenses, we had not yet acquired a single vending location. I asked Matt and Lin to focus on securing a spot in Tiananmen Square and another near the entrance to Silk Alley. Both would be ideal test sites.

Silk Alley was a massive flea market just off Embassy Row with hundreds of covered stalls lining the street. Within a hundred yards of the U.S. embassy, you could buy anything from T-shirts to fur coats, from Rolex watches to pirated computer programs. Trench coat–clad young

Lucky Dogs warehouse at 517 Gravier Street.

men would approach potential customers, and as they drew near say, "Mister, Mister, CD-ROM. You name price. Cheapa! Cheapa for you! You name price." Then, in the style of some perverted flasher, they would throw open their coats and reveal rows of CDs and DVDs hanging from the lining. Whatever you want, they usually have. In the rare case that they did not, they would run to a nearby stairwell, or reach under a car, or pull a bag out from some obscure hiding spot behind a bush, and within seconds the desired item would appear.

During my first visit to the Alley, one of the hustlers attempted to sell me a CD titled *History of the World*. When I inquired as to the price, the young man replied, "Only fifty renminbi," which, at the time, was equivalent to approximately six U.S. dollars. However, still suffering from jetlag, I was improperly converting the currencies. So I kept bartering and driving down the price. Finally, the seller looked at me with a pitiful face and said, "Mista, now only dollar quarter U.S. Gimme break, huh?"

The Chinese government allowed Silk Alley to flourish because it brought in millions of dollars in foreign capital. A mile or so away was a second Silk Alley, this one geared toward Russian visitors.

Vendors selling sweet potatoes off homemade grills at the entrance to Silk Alley.

Brand-name clothing manufacturers and computer companies vigorously complained to the Chinese government about the pirated products and the copyright infringements. Every few months, the U.S. embassy would make the obligatory formal complaint. The authorities would respond by staging a crackdown. It was as if some movie director yelled, "Scene one, take one, action!" Out of nowhere, the police would appear and do a quick sweep of the area. Ten minutes after they left, there would be even more sellers on the street than before the bust. Every hustler in town knew that it would be weeks before the next raid, so they had no fear. Some locals speculated that Party members and local authorities were receiving a cut of the proceeds.

While Lin persisted in her quest for a spot in the Alley, I asked Matt to approach the manager of A&W about the name of their bun and hot dog suppliers. If we bought from a common supplier, the larger production runs could result in lower costs for both companies. It was a long shot, but worth a try. If it didn't work, then Plan B would be put into action: corporate espionage, which meant that a hired lookout would sit across the street from the fast food restaurant and watch for the delivery trucks. The suppliers' names should be on the sides of their vehicles. First, however, we wanted to try the more honorable, direct, and businesslike approach.

A&W refused to divulge the name of their bun supplier. With the honorable approach out the window, we launched our covert operation. Expectations were high, and a stakeout was set up. The delivery van approached. Damn, it was unmarked!

There was an additional frustration: Matt and Lin were now predicting that the licensing would be in place before our five carts were shipped to Beijing. To them, this was unacceptable. They wanted the carts up and running as quickly as possible.

I understood their concern, but my thought was: wouldn't it be better to have the licenses and have to wait on the carts than to have the carts in Beijing and discover that we could not acquire the licenses? Plus, there were other setbacks we were still trying to overcome. Thus far, we had no secured locations, did not have a truly acceptable hot dog supplier, had not found a suitable bun, and, as of yet, were not legally licensed to operate. Matt understood, and said, "Things look difficult, but still look promising."

Then, a stroke of luck: The cavalry was on the way. Daniel Zeringue, a young Westerner whom Matt had met while studying in Beijing, had been living in Taiwan for the past year but was about to return to the Chinese capital. Matt had spoken with him, and he agreed to assist with the project. This was fantastic. Daniel's involvement would give Matt some help as well as someone besides Lin to bounce ideas off, and someone with whom he could share his frustrations.

Four days later, Beijing Lucky Dogs reached two major milestones. First, we received two more licenses. One allowed us to deal in foreign currency, making it significantly easier for us to convert renminbis, or yuan, to dollars. The other allowed us to import goods into China. With this, we could now ship carts from the States and Matt could clear them through customs in Beijing.

The second milestone was that we had been offered our first location, in the Museum of the Chinese Revolution on the eastern side of Tiananmen Square. Approval had been given for Beijing Lucky Dogs Fast Food Co., Ltd. to sell the All-American capitalistic hot dog in China's national museum honoring communism. Go figure.

We appeared to be making progress. Matt had hired our first employee. She was an accountant, and came highly recommended by the Bank of China officer responsible for overseeing all joint venture accounts. By law we had to have a Chinese bookkeeper, and this woman was more than qualified. Matt described her as "old, experienced, cheap, and competent." She was recovering from a serious leg injury and would only be available part-time, which would not be an issue for us. Before her accident, she had worked for a Japanese joint venture corporation. She appeared to be ideal. I just hoped that we would need her.

Also, Matt and Daniel had discovered a bread factory that was producing more than 10,000 hamburger buns a day for a state-owned company selling sandwiches in Beijing's subway stations. Daniel bought a variety of the sandwiches and reported that besides tasting horrible, they had given him food poisoning. But, he said, the bread was excellent.

We still didn't have the dog or bun that we wanted, but we did have at least one possible location and we had carts ready to ship. On Monday, April 28, 1997, I was scheduled to transport the five wagons to a company located a few blocks from the New Orleans International Airport. There, they would be crated and turned over to Schenker International for shipment to Beijing.

As I was delivering the last cart, Mark Talbot contacted me. He had just received an email from Matt, alerting us that the import tax would be approximately 80 percent.

Everyone had been insisting that the taxes would fall between 15 percent and 20 percent of the cart's retail price. Suddenly, there was a huge discrepancy. The taxes quoted were more than three times the anticipated amount. Thus, we postponed crating the units.

Matt felt horrible, but we all knew that in China, such problems occur. It is the nature of the beast. You believe that you have the correct answer. Everyone tells you that you have the correct answer. Then, at the last minute, you discover that what you had been led to believe as fact was actually fiction. Such occurrences were frustrating—inevitable, but still frustrating.

We were optimistic that the projected 80 percent import tax would be greatly reduced. However, in China, nothing is ever predictable.

McDonald's restaurants in Beijing had been charged thirty-one unexpected fees above and beyond normal taxes. An Associated Press writer reported that McDonald's had to pay for "family planning, flowers for city streets, and propaganda telling the Chinese to be more gracious." Other fees levied against the fast food giant went for river dredging, for displays placed on Beijing streets during holidays, and for the "spiritual civilization campaign," led by President Jiang Zemin, which blanketed Beijing in banners telling people to "be more cultured." In response to these additional charges, the *Chinese Economic Times* reported, "Some fees for foreign businesses defy understanding."

We were concerned that this could happen to us, and, more importantly, that we might not discover it until all five of our carts were operating on Chinese soil. At that point, we would be at the mercy of the local authorities. Time was another major concern. Ocean transport was going to be slow, and then there was the lengthy process of clearing customs. Months might pass, and we simply could not afford such a delay.

In addition, we were under the gun for both legal and practical reasons. The licensing procedure in China follows strict time limits and deadlines. According to Matt, we were in danger of losing our bank account. Regulations required that the $100,000 of registered capital be deposited within thirty days. If we missed the deadline, we would have to submit additional paperwork generated by a special accountant.

In spite of the potential problems, we all agreed that we needed to test the market before winter, so that realistic goals could be set for the following year.

So, I contacted Matt and informed him that after discussing the situation with Lucky Dogs' owner, I wanted a new approach. Instead of sending all five carts, we would send only one. This cart would be shipped via air instead of ocean freight. Thus, it could arrive in a matter of days. Also, it would mean that we would not have $50,000 of equipment in China and would not have paid shipping and import fees for four other carts if the venture failed. And, importantly, it would allow us to, as they say, "save face" with Lin.

The principle of saving face is extremely important in the Chinese culture. An article titled *China Business Etiquette* states that ". . . an individual's reputation and social standing is based on this complex concept." Take, for example, a situation in which you accept an invitation to an individual's home for dinner, but later, you find you are unable to attend. By not following through with your commitment, you are causing that person to "lose face." According to the article, "To save his or her face, as well as to save your own, you must apologize for not being able to accept the invitation, and then propose an alternative plan that is palatable to the person who has extended the invitation."

The article stressed that causing an individual to lose face is a guaranteed way to end a relationship not only with that person, but also with any of his or her friends and family, and probably with the person's employer.

We had agreed to send five carts; we were now proposing to send only one. This could present a problem with Lin. However, the fact that we were planning to ship the cart via air instead of ocean transport would allow her—and us—to save face. She could honestly explain to friends and associates that only one cart was being sent because of the tariff situation. She could also claim that we were shipping it via air, instead of ocean freight, because we valued her as a joint venture partner.

Our strategy was to put a cart on the street as quickly as possible and then, after a few days, move it to a new site. Then after a few more days, we would move it to another location. Once the cart proved that it could be profitable, the other wagons would be shipped. By the time they arrived, a manager would have been hired, locations would be under contract, and a labor force would have been trained.

Matt and Lin considered this to be a fantastic idea, and he ended his email: "I am going, next Friday, to a meeting at the Ambassador's residence [on] how to sell fast food in China. Based on your reply, I would like to set a departure date for our cart very soon."

Now that everyone was in agreement as to how we were going to proceed, I contacted Schenker International's air export manager. He predicted a shipping time of five to seven days.

With a cart about to be shipped, what we desperately needed was a test site. Finally, in mid-June, a possibility presented itself, as the result of a letter given to Lin by her former boss. His letter of introduction made it possible for Lin and Matt to secure a meeting with the managers of a shopping mall.

Matt was requesting a spot just inside the mall's main foyer. The site would put us in the area of greatest foot traffic as well as only about 150 yards across the street from two very successful Western fast food outlets, McDonald's and KFC. On Friday and Saturday nights, their lines spilled out of their doors and onto the sidewalk. Customers stood four abreast and fifty to seventy-five deep, each of them waiting for a chance to order Western burgers or the Colonel's original chicken. It was, to say the least, an encouraging sight.

Because of Lin's connections, it appeared that a lease with the mall would be forthcoming. Matt immediately rented an office—one far more modern than those previously considered. And he worked to lock down the mall site. As usual, progress was slow. The rental fee still had not been determined, though Matt believed that it would be finalized over dinner and karaoke. The mall's representative was insisting on hearing the young American sing in Chinese before agreeing to sign the lease.

In the meantime, I was finalizing the cart's shipping details. Its estimated date of arrival in Beijing was between the last day of June and July 2. That proved to be a problem: July 1, 1997, was the day the British were officially handing Hong Kong over to the Chinese. July 1 would no doubt be a huge national holiday. We decided to delay the shipment.

A few minutes later, I received an enlightening email from Matt about his recent night out on the town. He had taken the mall manager to an upscale restaurant where they apparently enjoyed a great meal and, after dinner, proceeded to drink themselves "into next week." Matt had brought along a three-star general he was close with, a high-ranking bank official, and a professor—all of whom were Chinese. He wanted the manager to see that we had local contacts in high places. After dinner, he wrote, "We did the big karaoke thing. All in all, it was a night for the books."

By July 6 it was official: we had a location in the mall. All it had taken was a letter of introduction from Lin's ex-boss and a young Westerner crooning Chinese love songs. Soon, that young Westerner would have the cart itself. It was being shipped via air freight from New Orleans to Frankfurt, Germany, where it would be transferred to another carrier for the final leg to Beijing. After six months of frustrations, at last there was light at the end of the tunnel. I emailed Matt that I would see him soon.

Everything was moving along flawlessly—then it hit the fan. In Frankfurt, our crate was transferred to the new carrier, but then it was offloaded because the plane was exceeding its weight restriction.

The aircraft headed to Beijing without our cart. I complained to Schenker. Schenker blamed the airline. The airline, in turn, blamed us for shipping such a large heavy crate. All the while, Matt was anxiously awaiting the wagon's arrival.

The size and weight of the crate was never a secret. We had been charged accordingly, but that didn't matter; though China-bound planes continuously took off from Frankfurt, our Lucky Dog cart kept being left on the tarmac. It was ironic that of all the places where this could happen, it was happening in the very city credited with creating the frankfurter.

Finally, we were assured that the crate would be on the next flight out of Frankfurt. Within twenty-four hours I was on board a triple-seven heading back to the land of the designated drinker.

There was more good news: we now had a bun supplier. Though Lin's husband's bakery had suffered fire damage and would not be able to supply the buns for some time, the company that was producing the 10,000 hamburger buns a day for the subway concessionaire agreed to bake our bread. Their quality proved to be comparable to the product served by A&W.

At the end of my first day back in Beijing, Matt and I left our newly rented office and returned to the mall for one more look. As we left the retail center, we hailed a taxi and gave Matt's apartment address—but the driver sped off in the wrong direction. Discovering his mistake, he immediately corrected it by making a U-turn onto a wide sidewalk. As we drove between the storefronts and the tree-lined curb, the cabbie laid on his horn, warning pedestrians to either jump back into the doorways or out into the street. At the end of the block, we went *Dukes of Hazzard*–airborne off the sidewalk, shot diagonally across the intersection between oncoming cars, passed a police officer standing on a box directing traffic, and headed in what the driver had finally determined to be the correct direction.

Aside from our misadventures with the Beijing cab system, we were not the only ones having problems. Rumor had it that Burger King was having difficulty acquiring a license. Supposedly, it was because the Chinese government wanted to stem the tide of U.S. fast food and give local businessmen a chance to develop their own brands.

Matt contacted Greg Wong, the U.S. embassy staff member we had met with earlier, and asked him about the rumor. Wong said that he, too, had heard that no new Western fast food businesses would be permitted in Beijing. Allegedly, an internal working document in the Ministry of Internal Trade expressed great concern over the rapid expansion of Western fast food. However, since this document had not been made public, no one could confirm its existence. Wong could only confirm that as of the moment, no one had officially been denied. The Chinese were smart; until there was an official denial, the embassy could not become involved.

However, the ruling would not hamper McDonald's, KFC, A&W, or others presently holding a license from expanding. If our cart ever cleared customs, we, too, would be allowed to expand.

Matt and I were of the opinion that in the future, if a major corporation had deep enough pockets and a Chinese partner with enough political power, they would still be able to acquire a license. If this proved to be the case, small companies like ours would almost certainly be frozen out.

But that was in the future. In the present, our cart had finally cleared customs, though not without a Chinese government-imposed 42 percent tariff on the wagon, then an additional 17 percent value-added tax. Matt had been led to believe that the VAT was included in the tariff. It wasn't. Our only option was to pay the 59 percent assessment.

Once the tax was paid, customs released the cart, and it was delivered to our office. Awaiting its arrival were our three new employees. Peter,

Lucky Dog cart just after it was unloaded in the mall's parking lot.

a local Beijing resident and a friend of Matt's, devised the pay scale. Each vendor was to receive a base salary plus a dollar a day for lunch. They would also divide a 13 percent commission on every dog sold. Peter figured that an hourly wage and a lunch allowance combined with an incentive program would attract the best employees and encourage the greatest effort. According to him, most of his fellow Chinese workers had no incentive, so it ended up taking six people to do the work of one. Plus, because the government took care of them, they didn't care how fast or how well something did—or did not—get done. We were hoping that the commission would give them a reason to hustle.

If the business proved to be successful, our plan was to hire Peter on a permanent basis. Otherwise, he would return to teaching English at a local school in mid-August.

While Peter was devising our pay scale, word came that the ambassador would not be able to attend our ribbon-cutting ceremony. Former President Jimmy Carter was scheduled to arrive in Beijing and would be requiring most of the ambassador's time. We would sell hot dogs, but the grand opening was scratched.

The trucking company arrived with our cart, and the next day, our first shipment of buns and dogs arrived. The quality of the bread was excellent. The hot dogs were not what we wanted, but they were all that we had.

At 3:30 p.m. on July 25, 1997, Lucky Dogs officially began operating in the People's Republic of China. Our first day's sales were a meager forty-three hot dogs. The number was disappointing, but we took into consideration that we hadn't opened until after the lunch rush was over. Plus, the Chinese weren't exactly certain what the strange-looking wagon represented.

Though the number was meager, the only reason we even sold forty-three dogs was because of a beautiful young woman. She was Chinese and one of Matt's friends. Her family had moved to the States when she was six years old. Now, having just finished her freshman year at Harvard, she was back in Beijing spending the summer with her grandmother.

Intelligent, outgoing, incredibly attractive, and able to speak both English and Chinese fluently, she was not the kind of hot dog salesperson to whom I was accustomed. As she taught our vendors how to hawk the dogs, she explained to those who walked by just what an American hot dog was. Even more, she encouraged our employees to smile and look friendly. She understood this was not the Chinese way—most workers in China were unenthusiastic. They had never been given an incentive to succeed. In fact, most did not fully understand what "incentive" meant. She translated the concept to our employees, and within minutes, we had the smilingest crew in Beijing. Not an hour after she had begun, she had them confident enough that they started stepping forward and explaining to passers-by that we were selling the "All-American hot dog."

With motivation under control, we needed to focus on the hot dog's identity problem. On day two, we sold seventy-two hot dogs. The price was a major issue, since we were in a non-tourist area. Potential customers walked away when they saw the price. So, we lowered it from $1.15 to $1.09. It seemed like a small reduction, but to the Chinese the six-cent drop was massive.

We were putting in thirteen- to fifteen-hour days with no time off. Making the long hours even more grueling was the summer heat and the fact that the Chinese did not believe in ice in drinks or truly air conditioning their buildings. The temperature inside the mall was at least 85 degrees.

Matt, on the other hand, had adapted well to China and the difficult temperature situations it sometimes posed. He had no choice. In the twenty-four-story apartment complex where he and Daniel lived, there was only one thermostat—and it was located in the manager's apartment. The Party paid the utility bill, so the Party's representative controlled the temperature.

Back at the mall, our sale figures failed to increase, but the food court on the fifth floor was booming. It was in an accessible location, not hidden away in a corner, and, as a result, it had better-than-average business. Its customers were well-dressed families coming for a low-priced family dinner.

It was easy to see that these parents went out of their way to please their child—child, not children, because in Beijing at that time, the Party's "one child per family" decree was in force. A local told me that any second child did not exist in the eyes of the State, and would not be eligible for government assistance. Thus, he or she would put a huge financial burden on the parents. As a result, most couples had a single child, and that child was usually spoiled rotten. Not only did the child have doting parents, but also the full adulation of two sets of grandparents, who each had only the single shared grandchild.

Thus far, my second visit had been non-stop. We had settled on a quality bun, revisited the meat factory, met with the mall manager, and purchased all of the basic supplies for the cart. We moved the cart to the site, located an electrical supply house that could build a converter overnight that was heavy enough to handle the cart, and applied decals to the wagon. We trained employees, continued looking for new locations, opened for business, and even had a four-by-six-foot sign made that stated, in Chinese, "Welcome, Please Try Our American-Style Hot Dog." Plus, we had survived food poisoning as we were trying to open for business. We might not have always been physically at the top of our game, but we were never out of the game.

In the States, hot dogs are an impulse item, bought primarily because they're something you eat on the run. Lucky Dogs carts have been successful back home because they fill a niche. But I was becoming less and less certain that the same approach would work in Beijing. The Chinese people are patient and slow moving; in general, they're not nearly as impulsive as Americans. Matt had pointed out that Dairy Queen had tables and chairs around their kiosk. That way, their customers could sit and eat. Western food was expensive compared to its Chinese competition, and often those purchasing it wanted everyone to know that they were affluent enough to afford it. Whenever possible, they wanted to sit at a street-side window so that those passing on the sidewalk could see them. Families would even dress in their best clothes and pose for pictures by the Ronald McDonald statue outside the restaurant.

We were attempting to sell these same consumers take-out food or food marketed for those on the go. We were denying them the ego boost of sitting in full view while they ate—an experience they coveted. Matt believed that we would have to modify our concept if we were to be successful in China. However, if we changed the concept, then the carts had to be replaced with true kiosks, and additional expenses would be incurred. Doug was not yet receptive to that idea. Before abandoning what had been so successful in the States, he wanted to be certain that it would not work in Beijing.

It was beginning to become obvious to Matt, Daniel, and me that the mall location would never be profitable. So far, the most dogs sold there in a single day totaled a meager seventy-two. We needed to gain access to other sites frequented by a more elite clientele.

In the meantime, we had a more immediate problem: a health inspector showed up. As he looked over the wagon, he asked, "Where do you wash your hands?" I almost fainted. Outside on the street, there were shirtless vendors cooking meat that hadn't been refrigerated for hours—and this inspector was worried about where we washed our hands! Originally, the cart had sinks, but we removed them because we were told they weren't required. Eliminating the sinks, plumbing, fresh water tank, and waste tank greatly reduced the cart's weight and thus lowered our shipping cost.

Matt explained that we washed our hands in the sinks provided by the mall. The answer was acceptable to the inspector, and he soon went on his way.

With the health inspector's departure, the cart opened for business, and Matt and I headed to Silk Alley. It was bustling. The Alley would be a great location, but so far, Lin had been unsuccessful in acquiring a spot.

Later, Lin insisted on taking us to the Museum of the People's Revolution bordering the eastern side of Tiananmen Square. Weeks earlier, Matt had tried to convince her that the location would not be profitable. However, she was adamant that we at least consider it. So off we went.

The Central Hall of the museum is "dedicated to the memories of Marx, Engels, Lenin, and Stalin," and their sculptured facial likenesses adorned the walls. Our location would be in the front wing to the left of the building's entrance, approximately thirty yards from the main door. On this day, we were there at lunchtime, and a major exhibit had recently opened. The museum, however, was empty. We wouldn't even sell five dogs a day with a stand here. The spot did have one advantage, however—if you stood where our capitalistic hot dog cart was to be placed and looked through the massive glass exterior wall, you had a great view of Chairman Mao's tomb.

After inspecting the site, Matt and I jumped in a taxi and headed to the office to meet Daniel, who had just returned from the States. Shortly thereafter, David Longacre, vice-president of Hormel Foods' Asia-Pacific division, called and invited us to join him for a drink. It would be early September before his new Shanghai facility would begin operating and he could supply us with hot dogs. Because of the delay, he wanted to give us the name of a local Chinese meat supplier that produced a quality frank. It was a generous gesture. And his assistance did not stop there—when we mentioned that we were having problems with our bread hardening after only two days, he contacted a baker friend in the U.S. to find out the softening agent used by his company. We passed the information on to our bun supplier. As soon as Hormel's plant was up and running, we assured Longacre that we would be his first customers.

Next, we headed to the office, where, we received a phone call from a U.S. embassy representative informing Matt that the director of the commercial division and a group of embassy personnel were about to head to the cart for lunch. After hanging up the phone, Matt exclaimed, "The embassy's on their way to the cart!"

Unfortunately, we were still selling dogs supplied by our original meat packer. Not wanting to disappoint the embassy personnel, we opened our small freezer and grabbed the samples that Hormel had dropped off. With dogs in hand, we raced out the door and down the gravel road to the main paved thoroughfare two blocks away where we were able to hail a taxi.

As our cab headed toward the mall, Matt happened to look back through the rear window. Rounding the corner and turning onto the wide tree-lined boulevard a hundred or so yards behind us was a large black limousine. Following it was another large black limousine. Both had small U.S. flags on their front fenders, flapping in the wind. They were going to arrive at the cart only moments after us. We had to buy some time.

Matt suggested that once we reached the mall that I immediately head into the building with the packs of wieners. He would stay in the parking lot and stall the delegation as long as possible. Daniel would form a second line of defense just inside the mall's door. Once the group entered the building, Daniel would go into a second meet-and-greet routine. By then, the dogs should have been boiling away in the hot water for several minutes. Normally, we steam our product, but under such time constraints, it wasn't an option. We had to resort to a faster method. After Daniel completed his spiel and the embassy members arrived at the cart, I would begin my dog-and-pony show. I would offer a brief history of the company, cover the cart's design, and conclude with what I found intriguing about China. All the while, the dogs would be getting hot and plump.

These were Americans, and we wanted to make a good impression. We wanted them to enjoy a true American hot dog, and what they were about to consume was as American as it gets. They were about to eat dogs produced in the United States; inspected by the USDA; and being served on Matt-, Daniel-, and Jerry-approved hot dog buns.

They stepped up to the cart and made their selections. Some wanted the regular all-beef hot dog while others requested our spicier turkey franks. We had a limited number of samples. Moreover, we did not have an equal quantity of each dog. By the grace of God, no one asked for thirds. I was about to suggest to Matt that we treat the delegation to lunch, but before I could, in true capitalistic fashion, he tallied up the tab and handed the bill to the embassy official who had refused to hire him.

Later, as I was emailing my daily adventure story back to the States, a major weather front was bearing down on Beijing. Rain pelted the city for hours. Smog had been keeping the sky a constant shade of gray. But on this night, for the first time, the air smelled clean.

From Matt's twenty-fourth-floor apartment balcony, all I could normally see was a haze in the distance. The Chinese were still burning coal in their factories and homes—one of the major reasons for their pollution. When added to the ever-increasing number of cars on the street, it was obvious that air quality was becoming more and more of a problem every day. It was not uncommon to see pedestrians wearing hospital-style masks.

However, the storm on this evening pushed out the pollution, and when I awoke the next morning, I saw clusters of massive skyscrapers being built and mountains in the distance. It was the first time that I had seen either from the balcony.

Under this abnormally clear sky, we headed out to a meeting with Beijing Western, the meat packer recommended by Hormel. The company was sixty miles outside of Beijing. Round-trip taxi fare, including the driver waiting for us during the meeting, was less than $50.

The head of Beijing Western's sausage-making division was a German named Wolfgang. Just hearing "Wolfgang," "German," and "sausage" all in the same sentence was exciting. Things were looking up. Wolfgang produced quality beef and pork American-style hot dogs. His equipment was state-of-the-art and his plant was immaculate. After the tour, the general manager invited us to join him for what appeared to be a twenty-five-course meal. Just like at the other plant, in the middle of our table was a massive lazy Susan overloaded with a variety of products. We tasted as many as we could, but it did not take long to become full. With lunch, we were offered a choice of Sprite, green tea, or the traditional warm beer. No one poured rice whiskey, and no obnoxious employee repeatedly shouted "Gan Bei." I was really beginning to like this place.

At the end of the meal, a large, round piece of flatbread resembling a thick pizza crust was brought to the table. Matt, sitting in the chair to my left, was handed the plate of bread. He tore off a small piece and passed the plate to me. I did the same and then passed it to the man directly to my right. He, too, tore off a small piece and then handed the dish to the gentleman to his right.

The plant's Chinese assistant general manager, sitting directly across the round table from me, watched in bewilderment. He was older, heavyset, and wore thick black-rimmed glasses. During both our tour of the facility and the meal, he had not said much, and when he did, it was in Chinese. His assistant translated.

As we tore off our pieces, the assistant general manager looked over the rim of his glasses and, in perfect English, asked, "Is this a re-enactment of the Last Supper?" It was priceless. I couldn't help but smile.

Up until this point, he assumed that none of his guests had understood the conversations that he had been having with his associates. In my case, he was correct, but not in Matt's. Matt had been listening, but never gave the slightest indication that he understood the language.

Then, in one of those priceless "gotcha!" moments, Matt looked across the table and answered his "Last Supper" question in flawless Mandarin Chinese. It was now the assistant manager's turn to smile. From that moment on, we all had a pleasant conversation in English.

Our host's name was George Lillie. He was Chinese, but had been adopted by an English couple, raised in British-controlled Hong Kong, and educated in British-run schools. Lillie was well aware of what it took to make a true American hot dog. During our discussion, he informed us that Beijing Western supplied 70 percent of the upscale meat market products in Beijing. A Hormel rep later said that Lillie was actually underestimating Beijing Western's market share. All that mattered to me was that we now had a quality meat packer that could supply us with franks until Hormel's plant was up and running. I have to admit, however, that I was puzzled as to why Lin had never made us aware of Beijing Western's existence.

That evening, Matt and I let the night shift close shop by themselves while we went out and celebrated our opening by eating Peking duck. You can't go to Beijing—which, in the past, was called Peking—and not eat the famed dish.

As we were walking toward the restaurant's entrance, several of the establishment's employees were tossing a drunken general out the door. I thought that perhaps another restaurant might be in order, but Matt assured me this was a common occurrence. The meal was excellent, and it was a pleasant evening.

Later, Matt and Daniel went out to meet friends. I was invited to join them, but they were young, single, and needed to relax. Plus, they needed time away from me. I headed back to the apartment where I spent the remainder of the evening writing emails.

To Jane, I wrote: "I will be heading home on the 5th. I have been eating broccoli, asparagus, and eggplant, and I've begun to like them. Obviously, I have been here far too long." After a few more emails I kicked back, turned on the television, and discovered the Star Channel. There, in living color and speaking the King's English, was Captain James T. Kirk of the Starship *Enterprise*. Suddenly, it dawned on me: the series had debuted in 1966. Mao didn't die until 1976. Was it possible the communist leader was a Trekkie?

The following morning, I boarded a plane home. As we cruised at 35,000 feet above the Siberian forest, my thoughts were focusing on what seemed to be an insurmountable task: how to sell more than fifty hot dogs a day to a potential consumer base of 1.2 billion people.

3

LAST CALL

McDonald's, KFC, Dairy Queen, and A&W all had giant corporate staffs to assist their China operations. They had legal advisors, marketing departments, financial departments, personnel directors, secretarial staffs, human resource branches, customer service departments, shipping divisions, and management training centers. They had hundreds of people in the States making plans and crunching numbers.

At Lucky Dogs, Matt, Daniel, and Lin were the entire boots-on-the-ground Beijing managerial workforce. In the United States the staff consisted of only Mark and me. When we weren't concentrating on international expansion, my time was devoted to the French Quarter operation, and Mark spent the bulk of his day overseeing our Harrah's Casino operation. We didn't even have a secretary; I did all of the required typing. We had no delivery person; if something had to be dropped off or picked up, I usually did it. Weekly, I would take the five-gallon propane tanks from each Lucky Dog cart to be refilled. I did the payroll, oversaw our day and night managers, ordered supplies, counted the previous night's receipts, took the money to the bank, and handled all personnel and company-related problems.

Mark would meet his suppliers at Harrah's loading dock, unload the order, stack it on a dolly, and haul it to the storeroom. He also handled the payroll, purchasing, daily management, and employee issues for our casino operation. In addition, he paid the bills for Lucky Dogs and provided any documentation that might be required by our accountants.

Throw in the fact that we also ran our New Orleans airport food concessions operation, our catering business, and numerous charity events, all from the same office, with no additional staff. I feel pretty comfortable saying that as a company, we were not management heavy. In fact, organizationally we were lean—so lean, that we were almost verging on starvation.

Entering the Beijing market was possible only because we had an American already in place who spoke fluent Chinese, and a Chinese joint venture partner who gave us a local presence. In addition, we had hired an accountant who was a resident of Beijing and had been recommended by the Bank of China. She knew the ins and outs of the country's bureaucratic system and proved to be a master at working through its seemingly endless roadblocks. What might have taken us years to accomplish, she achieved in a matter of months. Because of her help, Beijing Lucky Dogs Fast Food Co., Ltd. received approval from all of the twenty-eight necessary departments.

While we were able to overcome the frustrations of the licensing process, we were never able to improve on the 59 percent import tariff. Nevertheless, like the thousands upon thousands of Western companies that entered China before us, we still wanted a chance to hawk our wares in the Asian nation.

Everyone spoke of China as a billion-plus consumer market, but when we actually broke it down, the market for Western products was nowhere near that. Most of the country's population in the 1990s consisted of rural workers with an annual income of less than $250. The rural worker could not afford our product, or any other product produced by a foreign corporation. Our true target was the emerging urban Chinese middle class. The middle class, or *xiao kang*, represented roughly 20 percent of China's urban population, and in 1994, a middle-class family had an annual household income of approximately $2,300. It was this growing middle class that we had to attract if we were to be successful.

Defining the market was one problem; a second problem had to do with one of our young employees. Matt discovered that he was stealing cash from the register, and he let him go. The ramifications were unimaginable. Without hesitation, the boy's mother insisted that her son immediately enlist in the army. A bit drastic, we thought, especially since the total taken was less than $15. In the French Quarter, vendors would often come up short, and we would just allow them to work and pay it back. However, this was China. The issue of theft was being viewed through the eyes of a completely different culture.

The young man was handling what, to him, must have seemed to be an enormous amount of money. Temptation was great, and he was too immature to handle it. Matt tried convincing the boy's mother that forcing him into the military was a bit extreme. She disagreed. She reasoned that it was a blessing that he was still young enough to be set back on the right path. Her decision was immediate and final; there was no changing her mind.

The mother was concerned about her well-being as well as that of her son. In urban areas, where parents are under the "one-child policy," that child is their retirement package. It is their offspring who cares for them in their old age. If her son chose the wrong path, she would lack security in her later years. As she saw it, she had to correct the problem now before it doomed them both.

By now, it was mid-September. Children were back in school, the weather was turning cold, and sales had turned even colder. So, the cart was removed from the mall and transported to the office where it would be thoroughly cleaned and stored until a more suitable location could be found.

It was also decided that I should return to Beijing for a third visit. The plan was still to ship the remaining four carts, but before doing so, it was imperative that we find five profitable locations. None of us ever anticipated that it would be this difficult. In fact, what everyone had told Matt and Daniel was quite the contrary.

A few days before my trip, the cart was moved from the office to the Yue Tan Roller Skating Rink, the largest skating rink in Beijing. The patrons were young and affluent, and the property's manager was excited about being able to offer Western food to his clientele. He placed the cart in a prime spot next to the skating floor where it would be highly visible. Plus, several times a day, he advertised the "American Lucky Dog" over the rink's sound system, and he even recommended that Matt and Daniel hang posters featuring hot dogs. We could not have asked for a better landlord.

Still, the first day's sales totaled a dismal seventeen dogs. Most of the kids had enough money for admission and perhaps one drink. Few had enough funds left for a hot dog.

By October 28, Matt was ready to pull out of the skating rink. In his words, "We will lose money at this location." Though the cart would not be operating, our employees would still receive full pay. In China, workers are paid by the month, whether they work or not.

By this time, I was back in Beijing, and Matt and I went back to scouting for locations. The first site on our list was the "Dirt Market," an enormous outdoor flea market visited mostly by locals.

Upon arriving there, Matt and the taxi driver got into a heated discussion over the fare. Voices rose. People started staring. A uniformed officer wearing a red armband began walking toward us. I suggested to Matt that he settle the problem before the police got involved.

"Jerry, the driver deliberately took a longer route so that he could charge us more."

The red-armbanded man joined the fracas. He didn't look happy; no one looked happy. Visions of a bamboo cell, a wooden bowl of cold clumpy rice, and rats scurrying across a dirt floor began dominating my thoughts. The argument grew intense. Hands were waving; voices were interrupting voices. Suddenly, there was silence.

"I won," Matt announced in English. "The officer agreed that we'd been overcharged."

"How much?" I asked.

"A quarter."

"A quarter! All of this was over a freakin' quarter?"

Then it dawned on me: The street was Matt's language lab. It was his debate class. It was where he honed his skills and assessed his abilities. A local once told me that over the phone, Matt was undistinguishable from one of their own. In this instance, he had proven to be more than capable of handling himself in this different culture.

Now that the excitement was over and the cabbie had been paid, including a nice tip, we started touring the market. In US size, it was a couple of blocks long by a block wide. Part of it was just rows of tables set up on grass. The other section had a large roof and a concrete floor, but no walls. Under the roof, vendors were selling wares out of a hundred-plus stalls that lined several aisles.

The market had everything: paintings, clothing, Chinese artifacts from World War II, bronze items, vases by the thousands, shoes, belts, oriental rugs, and a large fossilized jaw with two massive teeth. It had to have come from something as large as a woolly mammoth. The heavily tanned, wrinkled, white-haired old man selling it looked as if he had just walked out of the most underdeveloped region of Outer Mongolia.

The market was interesting, but it was not our niche. We could never have competed with the low-priced noodles, stuffed dumplings, and other products being sold incredibly cheaply from several makeshift stalls. So, we headed back to the office where Matt took a moment to check his emails. As an American entrepreneur, he frequently received briefings from the commercial division of the U.S. embassy.

One of the topics in the latest briefing focused on fast food. It stated: "Problems currently existing in the fast food industry include the following: unstable quality; slow chain-store expansion; the lack of leading fast food chain enterprises; and the laggard development of fast food equipment, production, and supply." The Chinese wanted to solve these problems and, at the same time, promote the development of a Chinese fast food industry. In order to do so, the Ministry of Internal Trade developed a plan called the "China Fast Food Industry Development Guidelines." According to the plan, the Chinese fast food industry needed to grow at the rate of at least 5 percent per year. This could pose a problem for us: The Chinese now had an official policy pushing for the growth of local fast food. Freestanding walk-in restaurants probably would not be heavily affected. But we were trying to get into airports, subways, train stations, major shopping areas, on the street, and perhaps even in large skyscrapers. These were government-controlled properties that would likely be targeted areas, and the Party had just officially stated that they favored a growth in local fast food. This new policy would directly affect us. Our "difficult" situation appeared to have become a "virtually impossible to succeed" situation. Even so, we could hope.

The following morning before going to the office, we stopped by the residence of a man known to me only as Mr. Smith. This was the same Mr. Smith who had hired Matt as a translator when his embassy job failed to materialize. From what I understood, Smith had once been a professor at a major West Coast US university. He was now in China as an urban planning specialist and at the moment was in desperate need of a new laptop. Matt had promised to help him in its purchase.

The apartment was in a modern high-rise designated solely for foreigners. The suite had a living room, kitchen, and one bedroom. The monthly rent was approximately $7,000. Urban studies apparently paid well. It had to, because Westerners in Beijing were being charged an exorbitant rate when it came to housing.

Smith and I spoke briefly before the salesman arrived. My host suggested that I relax in his bedroom and browse through his bookcase while they conducted business.

As I looked around his room, a small, framed photo caught my attention. It was of Smith, but it had been taken when he was much younger. He was wearing military fatigues and standing on a dock next to a craft that resembled a World War II PT boat. The intriguing thing was there were no insignias on his uniform or any visible markings on the boat.

After the salesman left, Smith, Matt, and I sat and talked. Smith asked if I had found anything of interest.

"I did, and if it's not too personal, I was wondering about the small photo. You were wearing military fatigues, but there were no insignias designating branch of service or country."

He smiled and responded, "I speak fluent Vietnamese. I was one of the first five men the U.S. sent into Vietnam. That picture, however, was taken in Laos. I was there to facilitate the establishment of their Brown-Water Navy. Officially, I was never there."

What a coincidence. In 1994, after lecturing at the World War II in the Pacific conference in Washington, I was approached by the Naval Historical Center and asked if I would be interested in writing a book about the United States' Brown-Water Navy in Vietnam. I was flattered, but I turned down the offer. I had a family, a permanent job, and little free time. Had I accepted, one of the key players that I would have needed to interview would have been Smith. I would have never found him. Now, because of Lucky Dogs, I was sitting in his apartment in Beijing. I didn't say it, but I had serious doubts if urban planning was the real reason he was in China. I wanted to ask if the same agency that had funded him so many years earlier was still funding him, but I didn't. I knew that he couldn't answer.

The following morning, I boarded a plane back to the States. A few days later, I received an email from Matt. Mr. Smith's employer had lost his contract. In order for the ex-professor to remain in China, he had to be fully employed. Smith had come to Matt's aid when the embassy job failed to materialize. Now, Matt was returning the favor. The email was informing me that we had hired Smith as Lucky Dogs' "official bun taster." The papers had been filled out and the documentation submitted. The Chinese governmental agency in charge had stamped their approval. Smith would be allowed to remain in the country. My only question was how long it would be before Mike Wallace and 60 *Minutes* showed up at the shop.

The more time I spent in China, the more I realized the reality of the statement "you are only as strong as your minority partner." Our joint venture partner had become a nonentity. I liked her; she had a great smile, a friendly disposition, and seemed honest and hardworking. I believe that she did the best that she could. It was her contacts, not her efforts, that failed her. Her friends were either not high enough in the Party's pecking order to assist in acquiring locations, or they simply chose not to. If they would have just given us an honest assessment as to our chances of landing certain locations, that alone would have been invaluable.

I believe that as long as the idea of bringing Lucky Dog carts to China was theoretical, no one cared. Once a cart was actually on the ground in Beijing, we suddenly became a real threat to some bureaucracy's existing business.

Matt and I had heard rumors of a major fast food franchise whose minority partner was powerful enough that he had stopped his company's major Western rival from acquiring permits. Then, there was the businessman that I spoke with while flying to Beijing who told me that his company's minority partner helped oversee technology imports into China. According to him, his partner made certain that any potential competition never made it to China's shores.

We discovered that any way you looked at it, China did not now, and probably never would, have a level playing field.

Even so, Matt and Daniel worked tirelessly. They were not going down without a fight. Matt emailed in early December 1997, "We met with a friend of a friend today, who, of course, appears to have all the connections. We will wait and see."

We never found new locations. It was not because of a lack of effort or even a matter of price. It was more that everywhere we turned, doors never seemed to open. By mid-December, we came to the mutual consensus that we should liquidate everything. By the summer of 1998, a Western company operating in Beijing had hired Matt full-time. Daniel had also found permanent employment. Arrangements were made to ship the cart back to the States. By late summer, Lucky Dogs had left the country.

In looking back, there are several reasons why we never achieved our goal. First, as a company, our expectations were probably unrealistic. Second, we were in an unfamiliar market and relying on a Chinese joint venture partner who proved to be unjustifiably optimistic.

We were never able to procure the locations that would have made the company successful. We were never even able to place our street-vending cart on the street. The "official" reason was that the authorities suddenly had concerns about the cart impeding pedestrian flow. The underlying factor, however, was that numerous mobile food vendors were already selling a variety of products on the streets, and various governmental bureaus, including the police, owned many of those carts. By eliminating potential competition, they could maintain their own profitability.

Our third problem was that we were up against the widely held belief that any product sold off a cart was inferior, and thus, that it should be cheaper. This mindset was not going to change overnight.

There was also another problem. While A&W had walk-in restaurants with tables and chairs, and Dairy Queen, which, despite operating from kiosks, still had seating available, we offered a "grab and go" product at a price equal to our competitors—but we offered no tables. There was no ego boost derived from others being able to see that a customer was affluent enough to purchase a Western product. We were not giving our customers an experience; we were simply selling them food. Our eat-on-the-run concept was a benefit in the States, where everyone is in a constant state of motion; but in China no one was in a hurry, so our strength, quick service, had no value. Also, in America, the shape of the cart was an incredible marketing tool. People automatically knew what we sold. In China, most people had no idea what the strange shape represented.

It was obvious: If we were to be successful in China, we had to reinvent ourselves. We needed to shift from carts to kiosks. We would also need a new and much more powerful joint venture partner—someone influential enough to open the doors that, thus far, had remained closed.

Trying again was tempting because it would provide the chance to be on the ground when the growing middle class boom finally hit. Of course, every company that had been in China since Marco Polo opened the trade routes had been waiting for that, and there was no guarantee that it was going to happen any time soon.

Additionally, to continue operating would have required a massive influx of capital. We would have had to go deeply into debt or bring in major investors. Even then, success would not have been a certainty.

Some might consider the Beijing endeavor a failure. I disagree. Granted, the results were disappointing, but the one-cart test proved to be overwhelmingly successful. We were able to determine the pros and cons of expanding Lucky Dogs to the People's Republic of China not hypothetically, but by actually operating in the country. With a total net loss of less than $37,000, we acquired permits, air-shipped a cart, paid travel expenses, purchased supplies, opened bank accounts, paid legal fees, paid employees, and started steaming dogs on a completely different continent—all under a Communist regime with a workforce that did not speak a word of English. Without a major outlay of capital, we concluded that the risks were greater than we were willing to accept. So, we shipped the cart back to the States and said zai jian, or good-bye, to China.

4

THE GREAT VENDOR MIGRATION

From the time we closed in China in December 1997 until the late spring of 1998, we were contacted by numerous potential business partners: an interested party in Hong Kong; a businessman wanting to put carts in the Philippines; an attorney who thought we should take Lucky Dogs to Argentina; an entrepreneur in Austin, Texas; a politician wanting to operate carts in Houston's airport; a friend of Doug's who dreamed of lining Beale Street in Memphis with Lucky Dog carts; and the master concessionaire at the New Orleans International Airport who wanted us to expand our operation there to a third and fourth kiosk.

Most of the opportunities offered too great a risk with too little reward. One proposal even bordered on unethical. We decided to pass on everything except expanding in our local airport. There, we added new kiosks on two concourses. Things looked promising.

A few months later, it went from looking promising to looking downright exhilarating. *Playboy* magazine notified us that they were including Lucky Dogs in their 1998 4th of July issue as one of America's best hot dogs. I visualized shots of sensuous playmates pushing our carts down Bourbon Street, or perhaps a photo of the Playmate of the Year discussing management strategies with *moi,* but such was not to be. We were mentioned in the article, but no scantily clad, gorgeous women ever appeared at the shop. The magazine didn't even include a foldout of a Lucky Dog cart. Vendors and management were distraught.

1998 had been disappointing, but 1999 was a new year and with it came new hope. Unfortunately, instead of ringing it in with sumptuous Playmates, we rang it in with a slew of catastrophes.

The first disaster occurred early one January morning when a vendor was hit by a car while pushing his wagon back to the shop. The driver admitted that her windshield was fogged and her vision impaired as she pulled out of a public parking garage. As a result, she never saw the ten-foot-long hot dog cart or the vendor wearing a red and white striped uniform shirt and a reflective vest. In a split second, the vendor's Lucky Dog career was over. He was unable to walk for months, and when he finally could, he lacked the leg strength necessary to push a cart.

Then there was the woman who called and announced that she intended to sue the company. According to her, she had become deathly ill after eating what she deemed a "bad dog." I inquired as to how she knew that it was the hot dog that had made her sick. Her response was unbelievable: supposedly, she and a friend had made plans the previous day to visit the Quarter and buy Lucky Dogs, and so on the day in question, she refrained from eating breakfast and lunch. In her words, she "did not want to compromise her taste buds before devouring the first bite."

I was astounded. Never had it dawned on me that people would fast before consuming our product. Nor had it occurred to me that someone might wait more than a week to call and complain about a "bad dog." No medical reports, no documentation—just a woman on the phone declaring that if we refused to settle, she'd have her ambulance-chasing attorney take us to the cleaners. It wasn't long before I discovered that this wasn't her first rodeo. She was fully aware of how the system worked. We were being shaken down by a pro.

Before I could alert our insurance company, another call came in. On the line was a representative from *Live with Regis and Kathie Lee*, the popular network morning talk show. According to the caller, the show was broadcasting from New Orleans and wanted a Lucky Dog cart and vendor to briefly appear on the program. The vendor was to serve Regis a Lucky Dog, and the show's host would take a bite and follow with a favorable comment.

The decision to accept the invitation was a no-brainer. Millions of viewers would be introduced to the company's name and product.

Corporations pay a fortune for such exposure, and it was being offered to us for free.

The cart had to be backstage no later than 6 the following morning. I chose Jimmy Buckner, our longtime Jackson Square vendor, to work the wagon.

I awoke at 4 a.m. and was at the shop by 5. The cart and Buckner were on site by 5:45. Once backstage, the show's rep informed us of a "slight" change in plans. Someone associated with the program had decided that Regis should do a blind taste test. He would take a bite of a chili- and onion-topped Lucky Dog. Then, he would take a bite of his favorite New York frank covered with his special mustard. In fact, the mustard and dogs had already been flown in for the test.

It was obvious that this was not a spur-of-the-moment decision. "You asked us to bring a cart and vendor to appear on stage before a local audience and a national broadcast audience," I asked, "so that we could take part in a rigged taste test? I don't think so! This is not what we agreed to. It's probably best that we not participate."

The gentleman was stunned. It never occurred to him that we might withdraw from the show.

"But it was just meant to be fun," he insisted.

"Fun at whose expense?" I countered.

Someone overheard the conversation and brought it to Regis's attention. Regis sent word requesting that I trust him. At that point, I was comfortable that we would not be thrown under the bus and, despite the change of plans, decided to go through with the agreement.

During the broadcast, Regis was blindfolded and given both dogs to taste. The result? He could not decide which he preferred. "Both were excellent," he announced to the audience, proving that besides being a great television host, he was also a man of his word.

A few weeks later, more national attention came our way, this time in printed form. Leigh Buchanan, a writer for *Inc.* magazine, visited the Crescent City and spent several days observing our French Quarter operation. Her eight-page feature article, titled "The Taming of the Crew," was accurate and well written. She had taken the time to understand the company. She grasped the fact that in the Quarter, we can't eliminate the madness; we can only hope to manage it. She saw that we had rules, but that at best, they were selectively enforced, and because of the nature of those working our carts, we were fluid in their interpretation and extremely forgiving once they were broken.

Buchanan also witnessed firsthand that it was not a matter of "would the rules be broken?" but rather "how soon will it happen?" She understood that without forgiveness, we would have no crew. Some actions were forgiven in a day, others in a week. A few resulted in expulsion, but even that sentence was often commuted in two or three months, especially if we were short a few vendors. Serious transgressions, such as possessing drugs or weapons on a cart, however, resulted in a sentence of lifetime banishment without appeal. Other than that, we were extremely understanding.

While at the shop, Buchanan also witnessed a monumental event: Smitty moving out of the elevator shaft. I use the term "elevator" not in the modern sense of the word, but in reference to our old 1800s rope-pulled lift designed to haul freight to the upper two floors. Sheer muscle is the driving force; thus, it's seldom used.

Smitty had taken up residence on the shaft's seven-by ten-foot concrete floor. He could comfortably roll out a sleeping bag and still have room for an ice chest filled with drinks and snacks. He also claimed use of our shower, walk-in cooler, and washer and dryer.

It wasn't that Smitty was destitute. He had enough personal money locked in our safe to pay at least six months' rent. But he preferred living in the shop because it offered him around-the-clock companionship. It was not easy, but after much prodding and in-house counseling, he was finally ready to abandon the nest.

As Smitty was leaving the shaft, others were also on the move. Vendors were constantly drifting in and out of town, especially during the spring and fall. As one crew member took off, another would walk back through the shop door to take his or her place. The majority of the fall departures headed to Las Vegas or California. A lesser number ventured to southern Florida. All of those leaving were hoping to escape even the mildest New Orleans winters.

But other ex-vendors were leaving the North and returning to winter in the Big Easy, fleeing the snow, cold winds, and frigid temperatures.

They would become a part of our crew until the days grew longer and warmer, at which point they would turn in their tongs and head back north to the milder summers. Their void would soon be filled; those who had taken off for Florida and California were already on their way back to the Vieux Carré. It's a never-ending cycle I call the "Great Vendor Migration."

We don't need every vendor to return every year. To hope for such would be unrealistic. But what we do need is for a sufficient number to cycle back through to staff at least a medium-sized crew. We know that we'll always have vendors. We just can't ever predict who or how many.

Additionally, because of the transient nature of our business, it is vital to have trained backup in management positions. Thus, as managers leave, others can seamlessly slip into their place. All of this is possible because we're not a high-tech operation. Training is not difficult or time-consuming, though problems can arise. The unknown factor is how the replacement managers will interact with the rest of the crew. Some vendors, when promoted, suddenly feel empowered and attempt to use their new position to settle old grudges. Some have done things as childish as making an old adversary wait to receive his supplies, while others have been vindictive and assigned individuals they disliked to a less financially rewarding corner. The only way to control this is by constant oversight. Every vendor understands that my door is always open, and any perceived injustice can be appealed up the short chain of command.

One thing that we consciously try never to do is fall victim to the "Peter Principle." If someone fails in his or her new position, we don't fire them—we simply move them back to where they last had success. Buchanan grasped our management concept. She also discovered that though I had long since abandoned history as a vocation, I still enjoyed reading about (and in some cases, doing intense research on) the past. It serves as a form of mental relief from the madness of the shop.

Meanwhile, I had to deal with a new problem at Lucky Dogs. Some of our more recent hires were allowing the street crowd to hang around their wagons. These newfound buddies were what the old-timers called "pick-up drinkers." They would linger near our carts and wait for a customer to put down a beer or mixed drink. If the patron forgot it, the "pick-up drinker" would move in, scoop it up, and gulp the remaining contents. Having them lurking around the wagons was detrimental to business. They had to go.

Another problem was that vendors were coming up short of cash at the end of the night. Most were only $10 to $20 shy of being able to pay their bill. They wouldn't admit to it, but they had either lost the company's money playing video poker or had spent it on booze. They didn't view it as theft. Rather, it was a sort of unauthorized loan, which surely, the company wouldn't mind. They were mistaken.

An even worse occurrence was the more serious problem of a vendor skipping town with all of the cart's money. One such instance ended with a rather unexpected outcome.

As I walked into the shop one morning, a young man wearing a New York Yankees baseball cap and a very distinctive broad-striped shirt was sitting by the front door, filling out an application. Engrossed in the paperwork, he paid no attention as I walked past. Later that afternoon, I saw him again. This time, he was loading a cart with dogs, buns, and condiments. Like earlier, he barely glanced in my direction.

That night, I ended up working until after 10 p.m. Once I left the shop, I headed for the interstate via a downtown entrance ramp. Just as I was about to merge onto I-10, something caught my eye. Standing on the shoulder of the highway was a hitchhiker wearing a broad-striped shirt and a baseball cap. "It can't be him," I thought. "He's working a cart."

But it certainly looked like him. So, I pulled over and backed up. Sure enough, it was the new vendor, standing with his thumb out, hoping to catch a ride west. I obliged, but I explained that we had to make one quick stop. I exited the interstate, made a few turns and within minutes, we were parked in front of New Orleans Central Lockup. Sheriff's deputies and NOPD officers were constantly entering and leaving the facility. I turned and asked my rider if he recognized me.

"No," he replied. He couldn't say that he did.

"Think back to when you were filling out the application earlier today."

Suddenly, his face tensed. He started squirming in his seat. He would have bolted, but he had nowhere to run. I explained that I would like the money that he had just stolen from the company.

He was shaken. He looked at the police, at Central Lockup, and back at me. He quickly started pulling wadded-up bills out of his pockets.

I took what I estimated to be the company's portion and headed back to the office. As for him, he could walk back to the interstate or ask one of the nice officers for a ride. It was his choice.

By the time I arrived at the shop, Paul Hager, our night manager, had already located the abandoned cart and pushed it in. After taking into account what I had just collected, the thief had gotten away with less than $3. Within minutes, I was once again heading home.

Days later, I received a call informing me that my friend and mentor, Stephen Ambrose, had died. Cancer had taken one of America's greatest historians. Only because of his persistence had I turned my master's thesis into a biography of Andrew Higgins, a decision that resulted in my appearing in several documentaries. And it was Steve who first suggested that I turn my notes on Lucky Dogs into a book. The result was *Managing Ignatius*, for which I was interviewed by Terri Gross on her national NPR radio program *Fresh Air*. Because of Steve, I had had more than my fifteen minutes of fame.

I felt honored when asked to speak at his memorial service at the National World War II Museum in New Orleans. Others on the platform that day included former President George H. W. Bush, Tom Brokaw, former Sen. George McGovern, and Dr. Gordon Mueller, CEO of the museum and Steve's closest friend.

Though Ambrose is gone, his influence in my life and in the lives of all of those he taught will last forever. Because of him, my interest in history never waned, but rather grew stronger.

Shortly after Ambrose's death, I discovered that our night manager, Paul Hager, had been spending his time playing slot machines at Harrah's Casino, which was only two blocks from the shop. One evening, he hit for $4,000.

My two main concerns were: Is he addicted to gambling, and is he playing the machines on company time? At night, there was limited supervision, and often when I called the shop, there would be no answer. When I finally reached him, he would always say that he had been on the street checking on vendors or delivering supplies. Was he telling the truth, or had he been at the casino all the while? I had to find out.

If it turned out that he was playing the slots, it was possible that a losing streak might prompt him to finagle the nightly sales figures so he could cover his losses with company funds. Other than the potential gaming addiction, Hager had been doing much better than most of his predecessors. He was efficient at making the money collections, and he would run supplies out if a vendor needed them. He always checked to make certain that the crew wasn't selling store-bought franks and pocketing the cash. Plus, at the end of the night, he was finalizing the vendors' paperwork and getting them out of the building in record time.

Hager, however, wasn't the only one who needed to be watched. Longtime vendor Jack McCormick was presently handling the cart-washing duties. As long as he was sober, he did a fair job of cleaning both the wagons and the shop, but once he started hitting the sauce, productivity disappeared, and usually so did he—often for days.

One morning when I walked into the building, Jack was busily scrubbing the floor. Later, on my way out for lunch, he was still fine, but by the time I returned, he was smashed and out cold, but he wasn't lying on the ground; Jack had more style than that. He had passed out leaning backward over a flat-seated wooden barstool, right in the middle of the shop's entrance. His back was arched, his arms were gracefully reaching for the floor, and his head was dangling a foot above the concrete. A soft breeze coming in from the open doorway was gently blowing through his uncut hair. Looking at him made me think of *Swan Lake*. It also made me think that it was time to bring in a temporary replacement.

Later that afternoon, a second problem arose. This one involved a vendor who must have gone brain-dead. The vendor, Scott, was putting on an apron just before pushing his wagon out to the street. Aprons are not part of our company uniform. When he turned around, I could see that printed across the front of the apron in huge letters was the phrase, "Will Cook for Sex." Unquestionably, the apron had to come off. I explained that its wording was inappropriate and that we were operating on city streets in a tourist-heavy area. The city would object. He acquiesced and left the apron in the building. An hour later, I got a call from one of his co-workers recommending that I " . . . get to Scott's cart before the shit hits the fan."

I walked the eight blocks to his corner. As I approached, I could see Scott standing behind his cart, wearing yet another apron. This one read, "Don't F—k With The Cook."

"Scott, didn't I just tell you that you weren't allowed to wear aprons?"

"No. You only told me that I couldn't wear the other one. You never said I couldn't wear this one."

"You never told me that you had this one!"

"You never asked."

I tried a different approach. "Just so there's no future misunderstanding," I said, "let me make myself perfectly clear. You are not allowed to wear any apron or any shirt with any type of wording on it over your Lucky Dog shirt. If you do, I'll have you pushed in and your days of working for us will be over. Is that clear?"

"Yes."

"Do we fully understand one another?"

"Yep. But can I wear pants that have writing on it?"

He wasn't trying to be a smart ass—he was completely serious. So, I amended my statement to make it thoroughly clear: "No written words on your pants, socks, any type of head gear, coat when you wear one, gloves, any other item that you might wear, any item that you might have with you whether or not it is a piece of clothing, any accessory of any type that is in your possession at any time when you are in or around Lucky Dogs, or any piece of equipment that belongs to Lucky Dogs. Does that clarify it?"

"Yep."

"Now, please take off the apron. You can pick it up when you check in." He wasn't happy, but he complied.

The summer of 2003 was drawing to a close. Outside temperatures had been brutal, and as a result, our sales on the street had suffered. With temperatures reaching the mid- to high 90s and the humidity no lower, people weren't venturing into the Quarter until late in the evening. Even then, they weren't staying long.

Then, Hager's issue resurfaced. Vendors informed me that Hager was constantly playing the video poker machines at Chuck's Sports Bar across the street from the shop. I checked; he was, but only after he was off duty. What he did on his own time was out of our control.

That is, until on September 3, when a money run envelope containing $224 came up missing. Hager swore that he had deposited it in the drop safe only moments after counting it. According to him, the envelope must have gotten stuck in the drop cylinder and failed to fall into the safe below, and a vendor depositing his nightly check-in sheet in the drop safe must have discovered the envelope and stolen it.

Vendors are required to drop the last copy of their three-part check-in sheet in the safe. That way, we're certain that the night manager is not altering the dollar figures on the master sheet and stealing from the company. Hager insisted that a vendor had to be the culprit. I pulled the surveillance tapes, and there, in black and white, was Hager counting the run money. He laid the stack of bills on the desk and sat there tapping his pencil for a few minutes. Suddenly, he picked up the cash and stuffed it into his left pocket. The following night, I called him to the office and showed him the video. He denied doing it.

"How in the hell can you deny it? It's right there on the screen! You clearly stole the money. You forgot about the camera, didn't you?"

"I was taking medicine. I musta done it without knowing. I swear I don't remember doing it!"

"If that's true, then where's the cash?"

"It must still be in my pants."

"Great. I'll drive you home and you can get it."

"But if I took it without knowing, I must have lost it later."

"Cut the crap. You stole the money, gambled it away, and got caught. But don't worry. You actually never came up short. I've already cut your paycheck, deducted what you stole, and added it back into the night's receipts. The deposit is correct. All that's left is for you to endorse your check. As for the video, it will stay in the safe in case I need it in the future."

Hager didn't protest. He had been caught red-handed and knew better than to try and push his luck. Why did he get a break? At the time, we had no replacement. Plus, his *modus operandi* was to take money and then repay it as quickly as possible. A new manager might choose to take it all and keep on running.

Unfortunately, Hager wasn't the only one who ended up doing something dumb. One evening, David Straughter was scheduled to work the corner of St. Louis and Bourbon streets. While pushing to his spot, he ran his cart smack into the back of a Lamborghini Diablo. The cost of an imported replacement bumper was $13,500. Our guys never hit clunkers; they specialize in Mercedes, BMWs, Porsches, and, of course, Lamborghinis.

This was not David's first transgression. He had been given multiple passes for smaller infractions. Now, after taking the full body of his screw-ups into account, I decided it was time for him to take a long sabbatical. As David was leaving, Smitty was returning, luggage and all. New owners had taken over his rooming house and had decided to evict all of the tenants.

In need of a place to stay, we were number one on his list. However, the elevator shaft was locked, and I had the only key. That didn't deter him. He snuck upstairs and created a little bungalow behind a stack of napkin boxes. Every night after checking in, he would slip up to the second floor. Then, before I arrived the next morning, he would leave the shop. On several occasions, he forgot to roll up and hide his sleeping bag. I pretended not to see it. This cat-and-mouse game went on for weeks until he finally found a new place and moved out just before Christmas. So, one problem had been resolved. But a much greater one would soon require attention.

On Christmas Day, I brought two large baked turkeys with all of the fixings to the shop. Anyone associated with the company was invited to stop by for lunch. Most of the vendors had no local family, but they would at least be able to share a meal with one another.

Hager carved the birds and prepared the plates. After eating, a few vendors even chose to work the street. By doing so, they were less apt to feel lonely. Plus, on Christmas Day, tips were fantastic.

Kirk and Mark Talbot going over a catering contract in Kirk's office.

Everything was going so smoothly that the day after Christmas, Mark Talbot, his brother Kirk, and I headed to their dad's deer-hunting lease in Alabama: 1,700 acres of prime hardwoods. The deer were plentiful, the birds were singing, and the turkeys were roosting in the trees. The air was crisp, the sun was bright, and life was good. Then my cell rang. It was the day manager.

Hager had just informed him that he was quitting and leaving town. The day manager immediately called me. I climbed down from the deer stand and headed home as fast as I could—I knew where this was going. By the time I arrived, Hager was long gone, and so was $1,980. Apparently, he had stolen the 10 p.m. and midnight runs. The money from the 8 p.m. pickup, the 2 a.m. pickup, and the money collected at check-in had all been deposited in the drop safe.

It wasn't difficult to figure out what happened. Hager had dropped the first run's money in the safe. Later, the urge to gamble was more than he could control. At that point, he took the 10 p.m. run money to go play the slots at Harrah's and presumably lost it all. Then, like most hardcore gamblers, he believed that his luck was bound to change. So, he took the midnight run money and went back, but his losing streak continued.

He was smart enough to stop before he lost all of the night's gross. He dropped the 2 a.m. run money in the safe and later dropped the final check-in money. He even cleaned the kitchen and did the closing inventory. He had to have been torn between running with what cash he still had and staying and trying to work off what he had lost. In the end, he fled.

Several weeks later, I received a letter in the mail. The handwriting on the envelope looked familiar. It was Hager's. Inside was a $500 money order with a note stating that he would probably be dead by the time I received his letter, but he wanted to apologize for what he had done and explain that he just couldn't control his gambling addiction. He knew that he had to go where he would not be tempted. He was returning what money he had. He also wanted us to apply whatever he would have received on his final paycheck to his shortage. He had stolen more than $1,900. With everything taken into consideration, he had now repaid $1,000.

Shortly after I received the money order, a social worker called. She was spearheading Hager's effort to acquire Social Security disability benefits. According to her, he was seriously ill, and it was questionable as to whether he would recover. She knew about the theft, but wanted to verify the details. She also explained that if he survived and received benefits, his intention was to return the remaining portion of what he stole. No money ever came, and no additional letters ever arrived. As far as everyone else knew, Hager was still on the run with the police not far behind.

We were about to go into Mardi Gras season with no Hager, an undependable Jack as cart-washer, and a newly hired day manager who would miss the first big Carnival weekend because her cat scratched her and the wound had become infected.

Mardi Gras, under the best of circumstances, is difficult. The stress of working in the middle of the massive street crowds hour after hour is enormous. Plus, vendors are on their feet serving dogs anywhere from ten to fourteen hours a day for almost two weeks straight. They lack sleep, they become irritable, and by midnight, the streets are overrun with obnoxious drunks demanding discounted dogs. It's impossible for vendors to get away from their carts to eat or relax unless they

have a partner. It is a twelve-day endurance marathon. And even after
the Mardi Gras season passes, it takes several days before the body
begins to feel normal again.

After Fat Tuesday, it's always my hope that the craziness will sub-
side, at least for a little while. Such was not to be the case in 2004. A
few days after Carnival, I received a call from an out-of-control vendor.
A co-worker hawking dogs from a cart on the opposite side of Bourbon
Street kept walking over and tossing pieces of hot dog buns on and
around the caller's cart.

The bread-tossing vendor was trying to derail his competition. His
plan was warped, but effective: Potential customers began avoiding
the pigeon-laden cart and patronizing the antagonist's stand. The target of the attack was furious and demanding that management take
action.

I headed out to the corner, calmed down the victim, and ordered the
architect of the scheme to clean up the pigeon bait. No further action
would be taken as long as the perpetrator apologized to his co-worker
and refrained from tossing any more crumbs.

True to his word, the following night, no bread was tossed. However, this same vendor put his stool on top of his cart, climbed up on
it, and began dancing on the small wooden seat. Needless to say, he
attracted a crowd. Like at a NASCAR race, no one wanted to see anyone get hurt, but everyone wanted to be there to see the wreck. In the
vendor's case, he managed to pull it off.

Once the crowd size grew to his liking, he would jump down and
begin taking orders. It was a heck of a feat, but not one sanctioned by
our insurance company. I outlawed stool dancing. He wasn't happy,
but he complied.

Later that year, there was a vendor with whom I just could not reason. He walked off his cart on November 27 with $75 of the company's
money, then showed back up just before Christmas wanting to pick up
his ID. There was no way that he was getting his driver's license back
until he paid his shortage. He said he didn't have any money. I suggested that he take some time, work somewhere else, and come back
and pick up his license once he could pay what he owed.

"I'm not going to do that," he responded.

He didn't have another job, and he had no intention of ever repaying the company. "Look," I said, "it's almost Christmas. I don't want to put you in jail, especially for such a small amount. We have some cleaning that needs to be done in the shop. Why don't you do it and work off your debt?"

"I don't wanna work it off. Call the police."

"You don't want to be in jail for Christmas."

"I'm not leaving until the cops come."

He refused to pay, he refused to work, and he refused to leave. What he did do was calmly sit in a chair by the front door. Eventually, I called the 8th District station.

"You're not going to believe this," I said, "but I have a man here that insists on being arrested. He stole money from us and he'd rather go to jail than pay it back or work it off. There's no rush. He's sitting quietly waiting for you. He's no problem at all."

The officers came, and before I could get downstairs, the thief was already in the back of their squad car. The vendors figured the guy wanted to be arrested so that he would have a place to sleep and three meals a day. In street jargon, it's called "three hots and a cot." Combine that with not wanting to be alone on Christmas, and you probably have the reason as to why he rejected any plan that would have kept him out of jail.

The day after Christmas, we started preparing for New Year's Eve and the Sugar Bowl. Both days bring huge crowds to the French Quarter. On New Year's Eve, a vendor named Choya was working his cart at Conti and Bourbon streets outside the Royal Sonesta Hotel when a young college student walked up and ordered a plain Lucky Dog. Choya handed the steaming hot dog to the young man, who walked to the middle of Bourbon Street and handed it to his friend. His friend immediately struck the pose of a football center, at which point the purchaser backpedaled to the position of a punter. The center hiked the Lucky Dog to the punter, but once airborne, the dog flew out of the bun. Before it could be retrieved, the crowd had trampled it. Not discouraged, the young man calmly walked back to Choya and purchased a second Lucky Dog. Attempt number two also failed. The cycle repeated a total of four times until the punter finally received a dog in a bun and kicked it high above the massive crowd. With his hands victoriously raised over his head, he disappeared down the block.

Later that evening, a couple visiting New Orleans also stopped by Choya's cart. It was a tradition that they dine at his wagon when in town. After downing their dogs and chatting with their favorite Lucky Dog man, they hit the streets for a night of partying. Shortly after ringing in the New Year, the gentleman, an ophthalmologist, began displaying the effects of over-celebrating, growing loud and belligerent. An officer tried to calm him, but the man was argumentative. The officer grew frustrated, and he finally gave up and arrested him.

The man's wife, knowing no one else in town, turned to Choya for help. Choya knew that it would be several hours before her husband would be processed and ready for bond. He suggested that she go to her room in the Royal Sonesta Hotel right behind where his wagon was positioned and rest. Once he was off work, he would accompany her to Central Lockup, which is exactly what he did.

Choya is always neat, clean, and well dressed. The officer at the desk looked at him and asked the woman if this was her attorney.

"No, sir," the woman responded, "this is my hot dog vendor." It took a while, but the doctor was released.

Mardi Gras, like New Year's, tends to bring out the lunatics. The 2005 Carnival season proved to be no exception. On Fat Tuesday, at the corner of Bienville and Bourbon, just behind John Burris's Lucky Dog wagon, an inebriated reveler was leaning against the wall of a bar and babbling to no one in particular. Several times, Burris asked him to move on down the block so as not to hurt his sales, but the man refused.

Half a pint later, the reveler dozed off. As he slept, he swayed back and forth in an attempt to remain upright. The swaying caused his pants to slip farther and farther down until they finally dropped below his knees. Lacking undergarments, he would have been totally exposed were it not for his long shirttail.

It did not take long for the man to become one of the street's most popular photo ops. Passers-by would lift his shirt and take individual, and in some cases group, pictures with him. Burris, not wanting to miss out on a financially lucrative opportunity, put a tip cup on the sidewalk in front of the man. He figured he might as well make a few dollars before the guy ended up in the back of a paddy wagon.

The craziness on the street continued until midnight. Then, as is tradition, the police announced via bullhorns and car speakers that Mardi Gras was officially over, and they began clearing the streets. First to make their way down Bourbon Street were the mounted officers. They were followed by side-by-side squad cars, and then by water wagons spraying the streets, sidewalks, and anything or anyone that still happened to be out. The last of the die-hard partygoers got the message and headed home or back to their hotels.

By the following afternoon, life in the Quarter had returned to its normal state of abnormality. Everything was still crazy—just not on the scale of hundreds-of-thousands-of-intoxicated-people-crazy.

Even life at the shop was returning to its warped state of normalcy. It remained that way until Memorial Day. That afternoon, our day manager ran into my office claiming that Michael, our present cart washer, was threatening to stab a vendor with a screwdriver. I went downstairs to defuse the situation.

The frightened vendor accused Michael of getting in his face and threatening to "send him to see his mammy." It was hard, but I kept my composure. It was as if I was in a scene in a low-budget 1930s black-and-white movie. Unfortunately, this was real. The vendor believed that given the chance, "Little Mike" would run him through with the tool. Thus, he was quitting. While I was questioning Mike, the terrified vendor took off.

Naturally, Mike denied everything. A few minutes later, he, too, left the building. Within minutes, he returned with the recently frightened vendor. I was concerned that a screwdriver might have been used to help change the man's mind.

The shop was now calm, but the streets were deadly. A person we knew corroborated a story that a vendor had told us months earlier. The person and a group of friends had made a trip to the Quarter, and while they were standing on the corner of St. Peter and Bourbon streets, they heard what sounded like firecrackers. However, it was not fireworks—it was gunfire.

A middle-aged gentleman had just bought a Lucky Dog and was walking away from the cart when he was struck by a stray bullet. He fell against the wall of the club behind him and slid to the ground. As he descended, he held his right hand above his head as if he was trying to keep it above water. In that hand was his recently purchased chili dog. He had taken a bullet and fallen to the sidewalk, but the dog rested unscathed in his grasp. The ambulance arrived. Thankfully, paramedics diagnosed the wound as non-life-threatening.

The customer had taken a bullet but had refused to give up on life or his Lucky Dog. Now *that's* impressive. Not giving up the dog was either a reflex action or product loyalty. I prefer to believe it was the latter.

5

KATRINA

According to *Science Daily*, Hurricane Katrina was the eleventh tropical storm, fifth hurricane, third major hurricane, and second Category 5 storm of the 2005 Atlantic season. The storm formed over the Bahamas, reached tropical storm status a day later on August 24, and on Thursday night, August 25, the Category-1 hurricane moved across Florida's Miami-Dade County on its way to the warm waters of the eastern Gulf of Mexico. Once there, it was predicted that Katrina would strengthen, turn north, and make landfall in the Florida Panhandle. There were other computer models predicting a more westward track, but even those projected the odds of Katrina landing a direct hit on New Orleans at 17 percent or less.

My wife Jane, our twenty-five-year-old son Jeff, and I closely monitored the situation because we were planning to head to North Carolina the following morning for a twenty-fifth wedding anniversary party for Jane's brother, Tim, and his wife Cathy. Our oldest son, Chris, and his girlfriend Lizie lived in Asheville, so the trip would be an opportunity for our entire family to be together. After taking all of the various weather projections into consideration, we were confident that the storm was not going to pose a direct threat to New Orleans.

On Friday morning, August 26, we boarded a flight heading east. At 11 a.m. EDT, as we cruised at 37,000 feet, the National Oceanic and Atmospheric Administration announced that they expected Katrina to become a Category 2 storm by Saturday morning. The majority of projections still predicted landfall somewhere in the Florida Panhandle.

By 5 p.m., the forecast had the storm intensifying to a Category 3. Sustained winds would be in the 115-mph range. Moreover, for the first time, projected landfall was moved from the Panhandle to just west of the Alabama-Mississippi state line. This westward drift was a huge concern.

At 4 a.m. EDT on Saturday, Katrina was officially upgraded to a Category 3. At 5 p.m. that afternoon, the mayor of New Orleans began calling for a "voluntary evacuation" of the city.

An hour later, the National Weather Service announced that New Orleans had a 45 percent chance of being hit by Katrina, which would likely become a Category 4 or 5 storm. Depending on who you listened to in the media, the city had two possible fates: It was either going to become "a vast cesspool tainted with toxic chemicals, human waste, and coffins released from the city's legendary cemeteries," as reported by the Associated Press; or as some in the media were speculating, at the last minute Katrina, like numerous hurricanes before, would turn east and miss the city, and the resulting damage would be minor.

Several times during the Saturday night party, I slipped into another room and checked for updates. They were disturbing. New Orleans had become ground zero and was expected to feel the full impact of the storm.

I called the shop and recommended that anyone who had not evacuated do so immediately. At 11 p.m., as the North Carolina festivities tapered off, Jane, Jeff, and I discussed the possibility of returning home as quickly as possible. Those aware of our plans thought that we had lost our minds. We were safe and out of harm's way. The mayor had called for a voluntary evacuation. Why in the hell would any sane person want to fly into harm's way when everyone else was fleeing to get out of it?

We understood their concerns, but if the doomsday soothsayers were correct and the city was about to be obliterated, then everything we owned was about to be lost. All you had to do was look at the size of the storm, the potential 150-mph-plus winds, and the storm surges that could possibly overtop the levees to realize that the apocalyptic predictions could be dead-on.

After listening to the latest updates and taking everything into consideration, we decided that there was enough time to return home; grab important documents, photo albums, insurance policies, and everything else that we deemed irreplaceable; cram them into our two vehicles; and be back out of town long before Katrina's fury arrived. But we had to act immediately.

There were no early flights out of Asheville. The earliest available flight was out of Greenville, S.C., at 6:30 Sunday morning. With less than three hours of sleep, we were up and on our way. From Greenville, we flew to Houston, hoping to make a connecting flight to New Orleans. By the time we touched down in Texas, Katrina was a monstrous Category 5 hurricane with winds of 160 mph and a width of almost five hundred miles. The National Hurricane Center was describing it as "potentially catastrophic."

All commercial flights into New Orleans had been canceled. However, Continental Airlines had one plane specifically assigned to transport temporary staff to the Crescent City to relieve the company's local employees. This would give the New Orleans–based staff time to evacuate their families. Before conditions deteriorated and became dangerous, the replacements would be flown back to Houston. Because our older son, Chris, was a Continental Express pilot, we were eligible for the flight, if there was room.

As we sat waiting to hear whether we would be allowed to board the plane, a flight attendant sitting across from us broke into tears. We asked if there was anything we could do.

"No," she sobbed. Then she blurted out that she and her husband lived an hour or so outside of New Orleans. He was a high school football coach. She had been pleading with him all day, begging him to pack their belongings. She wanted him to be ready to evacuate as soon as she arrived home. Instead, he wanted to cut the grass on the football field so it would be ready for his upcoming Friday night game.

"Don't worry," he told her. "If things get really rough, we can just hunker down in the field house until it blows over."

She was crying. She loved him, but right now, she wanted to kill him. He, like hundreds of thousands of others who had ridden out storms in the past, anticipated intense winds, heavy rains, broken tree limbs, mild flooding, garbage cans being blown down the street, and an assortment of other non-life-threatening conditions.

After several hours of no electricity, he figured, the skies would clear, the streets would dry, the lights would come back on, and everything would return to normal. Then, as scheduled, on Friday night the whistles would blow, the cheerleaders would cheer, and his high school football team would take the field.

His wife didn't have quite the same vision. She had been following the news, and the storm's size and intensity frightened her. He, on the other hand, had not been listening to the news at all. Instead, he'd been busy getting his own plan ready: that is, his season-opening game plan.

As we spoke, the gate agent motioned for me to come to the counter. Jane, Jeff, and I had been cleared for boarding. As the agent handed me the tickets, she wished us the best and offered her prayers. A few minutes later, we were airborne and heading toward "ground zero." At almost the same time, the mayor of New Orleans was now calling for a mandatory evacuation.

The 737 hugged the coastline as it headed east. About halfway through the flight, the captain announced that the hurricane's feeder bands could be seen in the far distance off our right wing. To the south, out over the Gulf, was a never-ending cloudbank. Was this the storm that New Orleans had always feared? The "Big One" that would track up the Mississippi River, bringing with it such a massive storm surge that it would bury the city under a tsunami-like wall of water? I had no intention of being there long enough to find out.

By 11 a.m., we were home, and Jane and Jeff were stuffing boxes with what they deemed important. While they packed, I headed to Lucky Dogs to secure the building. Doug, his sons Mark and Kirk, and their families had all evacuated the night before. Our night manager and his wife had headed to Texas. Many of the vendors had also left town. However, a few were planning to ride out the storm in their apartments. As they saw it, the French Quarter had survived hurricanes for more than two hundred years, and there was no reason that it shouldn't survive this one.

At the shop, I discovered Bill, our day manager, and three vendors standing in front of the building. Their landlords had forced them to evacuate, and all four were reluctant to go to the Superdome, which had recently been opened as "a shelter of last resort." Instead, they wanted to take shelter in the shop until the storm passed.

I thought about it, and ultimately decided to give them permission. I couldn't force them to go to the Dome, and I certainly was not about to abandon them on the street. Our warehouse, in the middle of the Central Business District, is a three-story brick structure that was built in the mid-1800s. On three sides, it shares common walls with other brick buildings that are taller and stronger. Wind would not be a factor. In addition, the Central Business District and the French Quarter were constructed on the highest ground in New Orleans. The high ground, combined with the fact that our building is three stories tall, made danger from drowning a non-issue.

If the power didn't fail, those staying in the shop would have a microwave available. If it did, which was likely, they had access to 22 propane-heated Lucky Dog carts and an additional 30 propane tanks. In the walk-in cooler, there were more than 10,000 hot dogs. And, if the electricity went out, we had 1,500 pounds of dry ice on hand to keep things cold.

Because of the annual Southern Decadence festival held in the French Quarter every Labor Day weekend, we had anticipated huge sales. In the kitchen there were several thousand buns stacked in racks, ninety-seven cases of bottled water, and seventy cases of Coke products. It was obvious the four would never go thirsty or hungry.

I emptied the safe and made a final effort to convince them to evacuate. They were adamant that they were not leaving town and they were not going to the Dome. The only thing I could do was advise them to remain in the shop until after the storm passed. I wished them well and headed home.

Jeff, Jane, and I stuffed as many boxes inside the truck and car as possible, placed the remaining containers in lawn-and-leaf bags, and loaded them in the bed of my pickup. At 3 p.m., as we were putting the last piece of plywood over our home's windows, a fire truck came down the street, speakers blaring, "Evacuate now! By law, you must evacuate!"

God knows we were trying. We were tired and beat. We hadn't had much sleep, but we were doing our damnedest to get out of Dodge before Katrina blew into town. We wanted to be beyond the eleven-mile elevated section of Interstate 10 west of New Orleans before the

storm's fury arrived. There's nothing to the left of that section of interstate except swamp, and nothing to the right except the open waters
of Lake Pontchartrain. The hurricane-force winds, combined with the
lake's wave action, could cause driving conditions on the bridge to be
hazardous. If the hurricane didn't kill you, a frightened driver might.

By 3:30 p.m., we were turning onto a westbound I-10 access ramp.
We were easily on schedule to outrace the storm. Three minutes into
our journey, we hit gridlock.

Traffic was inching along so slowly that passengers were getting out
of cars and walking to an ice-cream truck in the middle lane. One ice-
cream man was selling Eskimo Pies and fudge bars from the back of
the vehicle while another walked ahead doing a booming delivery business. They had plenty of takers. State Police estimated that on that
Sunday afternoon, 18,000 people—per hour—were still evacuating
the city.

Feeder bands intermittently brought light rains and mild gusts,
but we were far up the interstate before the torrential downpours and
stronger squalls began pounding the metropolitan area. Eleven hours
later, at 2:30 a.m., we pulled into a north Louisiana rest area. Every
hotel and motel room along the way had already been booked.

Though we had been unable to find a room, we had been lucky
enough to find gas. With hundreds of thousands of motorists on the
road, stations were running out of fuel. Along with the gas, stores also
ran out of ice, drinks, chips, and everything else that a massive population on the move might devour.

We had been up for twenty-three hours. We were tired, hungry, and
in desperate need of sleep. Having finally found a rest area with open
parking spots, we pulled in, put our seats back, and crashed. Hundreds
of other evacuees were already there doing the same.

As dawn broke, the sound of cars starting filled the air. Added to
humans talking and dogs barking, it was impossible to continue sleeping. We sat in our cars and listened to the latest updates on the radio.

It appeared that the Big Easy had dodged a bullet. Acting on that
information, we drove west to Shreveport, then south toward home.
Then at 8 a.m., breaking news reported that water was flowing over
one of the levees protecting the city. That was a problem, but to what

extent? Because there was no mention of the situation being cata-strophic or uncontrollable, we continued driving south.

Later, at 11 a.m., an update reported that the mandatory evacua-tion order had not yet been lifted. Much later, we learned that the 17th Street Canal levee also had breached on Monday morning, and lake water was pouring into the city. Some neighborhoods, according to the report, were already under as much as eight feet of floodwater. Subsequent news flashes announced breaches at the London Avenue and Orleans Avenue canals; the Industrial Canal levee had toppled earlier. In addition, thirty-foot waves had topped the levees in St. Bernard Parish. All access into Orleans, Jefferson, St. Bernard, and Plaquemines parishes had been closed off by the police.

With no hope of returning home—if we still had one—and unable to find a hotel room, we reversed course and headed for my sister's house in Bridgeport, Texas, about an hour northwest of Fort Worth. All the while, we listened to the radio, hoping to get a clearer picture of what exactly was happening back in New Orleans.

Each new update brought more horrifying news. More than 90,000 square miles along the Gulf Coast had been devastated. The magni-tude of the destruction was mind-boggling. Thousands of people were trapped in flooded homes and on rooftops. The death total was pro-jected to be in the thousands, and hundreds of thousands of others were suddenly homeless. The destruction was catastrophic. We lis-tened in disbelief; Jane's life, my life, and the lives of everyone in the storm's path had suddenly been put on hold.

Thankfully, Jeff had been living away from New Orleans. On Tues-day, he headed back to Kingman, Arizona, and to his flight instructor's job. He wanted to stay and help, but there was nothing he could do. The only thing we were able to do was to watch the news in disbelief and wait.

By Thursday we were well rested and, as a result, extremely rest-less. We left my sister's house and headed for Jane's parents' home in Kentucky. As we drove, I was in constant contact with the shop. During Katrina and in the days just after, failed communications had crippled New Orleans' City Hall, the Police Department, and most of the first responders. Yet, the old-style wall pay phone in Lucky Dogs never lost service. I was able to speak with our crew as the hurricane's winds roared through the Central Business District and battered the Superdome. As horrific as things were outside, I knew that everyone inside the shop was safe.

Those in the warehouse kept me informed about the condition of the shop and the surrounding area. Our building had sustained minor roof damage, and wind-driven debris had destroyed the skylight in my office. Rainwater entered, though not in massive amounts.

On Monday morning, the winds had subsided, and Johnny Majoria, owner of Commerce Restaurant, located about a hundred yards from Lucky Dogs, surveyed the damage to his house and his adjacent well-manicured trailer park. A few trees had been uprooted in his back yard and a couple of trailers had been struck by falling branches. All in all, he considered himself lucky.

Johnny then headed to check on his restaurant at the corner of Camp and Gravier streets. After leaving his home on the west bank of the Mississippi River, he drove across the Crescent City Connection bridge and down the Camp Street exit ramp without encountering a problem.

Camp Street was dry, and traffic was nonexistent. Signal lights were out, but there appeared to be little damage in the seven blocks from the bridge to his building.

His restaurant was just as he had left it on Friday—minus, of course, electricity. The boxes of shrimp and fish, the roasts and hams, plus everything else in the freezer and refrigerators were still well within the safe-for-consumption zone. Wanting to keep it that way, he headed back home to pick up his portable generator. He figured his worst-case scenario was that he would reopen by Friday.

After loading his generator, he headed back to Camp and Gravier. Unfortunately, by then roadblocks had been set up at the bridge's onramps, and the police refused to let him through. According to the officers, the generator would be of no use; they told him that his restaurant must now be under at least four feet of water.

Commerce and Lucky Dogs are located only a few blocks from the river and in an area that, for thousands of years before the construction of the levees, had flooded when the Mississippi overflowed its banks. Because of the silt deposited by those floods, both buildings are located in one of the higher sections of the city. Johnny didn't know it, but his restaurant was not under water, and neither were we.

Meanwhile, I was on the phone with the shop, discussing the possibility of pushing carts eleven blocks to the Dome to help feed the evacuees. Our power was out, but the meat was being kept cold by blocks of dry ice. The ice blocks, however, would not last forever. Before the dogs spoiled, we hoped to cook and give away as many as possible.

Our plan failed. Floodwaters moved into downtown. Between the shop and the Dome, there were now areas where the water was waist-deep. In fact, between Lucky Dogs and the Dome, rescuers were using a section of roadway as a boat launch. Pushing carts to the stadium was out of the question.

What we were unaware of was that there were more than 20,000 desperate people congregated at the New Orleans Convention Center. The carts could have made it there. The Center is located only nine blocks from the shop, toward the river, and the streets between the two remained dry. However, upon learning about the stranded masses, we also heard rumors of shootings, rapes, and general lawlessness taking place there. Unless fully armed protection could be provided, the crew wanted no part in trying to serve hot dogs to thousands of people in such a volatile atmosphere.

Karl, one of those who rode Katrina out in the shop, later described the situation like this: "Right after the storm, you were on your own. There was no law. You didn't have no protection. Absolutely none, until the Guard got here. Up until then, we stayed close to the shop. Safety in numbers. We didn't venture out until the National Guard was here and had some type of control."

What our guys did do was dispense cases of water and boxes of hot dogs to people who passed down Gravier Street looking for food and drink. We also tried to get the police and the National Guard to transport our products to the Superdome and the Convention Center, but they refused.

The flooded streets prohibited the carts from getting to the Dome, but the rising water didn't seem to faze the looters. On Monday and Tuesday, retail outlets on Canal Street and throughout the city were vandalized. Thieves made off with everything that could be carried, dragged, transported by hand, or moved in stolen grocery carts.

On our block, Chuck's Sports Bar was broken into, but a police car happened to drive down the street and the looters scattered before any real damage was done. Commerce Restaurant on the corner did not fare as well. Sometime after Johnny left on Monday and before he was allowed to return on Thursday, the restaurant's glass front door was smashed. Thieves stole his register's opening bank, took a jug of half dollars, and cut the locks off his three video poker machines.

Theft is one thing, but besides taking the cash, they urinated and defecated in the building and in the refrigeration boxes, ice machine, soft drink coolers, and even on old photos of Johnny's ancestors that had been taken out of the cabinet drawers. One of the few parts of the building left untouched and still as clean as they had been at the close of business on Friday were the two restrooms.

Johnny's antique cash register had been shoved off the counter and it broke apart as it hit the floor. There was absolutely no reason to destroy it. Its cash drawer had been left open so that it would be obvious to everyone that it was empty.

No food, bottled water, bottled soft drinks, or bread were taken from the restaurant. The only thing missing was canned beer and a few bags of chips. Johnny understood the need to survive and would never have been upset with anyone taking food and drink, but the looters who wrecked his establishment weren't desperate people starving or dying of thirst. They weren't even seeking shelter. They were simply opportunistic low-class thieves.

Yet Lucky Dogs was not vandalized, and there was a reason. The manager and five vendors successfully rode out the storm in our building. In fact, they even invited two additional people to join them shortly after I left. One was the ex-vendor Karl. The other was his girl-friend. Karl had not worked for us for some time, mostly because of his explosive and often confrontational personality.

Shortly after taking refuge at the shop, Karl discovered a replica of a Bowie knife—a large, razor-sharp, heavy-duty Rambo model that someone had left behind. It shouldn't have even been in the building, but it was, and Karl happened to find it. Without question, he was the alpha male. Generally, when I called in the storm's aftermath, it was Karl who answered the phone. Seldom did I get to speak with our day manager, Bill.

According to Karl, he and Bill had gotten along fine. "Me and Bill," Karl once said of the situation, "took a family who lived over in the Quarter some water, bleach, and toilet paper. They had a Port-O-Let near their house that they could use. They had small children and needed help." On another occasion, Karl recalled, "Bill and I walked up to Harrah's [the casino near the riverfront, where the New Orleans Police Department had set up a command station] to let them know that we were here, how many, and our names. Hell, I knew the cop that we gave the information to 'cause he's arrested me a couple of times. As for the cops," he continued, "they mainly stayed at Harrah's. That was their base. The National Guard was the ones on the road. They had instructions: if fired upon, shoot. Until the sewerage [in the shop] backed up, it was cool. We'd take buckets down the block and get flood-water to refill the toilet so we could save the good water."

On Wednesday, two days after the storm, a few of those who had taken shelter in the shop decided that it was time to leave. Bill was one of the first to go. He was the only one of the group who had gone out wading through the floodwaters. "Bill went to his house to get some of the things he couldn't afford to lose," Karl later said. "Sentimental, can't-be-replaced type things. Like pictures—can't be replaced because the people in them are dead. There'll never be another picture of great granny cause she's done with. He just had it in his head he's goin'. I didn't know he'd left. He left that morning before I woke up, or I'd gone with 'em. When he came back, he had a big old bag full of stuff."

Of Bill's return, Karl said that they "scrubbed him down good because he had been out in that water. We used Dawn," he continued, "and then rinsed him off. He started 'hiving up' later. He said, 'I gotta go.' We said, 'Go.' Craig left with him. The only reason I didn't leave with them was because Jack [McCormick] wasn't feeling that well."

Bill was concerned because he believed that the swollen areas on his body were spider bites. No one else in the shop had any such marks. It is possible that the skin irritation was caused by the toxic floodwaters, or it's possible that floating spiders had indeed crawled on him and bitten him as he waded to his apartment.

No one else wanted to leave, so Bill handed the keys to McCormick and then headed for the Convention Center in the hope of finding medical attention and a ride away from the ungodly conditions.

As each day passed, I could tell through talking to the guys that the foxhole mentality in the shop, the "us-against-the-storm" feeling, was being replaced by an "every-man-for-himself" attitude. No electricity, no water, no AC, no hot food, no clean clothes, no workable toilets, no shower, and no way out were all contributing factors. Add to that August's heat and humidity, and the conditions were unbearable. People became irritable, and charged verbal exchanges occurred more and more frequently. By September 4, the day the authorities temporarily allowed residents back into Jefferson Parish, Orleans Parish's neighbor, for four days to check on their property, there were only two people left in the shop: Karl and Jack. Karl liked Jack, perhaps because Jack was older and not a threat to his alpha-male status.

Those who left the shop told me later that it was only because of Karl that the shop was never ravaged. On at least two occasions, street thugs walked up to the entrance and threatened to enter and take whatever they wanted. Karl responded by pulling out his Rambo knife, looking at them with his cold, steely eyes and asking, "Who wants to die first? I can't get all of you, but I sure as hell can take out a couple of you before you get me. I don't mind dyin'. Do you?" No one ever challenged him. They'd take one look at the disheveled, longhaired crazy man and say, "That motha f—ker's nuts."

In my calls to the shop after the storm, I repeatedly tried to convince Karl and Jack to lock the building and evacuate. They refused. By now, they had heard the horror stories about the Dome and the Convention Center and wanted no part of those locations. They rejected any suggestion about leaving, so I assured them that as soon as the State Police opened the roads, I would come for them. They didn't believe me. They figured no one would leave a comfortable air-conditioned place and drive into hell for them. Karl even remarked, "Cuz, I believe you're comin' about as much as I believe my ex-old lady's comin' back. And I know that shit ain't happenin'."

Like the US Marines, Lucky Dogs leaves no man behind. As soon as the official announcement was made that the barricades were being removed for four days to allow Jefferson Parish residents to inspect their property, I filled my truck with gas, filled seven additional gas cans with fuel, strapped them in the back of the pickup, and Jane and I headed home. Without electricity, even the gas stations that hadn't flooded would be incapable of pumping gas. Carrying backup fuel was a necessity.

The closer we got to New Orleans, the more crowded the roads became. We passed convoy after convoy of power company bucket trucks from all over the United States, heading south to help the over-whelmed local companies restore service. Just as prevalent were long convoys of military vehicles. Our car was but one in a massive move-ment rolling toward the hurricane-affected areas.

We arrived on the outskirts of the metropolitan area about 11:30 p.m. on September 4. There were already hundreds of cars parked on the shoulder of the road, waiting for the state troopers to remove the barricades.

My intent was to pull in line behind the last car, but in the dark, I passed it up and was unable to back up because another car was behind me. So, I kept driving. I continued until I reached the checkpoint. I figured the officers there would allow me to turn around and go back to the end of the line.

Instead, the trooper inquired as to our final destination. "Williams Boulevard," I responded. He thought for a second.

"Well, since that's as far as you're going, go on through."

Officially, the evacuation order was not scheduled to be lifted until 6 a.m. A few miles down the road, there was a second checkpoint. That officer also waved us through. There were no lights behind us, so I assumed the other cars must have been heading deeper into the par-ish and thus had been denied entry.

Jane and I drove east on Airline Drive until we were in the suburbs of a major urban area. There was nothing but total darkness. It was mind-boggling: no street lights, no house lights, not even lights from another car. We were the only ones on the road. We could see the silhou-ettes of mangled billboards and downed trees. Traffic lights were gone.

Stop signs had been blown down. Streets signs were missing. Piles of debris lined the sides of the roads. Smaller debris, such as shingles and leaves, covered parts of the roadway. Storm-damaged rooftops took on bizarre shapes in the night. Telephone poles were either leaning or were entirely on the ground; power lines draped across bushes and dangled from trees. The word "surreal" is often overused. In this case, it is an understatement.

Just after midnight on September 5, we arrived home. It was dark, but we could tell by the line of leaves and trash covering our driveway and extending across the front yard that the floodwaters had stopped about six feet from our front door. Like just about everyone else in our neighborhood, we were incredibly lucky. We had been spared major damage. We had a few missing shingles, our wooden fence had been blown down, and broken tree limbs covered the yard. Inside, there was some wet sheetrock, and the contents of the refrigerator's freezer had defrosted and oozed out onto the kitchen floor. The freezer in the garage suffered the same fate, but the stench there was even worse, because it had been filled with shrimp, fish, and raw venison. Other than the fact that the two floor areas looked like a chemical dump and a maggoty, gagging smell filled the house, we had been spared. We had a house, and we had all of our personal belongings. We understood just how fortunate we were. We were among the lucky few.

Using light furnished by a battery-operated lantern, Jane went to work cleaning up the mess while I removed the plywood from the windows. Sometime after 4 a.m., we called it a night, but the heat and humidity made sleeping impossible; there was no breeze blowing through the open bedroom windows. So we pulled the mattress off the bed and dragged it to the living room. At least there, we had a slight—albeit warm—cross-breeze blowing in through the living room window and out through the open kitchen window.

I was tired. I wanted to sleep, but I was somewhat concerned about possible looters in the neighborhood. Just in case, on the floor beside me were my Browning .380 semi-automatic pistol and my 12-gauge double-barrel shotgun. Just before dawn, I dozed off.

When I awoke, my focus was immediately on rescuing Karl and Jack. I tried heading downtown via the interstate. Floodwaters made

Airline Drive taken September 5, 2005. I was trying to make it to the shop to rescue Jack Mc-Cormick and Karl.

the roadway impassable. Next, I tried Airline Drive. It, too, was underwater. In fact, boats were using the highway as if it was a bayou.

My third choice was Earhart Expressway. I drove about two miles on the expressway toward the city before it turned into a lake. I wheeled around and headed back the way I came, eventually exiting through what would typically have been an entrance ramp. It wasn't a problem; no other cars were on the street.

After three routes failed, I tried Jefferson Highway. More water. I made a right turn and headed toward River Road. Along the Mississippi River levee, the roadbed was higher. Flooding there was not a problem, but the officer at the parish line roadblock was. He refused to allow me through.

I returned home. Then I thought about the West Bank Expressway. It was a last-ditch effort, but it was worth a shot. This time, Jane accompanied me.

We crossed the Mississippi River via the Huey P. Long Bridge in Jefferson Parish and drove on the elevated expressway toward town. Floodwaters were not a problem, but there was a checkpoint at the Orleans Parish line. Once again, I was informed that in order to gain access into New Orleans, I had to have an official pass.

The officer didn't care that I needed to rescue two employees or that I was worried about fifty propane tanks being abandoned in a building in the middle of the Central Business District. I tried to convince him that should the wrong person gain access to our warehouse, Lucky Dogs might be remembered as the New Orleans version of Mrs. O'Leary's cow. The officer didn't know any Mrs. O'Leary and he sure as hell didn't give a damn about her cow. Passage denied. End of discussion.

The officer was stressed and obviously had been working long hours. If he was local, there was a better than average chance that he had lost everything in the floodwaters. At the moment, his "citizen-friendly" skills weren't exactly his strong suit. I understood.

I finally got through to the New Orleans Police. They were no help. They had bigger issues. I was informed: "Don't worry about it. Your guys will eventually be rescued and chances are no one's going to blow up the tanks."

"Right," I thought. "Chances are no one's going to loot the city, either."

I drove over to the State Police's Troop B headquarters in Kenner. Maybe they could use the propane. All they had to do was go pick up the cylinders, but they, too, had more problems than they did staff. All of the possible channels had proven to be dead ends.

Desperate times called for desperate measures. If the truth didn't work, we had to try a not-so-straightforward approach. Luckily, a third party (who will remain unnamed) agreed to lend me his official police pass. His company had given him the task of delivering food to police stationed at a major downtown hotel. However, at the last minute, his employer reassigned the job to someone else, and he no longer needed the pass.

Though he did not need it, I certainly did. So I borrowed it and one of his company shirts. I made my way to a storage unit that Lucky Dogs rents in Metairie, a part of Jefferson Parish not far from where I live. Our unit was high and dry, and in it was the equipment from China along with products from our airport operation. Within minutes, I retrieved enough cases of napkins, paper towels, and outdated potato chips to fill the bed of my truck.

By now the sun was starting to set and curfew would soon be enforced. I would have to wait until the following morning before I could cross the bridge and attempt to get through the roadblock.

This time, I displayed my newly acquired police pass on the dashboard. The shirt, which was too small for me to wear, was strategically placed across the passenger seat with its logo showing.

The officer now manning the checkpoint must have assumed that the pass belonged to me. He must have also assumed that I worked for the company on the pass because of the shirt draped over the passenger seat. He never asked, and I never offered. He looked at the paper; he looked at the shirt; he looked in the back of my truck and saw the load of potato chips and napkins that he believed were being delivered to his fellow officers. And he waved me on through.

Once beyond the checkpoint, I was in no man's land. My truck was the only vehicle on a major roadway leading to the Crescent City Connection. I was the only vehicle on the bridge crossing over the

The corner of Camp and St. Joseph Streets, September 7, 2005. Nine days after the storm the Central Business District still resembled a ghost town.

Mississippi River, and when I came down the Camp Street exit ramp by the National World War II Museum, there was not a car, human, bird, insect, or animal in sight. There was no wind. There were no sounds. I stopped my truck, got out, and stood in the middle of what is usually one of the busiest thoroughfares in downtown New Orleans.

A city of 450,000 people was now a ghost town. It was as if I was the only person on earth. Then it hit me—what if I'm not the only person, and what if the other guy doesn't want company?

As a precaution, I had brought along my pistol and shotgun. Both were positioned within arm's reach. Being in New Orleans right after Katrina was like suddenly finding yourself in a hostile third world country. You hoped for the best, but you had to be prepared for the worst. I knew that I could protect myself, but I hoped to avoid any situation where it might be necessary.

I climbed back in my truck and continued toward the shop. However, before I made it all the way there, I stopped again. I decided that perhaps it would be a good idea to take boxes from the truck bed and place them on both the front passenger seat and the backseat. I didn't want either guy sitting beside or behind me, mainly because I had no idea as to their mental state. I wanted to take every precaution possible, especially since I knew that one of them was armed. The boxes would force the guys to ride in the open bed of the truck, thus eliminating almost any potential risk.

As I pulled up, Karl was standing on the sidewalk in front of the shop. Jack was off to his left leaning against the building. The rest of the street was deserted.

They hadn't shaved or bathed in days, their clothes were filthy, and their faces were expressionless. I wasn't certain whether, in their current mental state, they were friend or foe. As a precaution, I stopped about fifty feet short of where they were standing. This allowed me time to assess the situation. I knew Karl had the knife. He was my main concern.

I exited the vehicle, but left the door open. Both guns were accessible. I held my hands up and out and said, "Honey, I'm home." Karl smiled. Immediately, the threat level was reduced.

"Grab your bags," I told them, "you're heading for the airport. Before long, you'll be where there's air conditioning, cable television, clean beds, and cold beer."

Karl walked up to me. "It wasn't that we didn't believe that you'd come," he said. "It was how in the hell were you going to get in here. They weren't lettin' nobody in."

When Jack went inside to grab his bag, Karl said, "When you called this morning, Jack was to the point of going to the bathroom on himself. He wadn't movin'. He was conscious and that was as good as it got. If you would'na showed up, I'd a put him on the flatbed and pushed him to the Convention Center. He couldn't walk, brother. Just before you got here, I rode down there on the shop bike to see if they were still evacuating from there. Most of the people were gone. Then you pulled up. Done deal. I believed you'd try. I just didn't think you could get in."

At that point, I took the opportunity to ask if either of them had anything that might not make it through the airport's metal detectors. There was, of course, one specific object I had in mind. Karl pulled the oversized Bowie knife from under his shirt and handed it to me, handle first. "Maybe you oughta hold onto this," he said.

"Excellent idea," I thought. I immediately placed it under the seat of my truck.

Before locking the building, Karl and I took care of one final task. We loaded all of the hot dogs in the walk-in cooler into heavy-duty, sixty-gallon trash bags and stacked them outside on the sidewalk. With no electricity, the walk-in was now far above the food-safe temperature. The only option was to throw everything away, and it was better to do it while I had help and before it got ripe.

As we were hauling out the last of the dogs, a National Guardsman stopped his desert-camouflaged Humvee in front of the shop and instructed us to place the bags in the street beside the curb. He said he would send a truck to haul them off. I was grateful, first for the protection he provided, and second, for the assistance.

After dragging out the last load of dogs, I locked the shop. Before I had a chance to say anything, Karl and Jack had already climbed into the truck bed. Neither wanted to ride inside because of the way they smelled and the filth on their clothes.

I drove off with a sense of relief. The guys were heading for better days, the building was secure, the walk-in was empty, and the knife was safely stashed under my seat.

Upon arriving at the airport, we were immediately greeted by a medical team. Before Karl and Jack were whisked away, I handed each of them $300 in cash. Whenever they reached their final destination, they were going to need money.

After dropping them off, I headed home. Jane's cousin, April, and her husband, Wayne, were there. They were heading to Baton Rouge to spend the night with April's brother and his family, and they wanted us to join them.

Jane suffers from severe allergies. Two things that greatly affect her are mold and mildew. And two things that were everywhere in New Orleans, including in our house, were mold and mildew. We decided that she should accompany them. I stayed behind so that I could work until dark and then start again at first light.

The next morning, the trio returned. Jane went back to cleaning and scrubbing, and I devoted my morning to cutting up fallen limbs, raking leaves, clearing gutters, and bagging trash.

Later in the afternoon, I used my pass to go to Lucky Dogs, where I hauled out thousands of molded buns and wiped down the walk-in cooler's walls with bleach and water. The water came from twenty-ounce bottles that, at any other time, would have been sold from the carts. At the time, it was the only option, because New Orleans had no running water. As a result, almost everything took longer than normal to accomplish. My inevitable slower pace wasn't helped by the fact that in the windowless first floor of the shop, the only light I had to work by was supplied by a single flashlight.

Each evening, Jane would head back to Baton Rouge, and I would work around the house by candlelight. Around midnight I'd stop, lie on the mattress on the living room floor, and, in total darkness, listen to the never-ending sound of helicopters passing overhead. Day and night, they filled the sky rescuing the helpless, delivering supplies, and hauling troops. It is the sound of the helicopters that those of us who returned in the first days after Katrina will remember most.

There were other helicopters navigating the airspace with a different purpose than the rescue teams. Some of them carried huge buckets of water to be emptied onto fires that seemed to mysteriously spring up. Some blazes were accidental, caused by ruptured gas lines; others were the handiwork of arsonists. Rumor had it that some of those lacking flood insurance torched their property so the damage would be covered by their homeowner's policies.

Though people were temporarily allowed back into Jefferson Parish, there were no open groceries, no service stations, no hardware stores, and no mini-marts. In fact, there was virtually no commerce of any kind. Anything you needed was either hauled in, or you did without. I brought several cases of water home from the shop. I simply did not have time to sit and wait in the long lines in order to get ice and the MREs ("Meal, Ready-to-Eat") that were being handed out by the National Guard. I lived on peanut butter and honey spread on slices of wheat bread. It was in our pantry pre-storm, and it was still edible when we returned. We also had cans of beans and corn that we heated in pots on the barbeque grill. We made do with what we had and we were lucky to "have" at all; hundreds of thousands of others were not so lucky.

On the last day that residents could legally remain in the area, I reboarded our windows. Afterward, Jane and I headed back to Kentucky to wait for the permanent lifting of the evacuation order. For most portions of Jefferson Parish, that occurred six days later, but officials were urging everyone to stay away a few more weeks if at all possible. The evacuation orders for Orleans, St. Bernard, and Plaquemine parishes remained in effect. Their infrastructure was still far from being restored.

Home as we had once known it no longer existed. The metropolitan area, for the most part, remained powerless. There were no lights, no drinkable water, no AC, and no working sewerage transfer stations. Toilets could not be flushed without the risk of everything backing up into the house. Natural gas wasn't available because work crews still had thousands of miles of pipes to inspect. All in all, it was an uninhabitable and depressing environment.

On our first trip home, Jane and I had no idea what to expect. The second time was different. We brought candles, batteries, and a several weeks' supply of nonperishable food. We were ready for *Survivor: New Orleans*. We were back for the long haul, and we fully understood that it was going to be a long, long haul before the city and surrounding areas recovered.

Our first morning home, I awoke early, and, while Jane slept, I took an extension ladder and placed it in the oak tree in our back yard. My goal was to remove the top of a cypress tree that had snapped during the storm and landed in the canopy of the oak. Initially, I tried lifting the limb, but it was too heavy. So, I got out my trusty fully charged, battery-powered Dewalt Sawzall, climbed the ladder, and commenced to cutting.

I started by sawing off the smaller branches and tossing them to the ground. That seemed to work fine. Once a sizable piece was cut, I put the saw on "lock" and placed it in a cradle that was naturally formed by oak limbs. I even turned the blade away from me as an extra precaution. Only then did I pull the cut piece of cypress branch though the oak's limbs, free it, and toss it to the ground.

I was as safety-conscious as possible, and the task was just about finished when a gust of wind caused the limb holding the Sawzall to sway. As I was pulling out a cypress limb, the saw flipped, the blade turned downward, and the back of my left hand raked against the blade's sharp jagged teeth. Within the blink of an eye, I had a three-inch gash in the back of my hand.

I climbed down the ladder, calmly walked inside, and rinsed off the cut so as to not get blood on my saw. I applied several Band-Aids, but they failed to hold. By the time I got from the bathroom to the kitchen, blood was flowing again. So, I took a few paper towels, placed them over the cut, and tightly wrapped my hand with duct tape. Do-it-yourself triage; I was good to go.

After finishing with the tree, I started cutting the grass. Every once in a while I would stop, change my makeshift bandage, apply new tape, then go back to work. I was just about finished when the sound of the mower woke Jane. Things quickly went south. Like a bloodhound, she found the Band-Aids and red-soaked paper towels in the kitchen garbage can. Then, she stormed into the back yard to see what dumb thing I had done to myself this time.

I learned that my wife has absolutely no appreciation for the versatility of duct tape. She insisted that I needed stitches. I didn't think so. The tape seemed to be working fine, but to appease her, I agreed to consider it. First, though, I needed to go to the shop and check out the roof.

It had only recently dawned on me that the gutters might be clogged. Water could be trapped on the roof. If that was the case, the weight of the water combined with any coming rain might be enough to collapse the flat roof. Jane wasn't happy about the delay, but she agreed to accompany me—partly out of fear that I might bleed to death, and partly to see what I might do to myself next.

Besides cutting my hand, I had already gotten glass slivers in my eyes on earlier visits to the shop because of the broken skylight in my office. The only thing that made it worse was the fact that it happened not once, but twice. The first time, a pigeon was about to land on the skylight, and I instinctively looked up. The airflow from his moving wings disturbed the glass, and shavings landed in one of my eyes. A few days later, a similar situation occurred, which resulted in a shaving landing in my other eye. Thankfully, no permanent damage was done in either instance.

This latest trip to the shop would give Jane a chance to see the dev-astation between our home and the warehouse; thus far, she had only heard about it.

We headed downtown via Interstate 10. By now, the roadway had been reopened, though traffic still had to pass through a checkpoint on I-10 just before entering Orleans Parish. Officers wanted proof that you had a valid reason to enter the restricted area.

I pulled up and showed the police officer my business card. He glanced at it, then at me, and I swear, he said, "You're Lucky Dogs. Y'all are famous. Go on through." No sneaking in, no commandeering passes, no lying—just honesty and a friendly public servant doing one heck of a job.

Once at the shop, I discovered more than eight inches of dark, murky standing water on our third floor's flat roof. The drains were definitely clogged. I could see light storm debris floating on top and larger, heavier pieces sticking up.

I had no boots, and with the roof littered with windblown objects, I was concerned about stepping on a rusty nail—a risk made even more serious considering the fact that the city's medical facilities were not operational. It was best to avoid any risk. Still, the drains had to be cleared. What occurred to me next was what I consider my "Mac-Gyver moment." I went downstairs and got two 48-quart ice chests. I removed the lids and took the chests up to the roof. I put my left foot in one ice chest and my right foot in the other, and proceeded to shuffle-skate across to the drains.

Our shop is not one, but two buildings that were joined together sometime in the early 1900s. One side has a flat roof, the other side a peaked one. The buildings on either side are taller. The front and rear of our roof has a three-foot-high retaining wall. In the instance that our drains become clogged, our roof can trap a tremendous amount of water.

After making it to the drains, I stepped out of my pontoon slippers and onto the peaked roof. In doing so, I leaned to the right to bal-ance myself. Unknowingly, I placed my hand on a small piece of wood that had a rusty nail protruding through it. The nail penetrated my non-duct-taped palm. Instantly, I was aware that despite my efforts to avoid it, a tetanus shot would soon be in my future. But first I had another problem: while I was kneeling on the pitched roof and unclogging the drain, one of my forty-eight-quart boots had floated away.

As helicopters flew overhead, some reporter probably looked down and thought, "Why in the hell is there an uncoordinated white man bunny-hopping across a flooded roof in an ice chest? Poor son of a bitch must be delusional!" Admittedly, it was not one of my finer moments.

Once downstairs, I informed Jane that I was now ready to do as she suggested and have my hand examined. I failed to mention that I was talking about the one without the duct tape.

Not far from our home, an emergency clinic had opened. Since most of its doctors and nurses had evacuated and not yet returned, the clinic was currently staffed by military physicians.

When the nurse inquired as to why I was there, I explained the saw blade wound and the rusty nail. From behind me, a familiar voice blurted out, "I knew you gave in too easy!"

The doctor removed the duct tape and inspected the wound. Word quickly spread throughout the clinic about the doofus that had ripped open his right hand on a saw blade and proceeded to stick a nail in his left one. Everyone wanted a peek at the cut, because if the skin was moved just right, my bones were visible. I was an instant celebrity, but my fame was fleeting. Another guy came in with a huge rip in his armpit. Rumor had it that you could see right inside. Everyone gravitated toward him. I, however, was not the least bit impressed; he hadn't even used duct tape.

I was almost instantaneously a has-been, but at least I was a has-been with an up-to-date tetanus shot, twelve new stitches, and a wife who kept reminding me, "I told you that you needed stitches."

6

THE VENDORS' STORIES

While the antibiotics worked their magic, I tackled another problem. The 10,000 bagged hot dogs that Karl and I had moved from the sidewalk and into the street had not been picked up by a National Guard truck as promised. Instead, other Guardsmen must have rolled over them with their trucks and Humvees. For almost a block, 10,000 dogs were ground into the asphalt.

When I returned to Gravier Street on September 18, I was greeted by a swarm of flies in a magnitude that hasn't taken flight since the biblical plagues. Because of that, I convinced—though others might contend the term "bribed" would be more appropriate—two city workers on a garbage truck to help me clean up the mess. According to them, theirs was the only operational garbage truck in New Orleans.

After shoveling the last load of the rancid smashed wienies into their truck, they drove off down the street. Accompanying them were cases of water, boxes of outdated (but well-traveled) potato chips, and a cash tip.

For a long time, I was the only one from Lucky Dogs in town. Mark, Doug, and their families had evacuated to Toledo Bend on the Louisiana-Texas border to stay with a friend. Kirk and his family had headed north to his in-laws' house in Oak Grove, Louisiana.

Doug and his wife, Judy, later relocated to their country home in Camden, Alabama, where they stayed for several months. Kirk continued living with his in-laws; eventually, he and his wife enrolled their children in school there. Mark and his family moved into a mother-in-law cottage in the back of a friend's house in Baton Rouge.

New Orleans was no place for children. Hell, it was no place for adults. The city resembled something between a war zone and the aftermath of a tsunami. Even so, Jane and I were home for good, and my focus was on reopening the business. With a 100 percent commission-based salary, no sales meant no income. Nothing trumped reopening. Still without electricity, we had no lights and no working walk-in cooler. Without power, we simply could not reopen. In the end, it really didn't matter because our supply houses had also been devastated. It would be months before they could reopen.

Then there was the fact that hundreds of thousands of other homes along the Gulf Coast had been destroyed. Our local customer base had been, without question, greatly diminished. Aside from the loss of the locals, there would be no tourists and no conventions coming for quite some time. Adding to our dilemma was the fact that our roof had sustained damage, resulting in water seeping into our building in three or four areas.

Because of the seepage, mold grew between the shop's lower walls. Once the roof was repaired, we would have to gut, mold remediate, and re-sheetrock part of downstairs. However, nothing could be done until electricity was restored. Like hundreds of thousands of others, we were waiting for the next flood—one of contractors, carpenters, roofers, plumbers, and electricians.

Some of those who came were legitimate craftsman. Others were nothing more than scam artists—vultures preying on the desperate. They used fake business cards and disposable cell phones. With hundreds of thousands of people frantic to get their homes and businesses repaired, plus a huge shortage of building inspectors, there was little oversight. The bogus contractors had a field day. They had plenty of prey along the Gulf Coast.

We managed to avoid the shysters and reopened on February 16, 2006, almost six months after Katrina. During the time that the carts were off the street, my days were spent volunteering at the shop. I replaced damaged sheetrock, puttied and repainted walls, and restored broken carts to working condition. But most importantly, I answered the phone and informed the vendors who called that we intended to be up and running by Mardi Gras 2006.

As we were trying to reopen, so were thousands of other businesses. One evening, after leaving the shop, I stopped on the corner of Gravier and Camp and spoke with a construction supervisor working on several nearby buildings. I was curious about something: Every day at about 5 p.m., six to ten school buses would line up on Camp and depart soon afterward, packed with Hispanic workers. "They're probably all illegals," I remarked, "but no one seems to be giving you a problem."

"Everyone's using illegals," he responded. "That's who's rebuilding New Orleans. They're doing most of the mold and mildew remediation. In twenty years, if they develop lung problems, there'll be no proof that they were ever here."

It was one of Katrina's dirty little secrets. Someday, many of the laborers might end up being casualties of the storm, but no one would ever know for sure.

As for our vendors, they were scattered to the four corners of the country, but they all wanted to come home. Each had a Katrina story of his or her own.

Donald Plunkett was working the corner of St. Ann and Bourbon on the Saturday night before the storm. At midnight, NOPD officers insisted that he shut down and push off the street. He and fellow vendor Craig Martin headed to the shop, arriving with their carts around 1 a.m. By the time they checked in and finished discussing the approaching storm with their co-workers, it was after 3 a.m.

Plunkett adamantly refused to leave town. Like thousands of other New Orleanians, he figured Katrina would blow over, and by Tuesday, life would return to normal. Martin concurred and invited Plunkett to stay with him until after the hurricane passed. Sometime after dawn Sunday, they dozed off at Martin's place.

Both had worked long hours on Friday and Saturday. They were exhausted. "I slept most of Sunday," Plunkett recalled. "I knew the storm was coming, but I didn't know how bad it was. We weren't watching the news. Just workin' and sleepin'."

When they awoke Monday morning and looked outside, water was everywhere. Martin called the shop. Bill, the day manager, answered the phone and suggested that they make their way to the shop on

Gravier Street. He assured them the shop had plenty of food and drinks and that the building was high and dry.

The two vendors kept watching the floodwaters rise in the street. Finally, they decided they had to get out while they still could. A few of the intersections between Martin's house and Lucky Dogs were already under more than four feet of water. At times, they had to swim, but they made it—tired and wet, but alive nonetheless. They remained at the warehouse for three days.

Plunkett said that on the first day, he mostly stayed inside. According to him, "It was bad out there. The police were messin' with the young blacks."

Once, he was standing at the door when some black kids walked past. Simultaneously, a truck with two police officers in the front seat and four in the truck bed drove by. According to Plunkett, the cops looked at the kids and "just stuck their guns out and said, 'Y'all better get y'all's asses outta here.'"

He also recalled that Karl and Martin suddenly had a stash of about fifteen bottles of booze. He was uncertain as to how they'd acquired them, though he did recall guys walking by on the street selling looted cigarettes, alcohol, and drugs.

Plunkett stayed at the shop until Bill and Martin left to go to the Convention Center. At that point, he, too, moved out and returned to Martin's house, where he remained for more than a month.

Not wanting to freeload, he cleaned the house, picked up the storm debris in the yard, and guarded against looters. When Martin's landlord showed up, the man was so impressed with the condition of his property that he allowed Plunkett to remain there rent-free. It was a win-win situation; the property owner had a twenty-four-hour security guard, and Martin had a roof over his head and a bed in which to sleep.

Daily, as the National Guard patrolled Plunkett's neighborhood, they advised him to evacuate. In their opinion, he wasn't safe there. He ignored them.

At first, he lived off water and hot dogs taken from the shop. The wieners were heated on Martin's barbeque grill using gas supplied from a propane tank borrowed from Lucky Dogs.

Plunkett knew that the NOPD had grills set up at Harrah's Casino, but they fed only those working with them. He also recalled that there was plenty of food available on Decatur Street in the Quarter, but you could eat there only if you were a rescue worker. As far as he remembered, the first food offered to the public were MREs, which were distributed by the National Guard.

About thirty days after the storm, electricity was first restored to parts of Orleans Parish. It was then that Plunkett found work gutting houses and ripping out moldy sheetrock—a job he performed six days a week until we reopened. Proudly, he recalled, "I never asked the government for a dime."

John Burris, like Plunkett, kept his cart out Saturday night until the police ran him off the street at 2 a.m. According to Burris, people weren't concerned about the hurricane; they kept partying, so he kept selling. Once business slowed down, he planned on pushing in, checking in, going home, packing, and leaving town. Unfortunately, shortly after arriving home, he fell asleep and didn't awaken until after 7 a.m.

Immediately, he stuffed extra clothes in his backpack and made a beeline for the Amtrak station. He was too late; it had already closed. Frustrated, he turned around and walked the two miles back to his room in the Garden District, where he sat on his bed, watched the news, and pondered his next move. "Things were starting to look pretty scary," he recalled.

Even so, he once again nodded off, this time not waking for several hours. By then, his alternatives were drastically limited. As he saw it, heading to the Superdome was his best option. Staying at the shop never entered his mind because he had no idea that any of his fellow vendors were using it as a shelter.

Burris was streetwise and aware of what he might encounter in the Dome. He recalled the problems that had occurred when the stadium was used as a shelter in 1998 during Hurricane Georges. Many of those who had taken refuge there ended up trashing the building. Instead of being grateful for the shelter, the evacuees had destroyed bathrooms, stolen furniture, ruined stadium seats, littered the grounds, then had the gall to complain that they should have been served a better variety of free food.

Still, Burris reasoned that from a structural standpoint, the Dome was safer than the old two-story wood-frame rooming house where he lived. Besides, if Katrina ended up being as destructive as the media were predicting, power would be out for at least a week, if not longer. The Dome, he figured, would have food, water, and backup generators.

When he arrived at the stadium on Sunday afternoon, he discovered that the National Guard was in charge. For that he was grateful, even though he had to wait in line several hours before being allowed into the building. Every bag was being searched and every individual was being patted down. It was a concerted effort to keep drugs, alcohol, and weapons off the premises. For the most part, they succeeded.

Earlier in the day, as he was making his way to the Dome, he ran across a longtime street acquaintance. The man recommended that once Burris got inside the stadium, he should keep a low profile and stay out of places that he didn't belong. If he did that, he shouldn't have a problem.

As the storm winds blasted the city, sections of the Dome's roof peeled back. Rain fell onto the field. The Guard, along with a small contingent of NOPD officers, did their best to keep evacuees off the playing surface and out of the upper decks.

In spite of the damage, Burris never felt in danger. However, once the rain stopped and the winds died, he decided to move outside onto the building's exterior walkway. At least the air was breathable there—inside, the stench from backed-up toilets and overflowing urinals was sickening. Plus, the brutally hot August temperatures made staying in the powerless building unbearable.

Outside, he found an open spot on the walkway where he could stretch out and relax. As he lay there on the bare concrete, he could hear others talking. Rumors were rampant. One tale had people being murdered inside the stadium, and another told of women being raped. The truth, as people would later find out, was that the tales were just rumors after all. He also recalled hearing of guys breaking into storerooms, box suites, and stadium offices and stealing liquor and everything else they deemed to be of value.

For the most part, John adhered to his friend's advice. However, there was one exception: driven by boredom, he decided to go on a self-guided tour of the Dome. All was going well until he reached the lower level, where he came face-to-face with an unfriendly character who strongly suggested that he turn around and head back upstairs. Without hesitation, Burris complied. Burris figured that he stumbled upon an area where drug deals were going down.

After the storm, the number of evacuees in the stadium quickly rose as residents who could not or would not evacuate left their homes and headed to the Superdome. By Tuesday afternoon, the estimate had risen from 10,000 to more than 25,000, and still more people were coming. With auxiliary lights, limited supplies of food and water, and an indoor temperature exceeding ninety degrees, security was starting to have problems. Concerns were growing as to whether they could handle the situation if the numbers continued increasing. The decision was made to stop admitting evacuees.

Those turned away were in need of food and shelter and were desperate to get out of the water. Upon being denied entry, they weren't just upset—they were damn angry. Word began spreading on the street that the Convention Center had opened as a shelter. It hadn't, but that didn't matter; masses of people started bearing down on the locked building near the river.

As for the Dome, Burris recalled that the security forces began congregating in "a little tiny area on the outside of the building." Amazingly, according to Burris, food and water, at least in his case, were never an issue. They had been distributed before the storm and he never ran out. When additional troops arrived after the hurricane, the Guardsmen started passing out MREs. As someone who had served four years in the army, Burris knew that the meals were designed to give a combat soldier enough calories to last an entire day. That knowledge combined with the atrocious and unsanitary conditions of the bathrooms made him not want to eat more than one MRE a day. For Burris, the biggest problem was trying to combat boredom.

By Wednesday morning, the floodwaters had stopped rising. Throughout the stadium, the buzz was that rescue buses were on their way. People were anxious. They wanted to get out of the Dome, and they wanted to get out right then and there. Lines started forming, but the buses never came.

What those stranded in the building were unaware of was that Louisiana Governor Kathleen Blanco had, at the last minute, diverted the buses to a rescue drop-off point at I-10 and Causeway Boulevard in suburban Metairie. Her reasoning was that those at the I-10 drop off point had no shelter. After hours of waiting, the desperate people standing in line outside of the Dome gave up and drifted back inside.

Failure of the buses to arrive added to the evacuees' anger, but Burris said that "most people weren't violent; they were just frustrated." With their hope of leaving dashed, they felt more deserted than ever.

Soon after, a new influx of National Guardsmen rolled in, and the situation began improving. On Thursday, September 1, buses finally started transporting the masses out of the heavily damaged stadium. Col. Thomas Beron of the National Guard was in charge of security at the Dome. According to a statement he made to the New Orleans *Times-Picayune*, 828 buses participated in the stadium's evacuation. If each bus carried approximately fifty evacuees, he figured the total number of people transported from the site was around 41,400. The facility had been opened on Sunday as a "shelter of last resort." No one ever anticipated such massive numbers.

Burris ended up leaving on one of the final buses. "The last couple of hours I was there, Harmonica Chuck from the Quarter started playing music," he said. "Then some guys that had stolen liquor realized that they couldn't take it with them, so they gave me a bottle of Absolut Vodka." By then, he also had use of an abandoned cot. In his words, "Between the harmonica music, the vodka, and the cot, I didn't want to leave—at least not for a few hours."

Finally, it was his turn to board. He hadn't showered in almost a week and his clothes were filthy, but according to him, that didn't matter; everyone else on the bus smelled just as bad.

He took a seat and relaxed as his ride headed for its final destination: the Astrodome in Houston. This was the absolute ideal location for Burris, because a close friend lived almost in the shadow of the stadium. Unfortunately, his bus rolled right on through Houston. Updated instructions diverted it to Beggs, Oklahoma.

Burris spent three days there. Using his own money, he eventually was able to buy a Greyhound bus ticket back to Houston, where he stayed with his friend for several days before heading on to his sister's home in California. He was doing what hundreds of thousands of Katrina victims had to do: live with relatives, live with friends, live in a hotel, or live in a motel until they could find a way to get back on their feet. New Orleanians were citizens without a city, a population of nomads. God bless those who helped us—we will forever be grateful.

Burris, or John John, as his fellow vendors called him, returned to the shop and reclaimed his corner as we prepared to reopen for Mardi Gras 2006.

At the time of the storm, four of Burris's fellow vendors—Tammy, Thomas, Terry, and John—were all living in a house on Kerlerec Street, just a few blocks from the Quarter, that Tammy and Thomas were renting. Tammy and John were cousins, and John and Terry were close friends. Tammy had taken off the Saturday before Katrina, but her longtime companion, Thomas, worked and stayed out until 1:30 in the morning. The police never asked him to leave, so, like Burris, he just kept on selling.

All four knew that the storm was moving west, but none actually believed that it would hit New Orleans. If they had, they would have evacuated in Terry's van instead of just pulling it up on the sidewalk in case the street flooded—something that, in New Orleans, could happen after any normal heavy rainfall.

As the storm blew through town early Monday morning with Category 1 winds and heavy rain, all four were awake and watching. Tammy watched as pieces of awnings were blown down the street. She watched as the roof of the car lot office next door to her house tore away and slammed into cars. Tammy, Thomas, Terry, and John all gathered in their living room and raised the windows so the wind wouldn't blow out the glass. Rain shot through the openings, soaking the drapes and wetting the hardwood floors.

As dawn broke, they could see standing water in their courtyard. There was water in the street, as well, but no more than after a heavy rain. On the bright side, their house was an old New Orleans–style raised structure set a couple of feet off the ground on brick pillars, designed in the days before air conditioning to keep air circulating under the house and keep its occupants cool. Those pillars also served as flood protection.

Two blocks in either direction of their house, the streets, for the moment, were still dry. In the French Quarter, there was no water in the streets. But those areas were the exception. What they had no way of knowing was that approximately 80 percent of the city was, in fact, under water, and that the water was still rising.

Unaware of how dire the circumstances were, they left Terry's van on the sidewalk and headed to the shop to push out their carts. With the storm over, they figured people would pour out of the hotels and into the Quarter to eat, drink, and celebrate. They figured sales and tips would be phenomenal because most places would be closed. I was impressed by their determination and loyalty—maybe not their brains, but certainly by their determination and loyalty.

When I later asked Tammy about her walk to work that Monday morning, she said, "It was the wildest thing I've ever seen. We're coming up Rampart Street and everybody, all these street bums and homeless people, are all walking around with big bags full of whiskey bottles and beer bottles. They'd ask, 'Here, you want some?'"

"No, thank you," she'd reply. At first, she couldn't figure out where they had gotten such supplies. Then she heard about the looting. Many of those inebriated souls probably made their way to the Dome and, after being denied entrance there, on to the Convention Center. Others were happy to find something as simple as a dry doorway where they could crash.

After arriving at the shop, Tammy and her crew discovered that no carts were being sent out. Immediately, one of the group declared the time to be "beer-thirty," so they all took off for Johnny White's Pub and Grill on Bourbon Street. The pub had remained open throughout the storm, and its tap was still pouring.

As they downed a cold one, they caught up on the latest news, including the fact that the levees had been breached and the water was still rising. Dumbfounded, Tammy told Thomas and the rest of her crew that it was time to go.

Back at their house, the water had risen above the sidewalk, but it was still below the van's doors. If they hoped to escape, they had to do so fast. However, their gas tank was almost empty. Stations weren't open. They had to get it from anywhere they could; their neighbor's car seemed to be the perfect candidate. After all, he had supposedly gone to the Dome, so he wouldn't be using his vehicle—especially with waters rising at the rate they were.

Thomas cut off a piece of a garden hose and was just about to start siphoning gas when their neighbor's door suddenly burst open and they heard an angry shout of, "What the f—k do you think you're doing?!"

After a bit of negotiating, the neighbor agreed to sell the contents of his tank for $10 a gallon. The water was still rising, and so was the cost of gasoline, apparently. Price gouging had already hit the Big Easy.

Unfortunately, the car had only a gallon of gas. Even so, they packed everything they could into the van and drove off into the dark, murky water. Two blocks later, they reached Rampart Street. From there to the Crescent City Connection and beyond, there was nothing but clear, dry highway.

They drove until they arrived in the city of Ville Platte in the middle of Louisiana's Cajun country, about a two-hour drive west-northwest of New Orleans. The town was far enough away from the Gulf that it had not felt the power of the monster storm, and the municipality opened its undamaged campground free of charge to all Katrina evacuees. In addition, the evacuees were given free use of the city's community center.

During their time in Ville Platte, Tammy and Thomas frequently visited the community center to watch the news and listen for evacuation updates. Locals often stopped by to offer them food, clothing, pillows, blankets, and anything else they figured someone who had lost everything might require. One gentleman discovered that Terry's van had developed mechanical problems and fixed it for free.

"Those people were awesome," Tammy recalled. "They would come in the middle of the night and wake you up and see if you wanted to stay at their house. I didn't want to stay with anyone I didn't know, but they really were awesome people."

After living in the van for more than three weeks, the foursome was finally issued a FEMA voucher for a motel room. They stayed in a motel for a week before deciding to head east to Pensacola, Florida, where John's ex-wife and children lived. John wanted to see his kids. The rest of the group figured heading for Florida sounded like a pretty good idea.

The constant closeness and stress of never knowing what was going to happen next began to wear on everyone. Tempers flared, and in Pensacola, Terry and Thomas exchanged a few angry words. Shortly thereafter, the once-close friends decided to part ways.

Tammy and Thomas discovered an assistance program for Katrina victims fifty miles away in Daphne, Alabama. It offered a rent-free apartment, as long as they agreed to work wherever the program assigned them.

"We stayed there for about three months," Tammy said. "It was tough. They didn't have taxis. The nearest Wal-Mart was a mile and a half away. You had to walk there and back. Every week, I'd tell Thomas, 'Call Jerry. I want to go home.' Once we knew y'all were reopening and Thomas got his FEMA check, we rented a U-Haul and were on our way."

They arrived before we reopened, but Thomas was able to find a job on a truck hauling storm debris. It was hard, physical work, but the pay was good. His problem, like everyone else trying to return to New Orleans, was finding a place to live. Thousands of apartments and homes were now uninhabitable.

They were lucky in that their old landlord offered them a room in one of his boarding houses while he repaired their previous residence, but even then, there was a problem. The housing shortage combined with the huge influx of insurance adjusters, debris haulers, roofers, and construction workers meant landlords could get away with charging exorbitant rents. Housing now cost two to three times the pre-storm price. Large companies rented everything possible and, still facing shortages, brought in campers, RVs, and trailers to house key employees. Tent cities sprung up all over town to provide housing for construction workers.

Locals trying to return and put their lives and properties back together generally could not afford the high rates. Many ended up staying with family or friends whose homes had not been damaged, while others commuted from Baton Rouge or from across the lake to work on their houses. Some had no choice but to move back into their gutted homes, while those who were either not so lucky or affluent found shelter in abandoned buildings, in tents, under overpasses, or in their cars.

Tammy and Thomas ended up paying $750 a month for a single room in a boarding house. The common bathroom and common kitchen were down the hall. It was expensive, but they were thrilled to be home.

On the morning of August 29, while Tammy was watching the storm from her window on Kerlerec Street, fellow vendor Choya Smith was sleeping in a motel room on Airline Highway near the Orleans-Jefferson parish line, about four miles northwest of Lucky Dogs' warehouse. The night before, Choya had worked the corner of St. Peter and Bourbon outside the Krazy Korner club. "Some of the people on the street were panicking because of the storm," he said, looking back. "Some didn't care, and a whole lot still didn't believe that the hurricane was going to hit the city, so they just kept on partying. Some tourists even believed that riding out the storm would be fun."

As he worked his cart, he kept hearing hour after hour that Katrina's track had not changed. New Orleans was still ground zero. Just after midnight, he decided to push in and head out of town. On his way to the shop, he stopped at Smitty's cart and tried to convince him to do the same. Smitty looked at him and said, "But there are still people out here."

"I know, but we need to get the carts back to Lucky Dogs, and then we need to get out of here."

Smitty continued selling. Choya finally gave up, pushed in, then headed home. After eating and packing, he hailed a taxi and headed for the airport. It was 8 on Sunday morning and westbound traffic on Interstate 10 was heavy. By the time he arrived at the ticket counter, all outbound flights were already overbooked.

He had heard that additional flights would keep arriving until about 4 p.m. When that proved to be false, he walked outside, grabbed a cab, and asked to be taken to a hotel. The driver was on his way back downtown, so he dropped Choya off at a motel on Airline Highway, just inside the Orleans Parish line.

Choya had evacuated his apartment on St. Peter Street in the Quarter because he feared Katrina's surge might push water from the gulf upriver, causing the Mississippi to overtop its levees and flood downtown. What he didn't realize was that he had left an apartment in one of the highest sections of the city and was now at a motel in one of metropolitan New Orleans' lowest areas. If the Crescent City was a bowl, as many have described it, then the motel was in the bottom part of that bowl. Choya had been worried about water being pushed up the river. It never entered his mind that Lake Pontchartrain's levees might fail.

The woman behind the counter at the motel was in a hurry. Like hundreds of thousands of others, she wanted to evacuate. She handed Choya a room key and told him she'd collect when she returned. The motel's maintenance man was also in a hurry to leave, but he took a moment to warn Choya.

"I don't think you really want to be here," he insisted. "The lake's right over there."

"But this is far enough away from the river," Choya countered.

The maintenance man responded, "Forget the river. It's the lake that you gotta worry about."

Choya took the room anyway. He had been up all day Saturday and worked the street until midnight, and, once in his room, he stayed awake watching hurricane updates on television until he finally crashed and fell into a deep sleep. It wasn't until the floodwaters were high enough to wet his mattress that he awoke. Alarmed, he fled outdoors and discovered that the wind had died down. He also discovered that four people had already taken refuge on the flat roof section of the one-story motel building. Within minutes, he joined them.

One of the things he remembered most vividly was how quiet it was right after the storm. "The dead silence was incredible," he said. "The wind had stopped and it became absolutely still. I mean, there wasn't a single bird, not a sound. Then off in the distance, you would hear someone shouting from a rooftop in hopes of attracting attention."

Choya and a couple of the other guys decided to go out into the neighborhood and rescue those screaming for help. In a few cases, they brought both the people and their canned goods back to the motel roof. On one of their rescue missions, they came upon a highly over-weight, seventy-three-year-old diabetic woman stranded in her attic. It was 97 degrees outside. Inside the attic, the temperature would have been well over 100 degrees.

The woman had been stranded there for more than a day without her medication. Their plan was to rip out the louvers on the gabled end of the house in the hope that she would climb out. She refused because she couldn't swim. They kept trying to persuade her. They even found a huge chest that could be used as a raft. Still, she wouldn't budge.

Choya crawled into the attic and explained to her that if she stayed there, she was going to die. She was unwavering. He kept insisting that she jump out. He said she started calling him "everything but a white man." It didn't matter; he was not leaving her there to die.

So he got behind her and gave one big push, knocking the woman from her attic into the water below. Within seconds, the others had lifted her from the water and shoved her onto the makeshift raft. All the while, she was cursing Choya. Later, after she was safely on the motel's roof and had been given food and water, she thanked him.

To gain some relief from the hot August sun, the group took what looked like a clothesline cord and tied it to a tree near one end of the building and to a pipe at the other end. Sheets were strung over the cord creating an A-frame tent, which offered at least some shelter from the heat. The tent, added to a couple of cases of water and Gato-rade that had been "borrowed" from the motel's office, put the rooftop ensemble in good condition, at least temporarily. However, the flood-waters continued rising.

Early in the morning, Choya could smell salt in the air. Had the water been from the river, it would have been fresh and there would not have been a noticeable brackish odor. Because of the odor, he real-ized that the maintenance man had been right: He should have been more concerned about the lake. Lake Pontchartrain's drainage canals' levees had breached.

As the water continued to rise, more and more people made their way onto the roof. Choppers started passing overhead—Black Hawks, Coast Guard, police, and others that appeared to be taking pictures, not rescuing people. Eventually, Choya began hearing boats in the distance, but it was hard to tell exactly where they were because the sound of the motors was ricocheting off the buildings.

Two more guys made their way through the water and joined the rooftop community. They had just looted the nearby Circle K Mini-Mart. In their bags was a stash of Vienna sausages, canned beans, and crackers. They offered food in exchange for safety. In Choya's words, "It was a bizarre time."

During the day, he recalled, the tide fell about a foot. The first time it occurred they all thought, "It's draining off!" Then, about six hours later, it started rising again.

Even more people made their way to the motel. Then three dogs swam by and tried to climb up. They couldn't make it, so a couple of guys pulled them out of the water. He said they couldn't just stand by and let them drown. By the time help finally arrived, twenty-three people and three dogs were sharing the rooftop refuge.

At last, a group of five airboats arrived. They weren't manned by the police, or Coast Guard, or the National Guard; the owners were just average citizens doing what they could to help. "They didn't even have radios," Choya recalled. "Back at their makeshift launch, someone would say, 'At such-and-such a place, I saw some people that need to be rescued.' Whoever wasn't out of gas would go back after them."

Choya could have swum five blocks to a set of raised railroad tracks and walked out days earlier, but he didn't know it at the time. The only thing visible from his motel roof was water in every direction and an overpass a few blocks away with people stranded on it. The bridge was dry, but it provided no way to get out of the sun.

His group was lucky. They had food, water, cover, and enough room to lie down. "In the shade with a small breeze blowing," Choya said, "it really wasn't that unbearable." At its height, he figured the water to be almost seven feet deep, judging it against the motel's door frames. Summarizing the whole experience, he said, "All in all, we got along pretty well for a crowd of marooned people that didn't know each other."

In fact, he figured he had been better off on the roof than he would have been staying in his apartment and hanging out in the Quarter. When I asked him why, he responded, "Because I ended up getting rescued and sent to Houston."

Lindsey in front of the shop.

His friends who stayed in the Quarter later told him of the numerous problems they encountered on the street. According to Choya, "It wasn't a nice time. The Quarter didn't flood, but a whole lot of those that stayed behind were alcoholics or addicts. A lot of them were armed and not very rational. And there were no cops around."

After being rescued, Choya was evacuated by bus and transported to the Astrodome. Later that same afternoon, he received a ride to Bush International Airport where he bought a ticket. By early evening, he was in Florida with family.

Choya's fellow vendor, Darryl Lindsey, also kept his cart out on the street as long as he could that Saturday night before the storm.

By the time Lindsey pushed to the shop, paid his bill, and left, it was after 3 a.m. His hurricane plan consisted of riding out the storm in his room at the Dew Drop Inn on LaSalle Street, about three miles from the shop.

Sunday morning, as Katrina churned in the Gulf, Lindsey's brother called from Atlanta urging him to go to the Superdome. Lindsey started to take his brother's advice, but changed his mind. "I just had this gut-wrenching feeling that it was a bad idea," he recounted. "A very bad idea. Everything screamed 'red light—do not go.' It just wasn't right." So, he stayed at the Dew Drop, and, like Choya, ended up sleeping through most of the storm.

By morning, after the winds had calmed down, he went throughout the building checking on his neighbors. All were fine, but the structure had sustained damage. The intense winds had lifted part of the roof, leaving some rooms waterlogged, but for the most part, the building was sound. The aged structure next door wasn't so lucky. One whole side had collapsed, leaving it, in Lindsey's words, "looking like a doll-house where one side was left open." Fortunately, it was uninhabited. Lindsey believed that had that building not been there to block the wind, "the Dew Drop might have caved in."

His room, like the rest of the city, was powerless. However, it was dry. By early afternoon, the inside temperature became unbearable, so he went outside to sit on the curb and smoke a cigarette. While there, he noticed water seeping up out of a manhole cover in the street. He thought to himself, "That's not right. Water's supposed to go down, not come up. Something's weird."

Parked on the street in front of the Dew Drop was a red 4x4 pickup that belonged to one of the Inn's other tenants. A faulty starter had stopped its owner from evacuating. As Lindsey sat on the curb near the vehicle, he watched water continuously flowing up out of the man-hole. He promised himself that if it got halfway up the truck's tires, he would pack up and head out.

Overnight the water continued rising, surpassing Lindsey's criti-cal mark. When his neighbor asked what he intended to do, Lindsey responded, "I gotta go. I don't want to drown in this place." He grabbed an extra pair of tennis shoes, a change of clothes, and a pair of socks.

He figured that when he arrived at wherever it was he was going, he would need dry clothes.

As he walked out of his room, he picked up his cell phone and stuck it in one of the top pockets of his bib overalls. He picked up his camera and stuck it in the other. A few minutes later he, his neighbor, and a few more occupants left their second-floor rooms and headed down the stairs.

Water was knee-deep inside the building. By the time they reached the curb, the water was waist-deep. Lindsey led the group toward the Central Business District, believing they would find help there. The streets were void of moving vehicles; not even high-riding pick up trucks were attempting to navigate the flooded roadways.

Lindsey came across a man floating two elderly people to safety on an air mattress. Another desperate couple was pulling their two children behind them in a washtub. According to Lindsey, anything that could float had been converted into a raft.

As he waded through the murky water, he was fearful of stepping on submerged storm debris, or even worse, falling into an open manhole. His two other major concerns were downed power lines and water moccasins, poisonous snakes native to the Southeastern United States.

The electricity was out, so the power lines really posed no danger, and the probability of running into a moccasin was extremely slim, but in his mind, both threats were real. He described his journey through the black floodwaters as "a hellish nightmare."

While he was concerned about his own well-being, he was probably more worried about his mom in Kansas City. He knew that she would be frantic, and he wanted her to know that he was all right—wet, but all right.

As he waded toward downtown, he kept dialing her number. His problem, like hundreds of thousands of others along the Gulf Coast, was that he could not get a signal. Cell towers were down and systems were overloaded. After numerous attempts, he finally got through to his brother in Atlanta. He asked him to let their mom know that he was safe. His brother wanted him to call her, figuring that she would prefer hearing it from him. "You don't understand," Lindsey replied.

"I've got almost no reception and my battery is about to die. You've got to make the call!"

As he got closer to the Central Business District, he could see people walking on the elevated expressway leading to the Crescent City Connection. By doing so, they avoided the water. Lindsey and his group followed their lead, accessing the bridge via an entrance ramp just a few hundred yards from the Greyhound and Amtrak station and continuing on the deserted expressway until they reached the exit ramp leading to the Convention Center. Like thousands of others, he had heard that the Center had been opened as a shelter. It hadn't, but like everyone else, he didn't discover that until he was there.

People were descending on the building in ever-increasing numbers. They were tired, hungry, thirsty, and in many cases angry about having been turned away from the Superdome. Some were drunk, some were armed, and this time, they were not going to be denied. The building was locked. Someone grabbed a chair and hurled it through a glass door. The crowd poured inside. There were no security or National Guard troops stationed at the entrances. Only after the crowd had forced their way in did the police arrive, but even then, they stayed outside and they kept their distance because they were far outnumbered. At that point, no one had control over the mass of people.

When I was speaking to him about his experience, Lindsey was, at first, reluctant to talk about the horrific sights that he had witnessed. He paused, then quietly said, "While I was at the Convention Center, this lady's mother was having a heart attack. The daughter was begging some cops that had pulled up to 'please get help.' One cop was standing there with an AK-47. It didn't look like a police issue. They didn't even try to help the lady. Her mother died right there in her wheelchair."

Some of those seeking shelter in the massive building were needy citizens who had been flooded out of their homes. They had nowhere else to go. Others piling in were more deadly. There were armed drug dealers and street thugs. The mix of desperate citizens, among them a number of drunks and addicts high on drugs, created a potentially explosive situation, especially considering the fact that there was no law and order.

The actual number of displaced people that took shelter at the Convention Center was unknown, but 20,000 is a commonly used estimate—20,000 people with no working bathrooms, no food service, no beds, no communication, and no one in charge.

Lindsey said if something happened inside the Center, it was handled with street justice. "If someone had a dispute," Lindsey explained, "then—how do they say it in the Thunderdome?—'two men in, and only one walks out.' Problems were dealt with swiftly. It was wild. It was brutal. I tried to mind my own business, because I was just trying to stay alive. I had my camera, but if I had taken pictures of some of what happened, I wouldn't be here. They would have found my body lying out in the street."

Lindsey had heard that there were National Guardsmen inside the building, but he had not seen any. Then, something happened that caused the crowd to panic, and people started fleeing for the exits. He was pushed along in the stampede. Suddenly, at the top of a set of escalators, he came upon soldiers standing in front of an emergency exit. He said they had rifles in their arms and were refusing to allow anyone to exit through those doors.

Unbeknownst to most of the evacuees, there were, in fact, National Guardsmen in the building, but they did nothing to help control the crowd or curtail the violence. A total of 247 Guardsmen had taken refuge in the several-blocks-long building. They were debris removal specialists, not security personnel. Douglas Brinkley wrote in his masterful work, *The Great Deluge*: "They [the Guardsmen] did not even try to restore order; they ducked into a hall and locked the door. . . . On Thursday, they realized that the place was out of control, and they left for good." The actions of the Guardsmen exemplified just how out of control everything was. The Center was deemed too dangerous for armed Guardsmen, so they simply withdrew and left the elderly and the unarmed citizens to fend for themselves.

Lindsey recalled seeing police pass down the street, but in his opinion, their mission was to just keep everyone herded together at the Center. Once in a while, an officer would stop his car, get out, and hold his riot gun in his hand while resting its butt on his hip. According to Lindsey, the cops' only interest seemed to be in controlling what happened outside. If something went down inside, "oh, well." Lindsey said they were as stressed out as the rest of the crowd.

There were children and adults who, in some cases, had not eaten in almost two days. Word got out that the facility's generators were still working, and the food in the big freezers and coolers was edible. People began pouring inside and seizing anything that could be consumed. It was a matter of survival. The mass of people, who Lindsey described as "desperate, uncertain, mad, and unable to believe that this had happened to them," began cooking everything they could grab out of the freezers, after someone found electric skillets in the kitchen. Because the generators were running, the wall sockets still worked. Lindsey said the people at least had enough sense to pull the carpeting back and put the skillets directly on the concrete floor so that they wouldn't burn down the building. "I felt like I was asleep," he recalled. "You see it on TV all the time, but you never expect it to happen to you."

After eating, he went exploring. "The police had you at gunpoint," he explained, "and they didn't want you to leave, but they didn't have enough manpower to cover all the perimeters. So, people could walk away." After leaving the Convention Center, he walked the nine blocks to the shop to check it out. The doors were closed, so he assumed that no one was inside. He didn't need anything and had no real reason to enter the shop, so he never knocked. Lindsey's precaution was fueled by the word on the street—that the cops were shooting people. "I didn't touch anything unless I needed it," he said. "I wasn't going to try and open the door, because I didn't want no cop to think that I was breaking in and shoot me."

He walked across Canal Street and into the Quarter. It was only then that he discovered the Quarter had not flooded. The only damage he saw appeared to be caused by wind and rain. Even that damage he described as minor.

He left Bourbon Street and headed up to Jackson Square. There, to his amazement, he saw four mules huddled together on Decatur Street. Normally, they would have been pulling buggies loaded with tourists. They had broken out of their stable and walked the same route that they traveled every morning. They were at the Square reporting for work as usual. As they stood at their water trough, they had to be wondering what had happened to their buggies and drivers.

Lindsey said that as he made his way through the Quarter and the surrounding areas, he witnessed extensive looting. Any place that had anything of value had been hit or was being hit. People, including some police officers, were stealing all they could. He swore that all he ever took was food and water.

After surveying the damage in the Quarter, he headed back to the Convention Center. Once there, he made it a point to stay in the back of the crowd. He figured if the police ever felt threatened, they might start shooting into the mob of people. Thus, in his mind, being in the rear was the safest place.

There were swollen and rotting bodies on the sidewalk and inside the building, he said. Indeed, it was later reported that several people who died at the Convention Center were left there, to be collected later by authorities after evacuees were bused to safety.

Lindsey said he stayed outside most of the time because inside it was hot, unsafe, and, like at the Superdome, the bathrooms had overflowed and the building reeked of feces and urine. Outside was also hot and humid, and the ground was hard to sleep on, but he felt safer out there. "Even outside," he explained, "you never really slept, because you knew you might have to get up in a hurry in case something suddenly went down. It was bad. There were things that I didn't video because I feared for my life."

He constantly walked the grounds, checking to make sure that his friends were safe. He said one woman, who had her kids with her, couldn't go off and search for food because she didn't dare leave her children without protection. So, he went and found some chicken and ham and brought it back to them. "I didn't have a family," he explained, "so it was easier on me." He stressed that a father or mother might need to go look for diapers, milk, or food for their children, but they were unable to leave because they were scared of what might happen while they were gone. Those were the people he tried to help the most.

On the occasions when he did leave the Center and walk the streets, he only associated with people he knew. "There were crazy people out there. You made certain to stay away from them." He added that there were also those who just weren't too bright, such as one guy who had stolen a big-screen TV. Lindsey said to himself, "Dude, what are you going to do with that? There's no power."

When an influx of National Guard troops finally arrived at the Convention Center, Lindsey said he got even more nervous—mainly because he was uncertain what was going to happen next. At first, he said, it ended up being pretty much the same as before. They wanted everyone in one place. "The major difference," he said, "was with these guys, if you tried to leave, you might get shot. You could go outside, but you weren't allowed to leave." Again, Lindsey never remembered seeing troops inside the building. "Inside," he recalled, "was kind of a no man's land."

With the troops came food and water, but the people no longer wanted food and water. According to him, "All they wanted was to get away from there. They wanted to get their kids somewhere where it was safe. If people weren't scared for themselves, then they were scared for their kids. Some parents weren't watching their kids and bad things happened. It was frightening."

In addition to simply wanting out, everyone wanted the answer to a more specific question: If the troops could make their way in, why hadn't buses arrived to take the masses out? The buses did finally show up on Saturday, September 3, and the Guard attempted to load them in as orderly a fashion as possible. The soldiers announced that anyone with weapons needed to throw them on the ground, or they'd go to jail. Lindsey watched as guys got rid of .22s, .32s, and .38s. According to him, "guns had been all up in the Convention Center."

Unlike the Dome, where evacuees had been searched as they entered, the crowds who arrived at the Convention Center had forced their way into the building with no one there to confiscate weapons. However, as they boarded the buses that Saturday morning, it was different. The troops were there this time, and according to Lindsey, there was no doubt as to who was in control.

The Guard made certain that no one was in possession of guns, knives, drugs, or booze. Once checked, each evacuee was handed a bottle of water and some food and was allowed to board the bus.

Lindsey's destination ended up being an old military base in Arkansas. He figured it had been shut down but that a part of it must have been reopened to help process the evacuees. After being checked in, he said he was assigned to "one of them Bible, Jim-Jones-things. It was like a summer camp with cottages."

Shortly after arriving at the religious shelter, he contacted his mother, and he told her, "If I see any grape Kool-Aid, I'm outta here."

What surprised him the most was that husbands and wives were assigned different housing, and their children were housed in an entirely different area of the camp. In his words, "You just don't break up a family unit. It just didn't feel right. I called my momma back and said, 'Get the family together and get me a bus ticket out of here. These people are making me spooky.'"

In conversation with me, Lindsey thought for a moment, then continued. "I do appreciate what they did for us in Arkansas, but they don't know how to cook. That's one of the main reasons that I came back to New Orleans: the food. I don't know what it is. It's like [in New Orleans] they got a patent on it or something. They know how to do food right. It's just better down here."

After being in the Razorback State for only three days, he boarded a Greyhound bus bound for Dallas, where he stayed with his sister.

Lindsey, like a lot of his fellow vendors, arrived back in New Orleans a few weeks before we reopened for Mardi Gras 2006. But before returning, he tried to start life over in Fort Lauderdale, Florida. "I appreciate my family," he explained, "but I have always been self-sufficient and I wanted to be on my own. When I got to Florida, I was walking down the street with a nice size backpack on and a cop stopped me. He said, 'What the hell are you doing down here?' I replied, 'I'm from New Orleans. I had to leave because of the hurricane.'

"'So all y'all think you can just bring your asses down here?'

"I'm looking at him thinking, 'Y'all have hurricanes, you should understand. I'm not a foreigner. We're all part of the United States.' I'm looking at him thinking, 'How much more can we endure?' I told him, 'Man, I just lost everything that I own. I'm here just trying to start everything new. I'm not down here to rob nobody. I can work if you just give me a chance.'"

At that point, Lindsey said, "The officer just snapped. I couldn't believe it. He said, 'If I catch you down here later, then I got something for you.' In other words, 'get out.'"

Not wanting trouble, Lindsey turned back and headed to Dallas. Luckily, he could afford to do so: Some people in Atlanta who worked with his brother had taken up a collection and sent him cash and clothes to help him start over—exactly what he was trying to do in Florida.

After he arrived back in Dallas, he kept seeing news reports about New Orleans on television. He was not born or raised in the Big Easy, but he said, "I feel at home there. I've been to the east, to the west, up north, to New York, to California. I was born and raised in the Midwest, but I feel a lot more comfortable in New Orleans. I can't explain it. I don't know why. I just like it. Maybe it's the Southern hospitality. It's like putting on an old pair of flip flops or an old jacket. It's just comfortable. I didn't come down to New Orleans to get rich. I just came down here to live a quiet, peaceful life.

"I just couldn't wait for the city to open back up. As soon as they said that it was safe to return, I told my mom, my sister, and everybody that I'm going back. I couldn't wait."

When his bus pulled into the station on Loyola Avenue near the Dome, his first thought was, "I'm home."

The Dew Drop was still waiting for its roof to be repaired, so it hadn't reopened. Lindsey was lucky enough to find a room in an old, rundown hotel. It wasn't what he had hoped for, but it was infinitely better than sleeping under a bridge.

As for work, we weren't yet open, but the Tropical Isle bar on Bourbon Street was, and it needed a fry cook. Lindsey's formal training had been as a pastry chef, but if they needed him to fry, he was their man.

Lindsey paused for a second, then said, "In post-Katrina New Orleans, it's strange. Everything's changed, but it hasn't. People are kind of the same, but not exactly. Everyone's been scarred inside."

The Saturday before the storm, thirteen carts had pushed out to the street. Twelve were manned by what we consider "long-term vendors." All twelve of those regulars returned. The one vendor who did not come back had been on the job only two days.

There was, however, one other vendor who never returned: James Alexander Weathers. Alex had not pushed out on Saturday night. He had worked thirteen of the previous fifteen days. Burned out, he decided to take a few days off. About the time we expected him to return to work, people started fleeing the city to escape the storm. Later, when he failed to show back up, I figured that he must have gone home and decided to stay. If that was the case, though I hated to lose a vendor, I was happy for him.

Alex had potential, but if he had stayed in the Quarter and continued to hang out with people who didn't have potential, then his, too, would begin to wane. On more than one occasion, he and I had sat in my office and discussed what might happen to him—what kind of future he might have if he didn't leave. But he loved music and seemed enamored with the Quarter. He came to New Orleans looking for something. In his mind, he had found it. He wanted to live in the now. He didn't want to think about the future. It was his decision.

Alex was twenty-nine years old. He was a good-looking, good-natured young man. He had attended the University of Kentucky and had ridden his bike all over campus with his friends. He had an amazing laugh. As a kid, he had gone to Halloween parties and spent time hanging out at the ballpark. He loved ping-pong and playing the guitar. He had a caring family and long-term friends, some dating back to elementary school days. He had people who loved him and a girlfriend who missed him greatly. I learned all this in his obituary guestbook. James Alex Weathers was only one of more than 1,300 Katrina victims. His body was found not far from the Superdome. He had been beaten to death.

7

GETCHA LUCKY DOGS

More than two million Gulf Coast inhabitants evacuated to escape Katrina's wrath. New Orleans' mayor, Ray Nagin, estimated that 80 percent of the city's inhabitants heeded the warnings and sought higher ground. It proved to be the prudent thing to do, because in post-Katrina New Orleans, there was little dry ground.

According to Dr. Ivor Van Heerden, author of *The Storm*, 85 percent of the city—148 square miles of urban area—had been submerged under floodwaters. No major US metropolitan region had ever suffered such devastation. More than a million people had been displaced. Some had nothing to go back to. According to the state of Louisiana, 200,000 homes had been destroyed, 45,000 more were declared unlivable, and 15,000 apartments were deemed uninhabitable. Additionally, much of the Mississippi and Alabama coastlines were ravaged. The total amount of destruction was staggering—almost beyond comprehension. Those able to return were wondering if it was worth it.

When Jane and I arrived home, it was impossible not to be affected by what we saw, smelled, heard, and did not hear; one of the most unusual discoveries was that there were no birds. Even the most simple things were not as they had once been. For example, playgrounds were no longer playgrounds; many had been converted into staging areas for a variety of post-storm operations, or trailer parks for workers and residents. Lafreniere Park, not far from our home, was filled with towering mounds of broken trees that had been hauled in from the surrounding areas. Wood chippers worked from dawn to dusk reducing the limbs to mulch. The mounds never seemed to diminish; the tree haulers never seemed to stop.

The streets, highways, and interstate were all littered with trash that had fallen from trucks hauling off the millions of tons of storm debris. Roofing nails were everywhere. For months, getting a flat tire seemed to be the norm. Every vehicle on the road seemed to be a dump truck, trash hauler, military vehicle, or pickup truck pulling a trailer filled with old shingles.

The city officially reopened on October 4, and the destruction that we, the people of New Orleans, faced daily tore at our insides, but we had no choice but to move on—on past the neighborhoods where house after house had boarded-up windows and blue tarps nailed on their roofs in an attempt to keep out the rain; on past the flooded homes filled with people's memories, keepsakes now covered in mold and mildew and inches of mud and muck. The devastation was never-ending. We drove past mounds of furniture, appliances, and water-logged toys. The piles lining the curbs were stacked with belongings that people had worked a lifetime to acquire but now were nothing more than rubbish.

There were curfews starting at dark; constant dust in the air; deserted retail stores; blown-out windows; brown stain lines on buildings marking the height of the floodwaters; and large X's painted on doors or walls denoting who had checked the building, the date it had been checked, and whether there were any bodies found inside. There were shopping malls with no shopping. And then there was the "Katrina cough." Because of the mold and mildew, the airborne dust, the spilled toxic chemicals, and the caked mud that was lifted into the air as people's shoes made contact with the ground, the city's population hacked as if they all had tuberculosis.

Everyone had a story: when they evacuated, where they had gone, when they returned, and what they did and did not find upon returning. But at some point—and the point was different for each individual—you had to stop looking back and start looking forward. We all knew this. We also knew that it would take years before most people could return, but we New Orleanians always have been a resilient group. We knew what we had, and we knew what we could have again.

Houses could be rebuilt; families could be reunited. This was where our roots were. New Orleans was, and once again would be, our home.

There was never a doubt for Jane and me—we always planned on returning. Summer after summer when our kids were small, we loaded the car and traveled coast to coast on interstates and back roads. After they were grown, Jane and I had the opportunity to travel abroad. The more we traveled, the more we realized just how unique New Orleans is. It's compact and tightly knit, but it's an explosion of culture and character; it's red beans and rice on Mondays, beignets, jazz, great food, unique neighborhoods, wrought-iron balconies, marching bands, Mardi Gras Indians, bars that never close, and quaint tropical patios. It's a slow-moving lifestyle, with tree-lined streets, fine-shaved-ice snowballs, streetcars, crawfish boils, great architecture, and a live-and-let-live atmosphere. Like a good gumbo, it's a mixture of many things. New Orleans is a combination of diverse peoples and cultures, and we're proud of that fact. We have no desire to be like New York, Los Angeles, Kansas City, or Seattle. They're all great cities, but that's not who we are, and—no offense—it's not who we want to be.

Granted, we could use a few improvements: less crime, better schools, fewer corrupt politicians, a higher pay scale, and stronger levees would certainly be welcome, as well as a few more Super Bowl victories and a longer crawfish season. Other than that, though, we're pretty content.

Those who came back understood that there would be no quick fix. Recovery was going to take years, and there was no guarantee that New Orleans would ever be how it was before the storm. At Lucky Dogs, our customer base was gone. There were neither tourists nor conventioneers, and we were missing more than 200,000 locals. Even so, we were ready to move forward and get back to work.

On February 13, three days before reopening for business, we had no shop help. Our night manager stayed in Texas, and no one had seen or heard from our day manager since he handed Jack McCormick the warehouse keys and headed for the Convention Center. Our maintenance man, Little Mike, had ridden out Katrina in his apartment, but after martial law was declared, the National Guard forced him to evacuate. He and his wife ended up on a plane bound for Michigan.

In early November, three months before our reopening, Mike called wanting to return. I explained the condition of the city, but he didn't care. He desperately wanted to come home, and frankly, I was looking forward to having him back. He took pride in everything he did. Once back at the shop, he painted the walls, scrubbed the floors, and thoroughly cleaned every cart. He worked tirelessly. No matter what I asked him to do, he tackled it with enthusiasm and without question.

We worked in peace and harmony. The building looked better than it had in years—mainly because there were no vendors around to mess up what we had just cleaned and repaired. Mike was happy, but I could foresee trouble. He had become far too comfortable with just the two of us in the shop. Once our crew returned, I feared his territorial nature might become a problem. And our vendors certainly were trying to return, but most had no money and no place to stay. Their apartments had either been damaged by the storm or had been rented out at exorbitant rates.

If we were to survive, we had to be creative. I sent bus tickets to Dee and Raymond so they could return from Houston. I sent Choya a plane ticket—he could repay us later. Burris made it back from California on his own. Terry and John also heard that we were reopening, and they, too, wanted to work the street again. However, Terry's van had rolled its last mile, and they needed transportation. Their unique solution was to buy bicycles and ride back from Pensacola, Florida. When they reached the north shore of Lake Pontchartrain, they discovered that Katrina's storm surge had washed away several sections of both the Highway 90 and I-10 Twin Span bridges. After making it all the way there from Pensacola, they weren't about to let a couple of washed-out bridges stop them. They took the longer route west to Baton Rouge, then traveled east on Highway 61 to New Orleans. Their trip covered more than 500 miles and took several days, but they miraculously made it in time for our reopening.

On Wednesday, February 15, 2006, three days before the first post-Katrina Mardi Gras parade rolled downtown, our only shop employee was Little Mike. We still had no day manager, no night manager, and only two vendors, but that didn't matter. Carts were going to hit the street the following afternoon.

Later that day, Mark and Kirk Talbot returned to the office for the first time since the storm. Their homes, as well as Doug's, had been spared.

On Thursday, opening day, two people were added to the payroll: Tammy and Ivy. Tammy took over as day manager, and Ivy was hired to help out in the kitchen during Carnival. Our crew of vendors had grown to five.

On Friday, Red Lott showed up and came on board as our night manager. Red and I first met in the late 1960s when I was in high school and working at Orange Julius on Bourbon Street. Back then, he was young and just hanging out in the Quarter. Later, on various occasions, he worked for Lucky Dogs as a vendor, a day manager, and a night manager, though he never held any position for long. One day, he quit and proceeded to file for unemployment. We hadn't fired him; we hadn't even laid him off. He quit so he could enroll in a trade school.

He was hoping to attend class and simultaneously receive unemployment benefits. The state even awarded him the benefits. I lodged a protest with the Louisiana Department of Labor. As a result, we both had to appear before a labor judge. Outside of the judicial chambers, Red approached me and suggested that I not take the situation personally. He explained that he just needed the money. The judge listened to Red's side, then to mine. In the end, he reamed Red out for attempting to defraud the state. He even threatened to throw him in jail. As we walked out of the chambers, I turned to a distraught Red and said, "Don't take it personally."

Now, in post-Katrina New Orleans, neither of us was taking the past personally. Red needed work, and we needed a manager. Besides, at the moment, our potential managerial pool wasn't even a puddle. Sooner or later, someone more suitable would drift back into town, but until then, Red was our man.

We now had a full management team, but we were still in dire need of more vendors. However, they couldn't return without a place to live. To solve the problem, we decided to turn the shop's second floor into a barracks. Anyone who wished to stay was told to bring a sleeping bag or an air mattress.

By February 16, opening day, seven people were sprawled out and snoring just outside my second-floor office. Smoking was allowed, but only on the first floor by the front door. Drinking or bringing alcohol on the premises was taboo. That was the corporate line. Most tried to follow the rules—at least while I was in the building.

To prevent our vendor-tenants from getting into trouble, I called the shop each morning and asked about the previous night's sales. At the same time, I would let them know that I was on my way. I wanted them to have a heads-up that I'd be there soon. I did not want to catch anyone. If I did, I would have to send the violator packing so that order would be maintained—I couldn't make exceptions for anyone. Those staying in the shop needed work as much as we needed them as vendors. They weren't saints, and we knew it. So, for the time being, we played a game of cat and mouse, but in this version, the mice always knew when the cat was coming. As long as they didn't get out of hand or openly flaunt that they were breaking the rules, it was a controllable and workable situation.

During our first night back on the streets, the crew sold more than five hundred hot dogs. That was a good start, but it was the reception that the vendors received that was most rewarding. Total strangers walked up and gave them hugs. Customers purchased Lucky Dogs, handed the vendors $20, and told them to keep the change. Numerous calls came into our office from appreciative New Orleanians thanking us for not throwing in the towel.

Our reopening was seen as one more sign that the city was coming back, and believe me, everyone in New Orleans was looking for any kind of sign that the Big Easy was going to make it.

We cheered when the electricity was restored, and when a service station or grocery store reopened, even if it ran out of gas almost immediately or if it only stayed open for a few hours a day. Anything positive uplifted our spirits. We understood that businesses did not have enough bodies to cover every shift or enough customers to warrant regular hours, so we were grateful for whatever they could do.

Every positive sign was cherished because, day in and day out, all we heard on national television and radio broadcasts were talking heads debating whether they should even bother trying to rebuild the city. There were politicians and commentators from outside of our region arguing that federal funding should not be spent on a city below sea level. They proclaimed that "money should not be wasted on a lost cause." Less radical politicians called for the city to be rebuilt, but with a much smaller footprint.

It was an insane debate. New Orleans' port at the mouth of the river was invaluable—the US Department of Transportation rated it one of the country's top five ports when ranked according to tonnage. Additionally, New Orleans and the whole of south Louisiana were vital to the oil industry. It simply wasn't negotiable; the nation needed New Orleans to be rebuilt. Politicians could debate all they wanted, but while they talked, many of us were already here with our sleeves rolled up, getting the process under way. Joining us were church groups, college students, and thousands upon thousands of individuals who, out of the goodness of their hearts, had put their own lives on hold and stepped up to make a real difference in a city that could use all the help it could get.

Besides, we never bitched about people out west building their homes in the woods, where forest fires annually destroy thousands upon thousands of acres; or in Hawaii, where volcanoes erupt; or in San Francisco, which someday might be leveled by a major earthquake; or in Los Angeles, which some predict will eventually slide into the ocean.

You can make a case that no one should live anywhere. But that would be just as unrealistic as the headline-chasing politicians who, grandstanding in front of microphones, espoused that the nation should think long and hard before sending billions of dollars to the Gulf Coast. A lot of us in the devastated areas believed that those same politicians had close friends who were awarded major contracts to help rebuild New Orleans and the Gulf Coast, because God knows those contracts did not go to local companies. The local guys were hired as subcontractors and performed the bulk of the work, but the politically well-connected companies in other states held the master contracts and were the ones that reaped the real financial rewards. The big money never got to stay here, where it could have been turned over several times and could have made a real difference.

Like those who questioned whether or not the city should be rebuilt, there were those outside the region who questioned if Mardi

Gras should be held and if people should be partying so soon after such a tragic event. They saw Carnival as a waste of revenue.

To clarify, Mardi Gras is not put on by the city or state. It is privately funded by the various Carnival organizations called "krewes." Regardless, while outsiders debated, the parades were rolling, and we were selling dogs. On Mardi Gras Day, February 28, 2006, Lucky Dogs had twelve vendors on the street and a full managerial staff in the shop.

In the mind of every New Orleanian, the Mardi Gras tradition needed to continue, even if it meant throwing beads from the back of decorated trash haulers. Everyone in Katrina's path had spent more than five months engrossed in death and destruction. Others around the nation talked about it; we lived it. The people of New Orleans and the surrounding areas deserved, at the least, a few days of relief.

For our own sanity, we needed to get out the boom boxes, dust off the CDs, crank up the volume, and blast Al Johnson's "It's Carnival Time" through the streets of the Big Easy. We all needed to forget about Katrina, even if it was for just a couple of hours. After Fat Tuesday, we would have a lifetime to try and rebuild all that had been lost.

Amazingly, sales for the 2006 Carnival season were down only 25 percent from 2005's pre-Katrina season. We had fewer carts out and the crowd was much smaller, but there was also a lot less competition.

In comparison, on Mardi Gras Day 2005, eighteen carts had hit the street. In 2006 we had six fewer vendors, but it was twelve more than a lot of people ever thought that we would have. We were back. The company had daily sales. I was back making commissions. My personal checking account breathed a sigh of relief. Life wasn't great, but it was a hell of a lot better than it had been a few months earlier. Most importantly, we had hope. As for luck, we, like everyone else along the Gulf Coast, were making our own.

Yes, we were back, but we were struggling. From the mid-1970s until the mid-1990s Lucky Dogs had only two families in management that needed to be supported: Doug's and mine. In the mid-1990s, Doug's oldest son Mark entered the business, and a few years later his younger son Kirk came on board. In this post-Katrina world, the company was management-heavy and profit-poor. Something had to give.

On Christmas Day 2005, Joe Kimmel of Kimmel and Associates offered me a job in Asheville, North Carolina. My brother-in-law, Tim, had worked for Kimmel for years. On at least two previous occasions, Tim had tried to convince me to join him there, but Jane and I were too entrenched in New Orleans to pick up and move.

Now Joe was offering me an opportunity to start over in a non-devastated city. It was tempting. However, before Joe's invitation, Tim had introduced our oldest son, Chris, to one of Joe and Cynthia's daughters, Lizie. They had started dating, and their relationship seemed serious. While Joe's offer was sincere and greatly appreciated, I couldn't accept it. Lizie served as the company's office manager. Relationships are tough enough without adding a boyfriend's father to the mix. I liked Lizie, and there was no way that I was going to be responsible for mucking things up. Besides, I felt obligated to get Lucky Dogs back up and running.

It was now March 2006. With the company struggling and having just turned down a job opportunity, I offered to lighten the financial load by resigning. I had a degree in education and a master's degree in history. I figured I could find a teaching job, but Doug was adamant. He did not want me to leave. In fact, he suggested that we draw up a contract to assure that I would remain at Lucky Dogs until I was at least seventy. We hadn't had a contract for the past thirty years; I did not see the need to have one now. We trusted one another. I let the idea die.

When Mark and Kirk came back after the storm, our airport business was nonexistent, Harrah's Casino was closed, and the French Quarter operation was but a fragment of what it once was. As a result, Kirk took a job gutting houses for a local contactor. A few weeks after that, he landed full-time employment inspecting properties for Fannie Mae. The job paid more than he would have been making working for his dad, and the move reduced Lucky Dogs' payroll and eliminated one family from the company's insurance policy. It was, in a way, a sort of "win-win" situation. Even so, Lucky Dogs was struggling—hanging on, but struggling.

Life in post-Katrina New Orleans was different. Lucky Dogs was different. I was different. In this new environment, competition for employees was fierce. Burger King and McDonald's were offering $500 signing bonuses for counter help. They were paying $10 an hour for entry-level positions. Construction jobs were paying unskilled laborers $20 an hour.

Even amid this employee free-agent frenzy, our pre-Katrina crew returned in force. Though we couldn't match the guaranteed salaries of other companies, we could offer them a place to crash and use of a shower, a washer and dryer, and refrigeration. Plus, we could offer them a cart, a corner, and a connection to what once was.

We were attempting to reopen in a city of glazed, staring people; tough times; few amenities; and inhabitants whose tempers often flared for no apparent reason. Depression was rampant. Some problems we could solve; some we could not.

We had solved our vendors' housing problems by creating a second-floor "corporate commune." Everyone was allowed to pick out a place on the floor to call his or her own. Additionally, I gave our boarders a voice as to who should be allowed to join them and who should be asked to leave. In essence, we instituted *Survivor: Lucky Dogs.* For the most part, it worked well, and the crew policed themselves. Everyone worked to get along, and eventually, an "us against the world" mentality developed. The result was a more harmonious group. We didn't have much, and things were difficult enough, but, as they say, "at least we had each other." From a management perspective, we were glad that our vendors had returned, and, because they felt appreciated, they were more willing to endure the extra hardships and the reduced sales, which translated into reduced commissions.

Vendors get a 16 percent commission on their sales, plus tips, and they set their own schedules. As long as they worked two or three days a week, I said nothing. On Mondays, Tuesdays, and Wednesdays, there wasn't enough business on the street to support more than three or four carts. In pre-Katrina times, ten to twelve carts would have rolled out on a weeknight, but in this post-Katrina period, there were, as previously mentioned, no tourists and no conventioneers. Our customers after the storm were mostly construction workers, off-duty National Guardsmen, and a few locals. The vendors decided who would work and when. Sending a full crew out during the week would have been counterproductive. Guys would have been sitting on corners growing disgruntled, because they would have been putting in long hours and taking home little money. On the weekends, when the construction crews had pockets full of cash and all night to party, we put everyone we had on the street.

I was honest with the guys about what they should expect. Predictions were that the city would not recover for five to ten years. In the meantime, they were working in what many considered to be a third world environment. To work in those conditions was difficult and stressful, and there were times when they needed to get away, just so they could get back in touch with what it felt like to be normal. Every now and then, they would take off for destinations where stores weren't boarded up and city buses actually ran—somewhere where people talked about something other than "the storm"; where there were no blue tarp roofs, no government-supplied FEMA trailers, and no watermarks on buildings. Once mentally recharged, they would return and work the streets for a few more months. Some, however, would end up spending more than they should, and I'd get a desperate call from a stranded vendor wanting me to buy him a bus ticket home.

There was, however, one vendor for whom I purchased a bus ticket so that he would leave. Around the shop we fondly remember him as "Lucky Dogs' Last Samurai."

We had been operating for almost a year after Katrina when we hired Shadowhawk. That wasn't his birth name; it was, according to him, his adopted Native American name. In this desperate post-Katrina world when he came to the shop wanting to be a vendor, "The Shadow," as we called him, met our most important qualification: he was breathing.

The Shadow had potential. As a result, we allowed him to join the second-floor commune. He rewarded us by coming up short of cash twice at check-in. To pay off what he owed, he helped clean the shop. He swore on his mother's grave that he'd never again come up short. In hindsight, his mother was probably still alive.

At any rate, like the Indian agents of old, Shadowhawk spoke with a "forked tongue." In modern terminology, he flat-out lied about never again being a problem. First, there was the incident when he refused to push in. Thomas Bickle, our relief night manager who went by the nickname "Snake," could not, on this particular evening, get The Shadow to call it a night and push to the shop. The rest of the crew had checked in hours earlier.

The Shadow kept ignoring Snake's demands. Finally, at 5:30 a.m., Snake called me begging for help. I got out of bed and was on the corner of Toulouse and Bourbon by 6 a.m. The street sweepers had already made their morning pass through the Quarter and the bars' cleanup guys were out hosing off the sidewalks in preparation for a new day.

The new day was dawning, and all the while, The Shadow was peacefully leaning against his cart and watching the sun slowly rise in the east. He wasn't drunk, but he also wasn't sober. Meanwhile, back at the shop, Snake was fuming. His shift couldn't end until he checked in the last vendor and closed out his paperwork, but his last vendor was refusing to leave his corner.

As I drove up, I could see The Shadow on his cell in deep conversation. I walked over and insisted that he hang up, make a money drop, and start pushing his wagon to the shop. He complied, and once his cart started rolling in the right direction, I drove back to our warehouse. Thirty minutes later, The Shadow still had not arrived. By now, the Quarter was basking in sunlight.

I drove back to Bourbon where I discovered that he had pushed only a block, and then stopped and reopened. This time, I was prepared. Not wanting to spend my entire morning coaxing him to come in, I had brought Thomas Porter's grown son T.J. with me. His job was to push the cart to the warehouse. The Shadow and his money would ride back in the truck with me.

Snake wanted to kill The Shadow, but the vendor lived to work another day. On second thought, it might have been two—but no more than that.

In down-and-out post-Katrina New Orleans, every business owner and manager tended to overlook employee flaws. If you didn't, you would end up working alone. However, on the particular morning that I'm about to mention, The Shadow crossed the line.

It was a little before 8 a.m. I had just arrived downtown and was walking from my truck in the Whitney parking garage to our shop. As I passed Commerce Restaurant and started rounding the corner onto Gravier Street, a young man flew by like a gazelle. Seconds later, Shadowhawk passed at full speed, waving a two-foot-long Japanese sword above his head. As both men rounded the block, recovery workers standing on the corner watched in disbelief.

Moments later, the duo reversed field and headed back toward me. I let the young man pass and then jumped in front of our vendor. By now, The Shadow looked more tired than menacing. His sword was hanging lifelessly by his side. He might have wanted to run the guy through with his blade, but he was too out of shape to catch him.

According to our gasping and heavily perspiring vendor, he had been sitting on the sidewalk in front of the shop waiting for Tammy to arrive and unlock the door when he dozed off. It wasn't until he felt someone tugging on his watch that he awoke.

The thief, a twenty-something-year-old man, suddenly realized that his mark's eyes had opened and he fled. Shadowhawk grabbed the sword—from where, I do not know—and followed in hot pursuit.

I tried to explain to our sword-wielding vendor as best I could that even in post-Katrina New Orleans, the authorities frowned on beheadings. "Besides, I know for a fact that decapitations are against company policy."

The Shadow responded that he was "just trying to execute justice." The word "execute" bothered me. So did the sword. I asked him if he could be anywhere in the U.S. other than New Orleans, where he would be.

"Orlando," he shot back.

"Orlando! Sound the horn and ring the bell, you said the magic word! We're giving you a free ticket to the home of Disney World and the Magic Kingdom." Within minutes, he and his belongings were in my truck, bus station–bound. He couldn't believe that we were willing to pay for his fare. I couldn't believe that I hadn't thought of it earlier. This was our contribution to the city's rebuilding effort. This was good citizenship, a humanitarian effort, and corporate responsibility all rolled into one. As I handed him the newly purchased, one-way, non-refundable ticket, I thought to myself, "Sorry, Mickey."

Gold bullion could have been left unguarded outside of the shop for days and it would have remained untouched; word of the saber-wielding madman had spread up and down the street, and no one wanted to incur the wrath of Lucky Dogs' "Last Samurai."

With The Shadow gone, Gravier Street was quiet. Unfortunately, so was the Quarter. Sales were down, but in post-Katrina, that was expected. It was part of the "new normal," since New Orleans' pre-Katrina normalcy no longer existed, having been washed away by the storm. We now spoke of things in terms of "pre-Katrina" or "post-Katrina."

In this early post-Katrina period, you had to try to not look back. You wanted to stay focused on the now, or, even better, on the future. In the now, The Shadow was gone, but Smitty was still here. He had ridden out the hurricane on the west bank of the Mississippi River in a rental house owned by fellow vendor James Hudson. The hurricane-force winds had ripped shingles and felt paper from the roof, but other than a small amount of interior sheetrock damage, he still had a comfortable place to live. His electricity had even been restored within a few days.

Smitty's major concern was not storm-related at all. He had just turned sixty-two and had applied for Social Security. His application had been rejected, and it stemmed from the fact that he had been adopted, but his name had never been changed on his birth certificate. So his birth records showed the name of his biological parents, while his Social Security card showed his adoptive last name. He was caught in a bureaucratic snafu. The Social Security Administration would not approve his application until the documentation matched. The only way to achieve that was to petition the state in which he was born to officially change the name on his birth certificate. The fact that both sets of parents were deceased complicated the matter.

Smitty is kind, gentle, and good-hearted. He is also very simple. He had no idea what to do, so he asked for my help. Without hesitation, I agreed.

The first problem we had to confront was that he had no idea what had happened to his original birth certificate or his adoption documents. Living as he had over the years, that was easy to understand. I contacted the state in which he was born and explained his plight to official after official, but no one seemed to care. According to them, without proper documentation, nothing could be done. After all, they had rules.

So, the next time I called the state's Department of Records, I presented the problem in a slightly different manner. Granted, I might have been a bit vague, but I was never dishonest.

I explained to the new official that I was calling from New Orleans. I informed her that Smitty no longer had his original documentation. When she asked why, I explained that New Orleans had flooded during Katrina, and that some areas had been under more than ten feet of water. I also mentioned that Smitty could not swim. I told her that at the moment, we had no idea what had happened to his documents, and we had no hope of ever recovering them. All were true statements. She must have assumed that Smitty's house had flooded and that that was why his documentation no longer existed. She never asked for confirmation, and I never offered.

Because of those assumptions, she was willing to help, and we were more than willing to accept it. With her incredible assistance and guidance, the red tape was cut within thirty days and the necessary forms were filled out and notarized. I mailed them directly to her, and a few days later, Smitty received a new birth certificate with the name matching that on the rest of his documentation. The following morning, he filed again for Social Security. The state official believed that she had been of great help to a Katrina victim. The truth is, she had.

In the meantime, business throughout the summer was dismal, and the number of vendors working each night continued to range anywhere from two to thirteen, depending on the day of the week. Overall, sales were down 34 percent when compared with the same period pre-Katrina. I was surprised that it wasn't worse.

As a business, we were operating as lean as possible. We were in serious condition—on life support—but not yet dead. To recover, Lucky Dogs was going to need more time, more tourists, more conventioneers, and a close rein on the purse strings. The best diagnosis was that the city would not see marked improvement until 2011 or 2012. Like a recovering alcoholic, we were just trying to make it one day at a time.

In a 2006 study compiled for the city, GRC and Associates reported the New Orleans pre-Katrina population as 454,000. It reported that by the fall of 2005, the number had declined to less than 70,000. By the first anniversary of the storm, it estimated that the number of inhabitants had increased to 230,000—approximately half of the city's pre-storm population. The study also discovered that while 50 percent of the city's bus routes were operational, ridership was at only 17 percent of its pre-storm numbers. Aviation fared somewhat better, but it, too, was suffering. Enplanements at Louis Armstrong International Airport were 66 percent of their pre-Katrina level. In health care, only four of the city's ten full-service hospitals had reopened, and in commerce, the number of occupational licenses had dropped by 50 percent. The study additionally found that just one-third of the city's restaurants had reopened; approximately 44 percent of the schools had reopened; and the police force was at 72 percent of its pre-hurricane strength. We were improving, but anything resembling a true recovery was still years away.

In this atmosphere, vendors tended to drift in and out. One of those drifting back into town was Karl. I hadn't seen him since I dropped him off at the airport. He was back, and I couldn't say that I was overjoyed. But we were nearing the end of August and expecting a boost in sales with the return of the annual gay pride festival, Southern Decadence. We needed all of the vendors that we could muster, plus we needed someone to wash carts on Little Mike's days off. As long as Karl behaved, he would be welcome. As for the Rambo knife, neither of us brought it up.

On Thursday, August 31, 2006, Southern Decadence began. The 800 block of Bourbon looked like the French Quarter of old. Crowds were packed into the street at the corner of St. Ann and Bourbon, which was the heart of the festival. Hudson's cart was set up on St. Ann near the curb just outside Napoleon's Itch bar.

Lucky Dogs' carts had legally worked the spot since the 1940s, and it had never been a problem. However, this year, Chuck Robinson, one of the bar's cofounders, decided to sell food from a temporary counter that he set up in his bar's open doorway. Because of that, he wanted Hudson to move thirty feet back from the corner. Hudson was not fond of the idea.

If he pushed his cart back the requested distance, he would lose the cross traffic, and his sales would plummet. Seeing Hudson's reluctance, Chuck suggested that he move his wagon to the other side of Bourbon. That way, he would still be on a corner, but not directly competing against his bar's doorway take-out.

To help keep the peace, Hudson gave in and relocated. Instead of peace, war broke out. A girl on the new corner passing out free condoms to festival-goers went ballistic. According to her, she "wasn't gonna share no spot with any weenie man!"

Hudson figured that was *her* problem, not his. He went ahead and opened for business, later turning the cart over to his helper. Shortly after Hudson left, the condom distributor shot across the street to one of the businesses and voiced her displeasure to her friends. That business then decided that, like her, it "didn't want no weenie cart on their side of Bourbon." Within minutes, an off-duty police officer was ordering Hudson's helper to move to another location. She informed the worker that if the cart was there when she came back on duty that night, "there would be trouble." The fact that we were legal and that she was sworn to uphold the law didn't seem to matter in the least.

It was obvious that I needed to walk over to 8th District police headquarters and speak with the captain. He wasn't in, so I spoke with his administrative assistant. The assistant requested that I try and rectify the problem without getting the police involved. I agreed to try.

I went back to speak with the business owners and managers. First, I spoke with Chuck, then with the others. It appeared that we were now all in agreement as to where our cart would set up, so I headed back to the shop. I was almost there when Hudson's helper called. A night manager from one of the establishments who had just come on duty was livid because of our cart's location.

I asked to speak with the gentleman. I explained the agreement. He shouted a few obscenities, then slammed the vendor's phone down onto the pavement.

I walked back to the 8th District station and explained what had just taken place. Unbelievably, they asked if I would try to reason with the unhappy manager in person.

I went back to St. Ann Street and approached the disgruntled manager in a friendly and civil manner, hoping to find a workable solution for all involved. The manager informed me that he had spoken with the city permit department and that according to them, we had to keep moving; our cart could not stay in one location for more than fifteen minutes.

That was an old ordinance that strictly applied to temporary Mardi Gras vendors working the parade routes. I explained that the ordinance did not pertain to us and offered to show him our permits. I suggested that he call the police station and speak with the captain's assistant. Instead, he grabbed my business card out of my hand and slammed his office door.

A few minutes later, he and some friends appeared with a number of metal police barricades and began placing them around Hudson's cart. I called the 8th District and informed them that I had tried to reason, but it hadn't worked. The captain's assistant agreed to send a car.

By the time the officer arrived, our cart was surrounded by NOPD barricades that had been placed there by non-police. Their action was illegal, but humorous. The result was the exact opposite of what was intended: the vendor now had his own little protected island in the crowd. The mass of people couldn't get close to the cart, but the vendor could still sell to those standing on the other side of the barricades. The perpetrators looked frustrated.

A young officer arrived and wanted to discuss the situation right in the middle of the intersection. I asked if we could possibly step around the corner. He demanded to know why.

I pointed to the television news crew that had just pulled up, obviously looking to do a story on the festival. His uniform and the barricaded cart were bound to attract attention, and unless he wanted to be featured on the five o'clock news, we needed to get out of sight. He agreed.

Once the camera crew left, the officer calmly walked over to the other side of the street and ordered those responsible for placing the barricades there to remove them. If they didn't, someone was going to jail.

This time, the upset manager called the mayor's assistant. The manager walked over and handed the phone to me so the assistant could inform me that we had to move. At the same time, the officer was calling his captain asking for guidance. Not wanting to be left out of the "who has the biggest gun" contest, I called a New Orleans city councilman on his cell to let him know what was happening.

I explained to the mayor's assistant that we were legal and asked if he wanted to speak with the councilman. Serious city problems seldom received this much attention, let alone petty issues such as the one currently on our hands. Things were ratcheting up.

The captain requested to speak with me. He asked if I would do him a personal favor and move the cart back across the street in front of Napoleon's Itch—the location where Hudson had originally started out. I explained that we would be happy to do so, but I wanted all parties concerned to understand that we were completely legal in both locations. Plus, I requested that the officer accompany me into Napoleon's Itch and explain that we were moving back at the request of the 8th District. Chuck was extremely polite and very understanding.

In my opinion, the entire incident was sparked because in this post-storm period, everyone was on edge. Sales were down, the cost of doing business was up, the Southern Decadence festival failed to attract as many visitors as it had in past, and thus profits were less than anticipated. As for the girl promoting safe sex, God only knows what her objection was.

When I arrived back at the shop, there was a letter waiting for me from Larry Griffiths. It was the perfect end to a very imperfect day.

Larry had worked for us on and off for years. By trade, he was an engineer. Earlier in life, he had been part of the military-industrial complex, and his résumé included working on designs for a US Navy minesweeper and on the booster assembly project for the Apollo spacecraft. But, overqualified and taking lithium, Larry had been bypassed by companies looking for younger engineers willing to accept smaller salaries and apparently representing less of a risk. Thus, he joined our ranks.

In the past, when Larry failed to take his medication, he had done some pretty irrational things. Once, he was picked up for standing in the middle of a busy intersection and directing traffic. Another time, he believed that he was a baseball manager, and he came to the shop looking to recruit players. Then there was the occasion when he wrote a note saying that he was "going to kill Jerry the Lucky Dog man." I didn't take it personally.

His landlord found the memo in his apartment along with several bullets, but no gun. At the time, Larry was a guest in Charity Hospital's lockdown observation ward. He called from the ward's pay phone wanting to know if I would lend him money so that he could buy soft drinks and cigarettes. I sent him $40. I figured once he got out, he would repay either me or my estate.

Larry's letter confirmed that he had survived Katrina. For that, I was thankful. But the letter also confirmed that he had not been taking his medication. It was addressed to "General Blink, A.K.A. Jerry Strahan c/o Lucky Dawg, Blink, Inc., or Markovich Talbuttinsky (Lt. Gen., J.G) ?! or Dad, 517 Grave?ier St., New Orleans, LA 70126." His return address was "Robbed Twice, thrice," then his actual address, followed by "Heal, dammit, Heal!" Even with the wrong ZIP code, I received the letter.

Inside was a card that stated "Dear Fred." After that, it was incoherent. There had been other occasions when Larry had sent me strange letters, including one he closed by signing, "Zorro!"

I did not respond to this latest note because I feared he would mistakenly believe that I was suggesting he return, and in his case, he was far better off in a city where the medical facilities were fully functional. New Orleans had few working hospitals, and those that were open were understaffed.

Medical care was nowhere near its pre-Katrina level when, on September 22, 2006, we required emergency assistance at the shop. Louis Willis Jr. had shown up at Lucky Dogs earlier in the summer and since then had made a living pushing vendors' carts out to their corners for the day and back in at the end of the night. He was a tall, gentle, quiet, and soft-spoken man. Because of his size, he could easily have been mistaken for a physically fit, bulky, professional basketball center.

On this particular afternoon, Louis pushed out Tammy's cart and then pushed out Dee Dee's. Afterward, he returned to the shop and was resting in a chair by the front door when he suddenly fell forward onto the shop's concrete floor. Jason quickly dialed 911, but by the time the ambulance arrived, it was too late. Louis had died from a heart attack.

In the months that Louis had been around, I never heard him utter a single derogatory word about anyone. He was the kind of guy you couldn't help but like. In pre-Katrina New Orleans, I believe the ambulance's response time might have been quicker. Would it have made a difference? There's no way to know.

On a less serious note, three days later, something occurred that affected the spirit of all New Orleanians and broadcast to the world that the Big Easy was alive and improving. To the average fan looking at an NFL schedule, the Saints/Falcons Monday night contest was likely just another football game, but to New Orleanians, it was our chance to welcome the Saints back home and to showcase to the world a completely renovated Superdome. It was a chance for the stadium to be reborn and to put behind it the fact that most recently, it had been seen as a symbol of death, devastation, and all that had gone wrong during Katrina.

This would be our first game in the Dome since the hurricane. Half of the Saints' 2005 home games had been played in Baton Rouge, seventy miles upriver from New Orleans, and the remainder took place in San Antonio, Texas.

Days before the September 25 Monday night game, you could sense a change in New Orleans. As I was having lunch at Commerce Restaurant, the topic revolved around the Saints—not levees, not insurance adjusters, not even the dysfunctional FEMA (local interpretation was "Federal Employees Missing in Action"; if an argument really got hot and heavy in early post-Katrina, you might hear someone shout "FEMA you"—everyone understood the implied meaning). However, at Commerce and in coffee shops and offices all over town, the talk now was not about FEMA but about the 2–0 Saints.

On game day, the city became a sea of Saints' black and gold. You could sense the excitement. In the parking lots near the stadium, tents had sprung up, beer was being iced down, jambalaya was steaming in pots, and red beans and rice were heating up. Cajun smoked sausage, alligator sausage, and andouille sausage were cooking on the grills. Tailgating was in high gear.

Most businesses closed early that day, as did City Hall. Chants of "Who Dat! Who Dat! Who Dat say dey gonna beat dem Saints?" echoed through the streets of the Central Business District and the French Quarter.

Our carts were out early, hoping to capture as much business as possible before fans headed to the Dome. The atmosphere was electric. Not even Super Bowls brought this kind of excitement. Stages had been erected in parking lots near the stadium, and the crowd listening to the band at the corner of Loyola and Poydras, just a block from the Dome, was so large that it spilled into the street, causing a traffic jam. Even in a financially strapped metropolitan area with only half of its pre-storm population back home, the game was a sellout.

At kickoff, the noise was deafening. Saints coach Sean Payton was quoted in a New Orleans *Times-Picayune* article as saying, "It was as loud as I've ever heard a stadium, ever . . . and [there is] a big gap between second."

The article's author, reporter James Varney, quoted Saints offensive lineman Zach Strief as stating: "That game was so little about football. . . . You look into the stands that game and there's people crying, there's guys on the sideline crying. It was finally a chance for people, I don't know, to not think about what was going on in their lives and because of that, it wasn't football. It was like a release, and that's what made that game unique."

ESPN broadcast the game to the world, and 14,999,000 viewers tuned in. It dominated the prime-time ratings for the night on both cable and broadcast television.

In addition to Sean Payton and Zach Strief, ESPN's Monday Night Football play-by-play man Mike Tirico was quoted in the same *Times-Picayune* article as saying: "When people ask me, of the games you've broadcast, what one is the most memorable, that's the one for me, because it was so much more than a sporting event. I've been to Super Bowls and other sorts of events like that, but championships are won every year, records are set every year, comebacks happen every year. But a city doesn't announce its return to the world very often. And that's what happened that night."

In the game's first series, Saints special teams ace Steve Gleason blocked a Falcon punt. Teammate Curtis Deloatch recovered the ball in the end zone for a touchdown, and the crowd went berserk. The Black and Gold never looked back on their way to a 23–3 rout. After the victory, the long-suffering Saints fans weren't ready for the evening to end. They poured out of the stadium and headed en masse for the Quarter. Sales that night were phenomenal—ten times greater than the previous Monday's.

Several weeks later, on Halloween night, business was once again outstanding. However, on this occasion, it wasn't the number of dogs sold but rather what happened on the street that made the evening memorable.

Five costumed characters ended up in a street brawl next to Choya's cart at the corner of Conti and Bourbon, just outside of the Royal Sonesta Hotel. Three were dressed as the Three Little Pigs and a fourth as the Big Bad Wolf. The fifth participant was wearing a Big Bird costume.

The pigs were acting more like wild boars. They were all over the bird, with punches being thrown and feathers being plucked. It was a fairy tale gone awry. In the heat of the scuffle, one of the pigs ripped off Big Bird's head and tossed it into the crowd. Like a beach ball at a concert, it started being tapped into the air until it disappeared down the block. In the middle of the ruckus, two police officers arrived. As they focused on rounding up the pigs, the Big Bad Wolf took advantage of the situation and slipped away into the crowd.

The officers had the pigs spread-eagle against the Royal Sonesta's wall. Big Bird was ordered to do the same against the hood of the police car. With everything now under control, the officers began taking the testimonies of those who had witnessed the fiasco.

Choya overheard the officers come to the conclusion that under no circumstances were they hauling the pigs and their feathered adversary to jail. They had no desire to invite the humiliation back at headquarters as the duo that had collared the ferocious Three Little Pigs and the notorious Big Bird. That kind of collar would follow them their entire careers. Nor would their fellow officers ever let them forget that they failed to prevent the infamous Big Bad Wolf from slipping away.

Their solution? Threaten the costumed characters with jail, unless they agreed to leave—in opposite directions—and not stop walking until they were out of the Quarter. Big Bird took off down the street to retrieve his head, while the Three Not-So-Little Pigs wandered off in the opposite direction in search of their furry friend. All in all, it was just your typical Halloween night on Bourbon Street.

8

POST-KATRINA

Early New Year's Eve morning, James Hudson showed up at the shop tired, grouchy, and a couple of beers over the legal limit. Minutes after walking through the door, he lit into Jason for supposedly doing a "half-ass job" of cleaning his cart. He followed with a long rant about a number of perceived problems with his wagon. Making matters worse, he kept repeating his criticisms, gradually growing louder and louder. He wanted to make certain that everyone in the warehouse could hear him.

Hudson's grievances were not factual—it was the booze talking. I escorted him upstairs to my office where I made it clear that he was to leave Jason alone. Then I recommended that he head home and sleep it off.

During New Year's, the Sugar Bowl, and Mardi Gras, we all work long hours for days on end. Inevitably, everyone becomes irritable and impatient. Even so, Hudson had been out of line, and he couldn't be allowed to disrupt the shop. His behavior could wreak havoc in a building where everyone was already stressed out and surviving on adrenaline.

If Hudson's attitude didn't change, Choya was standing in the wings ready to take over his cart and corner. He had informed me earlier in the week that he would be back in town and ready to push out on New Year's Eve.

Wisely, Hudson headed home and slept it off. When he returned later that afternoon, he was rested, sober, and in a better frame of mind. After apologizing to Jason, he pushed out like normal to the corner of Toulouse and Bourbon. Choya worked a cart at his old spot in front of the Royal Sonesta Hotel.

2006 was drawing to a close, and all I could think was, "thank God!" Sales for the year were down 40 percent compared with the pre-storm figures of 2004. Maybe with the dawning of a new year would come better times and better business. We could at least hope.

Unfortunately, it didn't take long to discover that hope just wasn't going to cut it; 2007 started out no better than 2006 had ended. On New Year's Day, Hudson's twenty-something-year-old grandson worked the cart with him. Tempers flared, words were exchanged, and the grandson stormed off. Hudson responded by declaring that his dog-hawking days were over. He pushed his wagon back to the shop and retired. I knew that within a week, he would change his mind, but for the moment, we were short a vendor.

In the shop, things weren't much better. With a full crew of twenty-two vendors going out daily, Jason needed help. To assist him, we hired Bob, a man who had wandered into our warehouse looking for work.

Bob did great his first day. Unfortunately, a darker side surfaced on his second day. Jason had had trouble with Hudson the day before, and now Bob was exhibiting an in-your-face argumentative attitude. He was questioning everything Jason asked him to do.

I was out of the building picking up supplies. Instead of calling me on my cell to report the problems Bob was causing, Jason continued washing carts, growing more and more frustrated all the while. Finally, he reached his breaking point, and he quietly picked up his backpack and walked out the door.

Jason has a passive nature. He prefers avoiding confrontation. We owed him a week's pay, but his stress level was so far beyond what he could handle that he didn't care. He walked out before I returned. I knew that like Hudson, he would eventually return, but with Jason, I couldn't predict when that might happen.

It was New Year's Day, Hudson had burned out, and Jason had walked out. I would have loved to have thrown Bob out, but I needed him to wash the rest of the wagons. We were already down a man. To replace Jason, we needed a new recruit, and we needed him fast.

I drove up to the Exxon station at Lee Circle, not far from the shop, and discovered a guy named Johnny hanging around out front. He was looking for work, and we needed a worker. It was a win-win situation.

In this post-Katrina period, guys often drifted into town in hopes of finding employment. They'd hang out in front of Home Depot, Lowe's, or, like Johnny, a service station. In this case, I happened to find him before some construction foreman did. Johnny had a friend staying at a nearby homeless shelter who was also looking for work. Within minutes, he, too, was in my truck and on the way to the shop.

I assigned Johnny to be Bob's cart-washing and floor-sweeping assistant. His friend was assigned the job of helping Todd, our present day manager, in the kitchen. Todd had taken over the position when Tammy decided to go back to working a cart. Having to deal with the vendors had mentally burned her out.

Johnny's friend did well the first day, but the following morning, he failed to show. Then on January 5, Johnny and Todd had words. Johnny, like Bob, resented being told what to do, despite the fact that Todd, as the day manager, was his direct boss.

Like Jason had done only a few days ago, Todd got frustrated and walked out. Once I arrived, it didn't take long to assess the situation and to send Johnny packing. After hearing from a vendor that "Jerry axed Johnny," Todd returned as if nothing had ever happened.

On the security monitor in my office, I noticed Todd hard at work trying to make up for lost time. Later, when I saw him in person, I never mentioned the incident. Sometimes it's best to just leave things alone. We could discuss the matter after the holidays were over and the shop had returned to normal.

In post-Katrina New Orleans, the dependability of newly hired employees like Johnny was nonexistent. They figured that if they got fired, they could easily find work on a trash hauler or with some contractor gutting houses, and they were right.

Even so, certain rules had to be enforced. On May 23, 2007, Lucky Dogs officially made a statement that storm or no storm, theft was unacceptable. Charges were filed and arrest warrants were issued for three new vendors who had come up short and refused to pay their balances. They all had been given numerous opportunities to make amends, but instead, they had chosen to walk up and down Bourbon Street, bragging that there was nothing that Lucky Dogs could do to them. Sadly, they had mistaken kindness for weakness. The judge explained the difference and gave them each ninety days to think about it.

Up until now, it had been virtually useless to try and get a warrant put out, and the vendors knew it. In the still-ravaged city, the police force and the courts were understaffed. Neither group wanted to be bothered with what they considered petty theft. They wouldn't admit it, but they had their hands full trying to capture and convict the thieves stealing truckload after truckload of roofing material and lumber from construction sites. Plus, crooks were ripping copper out of houses and buildings faster than plumbers could install it. They could sell the metal to scrap yards for pennies on the dollar.

Thieves were making it difficult for the city's rebuilding effort to make headway; and with violent crimes increasing, law enforcement viewed our problems as minor. Even so, we had to take a stand. The two arrest warrants were issued, and the word quickly spread on the street. Shortages came to an abrupt halt.

Thankfully, the summer and fall of 2007 were relatively uneventful, and for the most part, our crew remained intact, as did our second-floor commune. Then finally, as rooming houses and apartments reopened and rents started to drop, our boarder total declined until finally, the last vendor moved out.

By August 29, 2007, the second anniversary of Katrina, approximately two-thirds of New Orleans' population had returned. That was a positive sign. However, on the negative side, we were still missing more than 100,000 residents, and several neighborhoods continued to resemble ghost towns. Additionally, only eleven of the area's sixteen hospitals were operational, and the city seemed no safer than it had before the storm. The thugs had returned in droves. By late August, 154 murders had been recorded. The Big Easy's homicide rate was higher than New York City's.

The good news was that 2007's sales ended up being only 14 percent behind those of pre-storm 2004. The reduction in the size of the percentage looked promising, but it was deceiving, because the cost of doing business in post-Katrina New Orleans was much higher than in pre-storm New Orleans. Costs of both goods and labor were up, and insurance rates had soared beyond belief. Like the city, Lucky Dogs was just trying to survive until true recovery occurred.

Even with all of the city's continuing problems, the hotels, the Dome, and the French Quarter were ready and eager to host the Sugar Bowl. On New Year's Eve of 2007, thousands of University of Georgia and University of Hawaii fans hit the streets in a partying mood. They were boisterous, loud, and thirsty. Takeout windows along Bourbon were doing a brisk business serving beer, and at the corner of Orleans and Bourbon, a line had formed at Todd's cart.

Todd, like Tammy, had burned out in the shop and decided to return to the street. On this night, things were going well—that is, until, as Todd recalled, a large man wearing a University of Hawaii baseball cap broke in line and demanded to be served.

Despite the customer's rudeness, serving him was literally impossible, as Todd had just sold his last dog, and his new batch wasn't quite ready. The Hawaii fan didn't want an excuse. He wanted a hot dog, and he wanted it now. Todd once again explained that it would take a few minutes; besides, he told the man, there were others that had to be served before him.

The line-breaker profanely disagreed. Todd politely asked him to go to the back of the line, but at that point, the drunken fan leaned over the cart and took a swing at Todd. The attacker's fist hit the tip cup and sent it flying. Money spilled everywhere. Todd was upset, but not looking for trouble. He remembered saying, "Look, there's a vendor on the next block no matter which direction you go. Just go buy a dog from one of them. Mine are still cold."

But the fan didn't want to go anywhere else and apparently resented the fact that a street vendor was telling him to do so. Now more than ever, he was determined to get a dog from Todd's cart. He attempted to push his way through the crowd to get behind the wagon. Three large bun boxes were in his way, but that didn't stop him; he grabbed the top two boxes and tossed them into the street. Buns landed everywhere. He kicked the last box aside, and with nothing now in his way, he aggressively headed for Todd. Todd backpedaled, but he slipped in his attempt to escape.

He jumped back up and, out of instinct, grabbed the small paring knife that he used to cut the large quarter-pound Lucky Dogs in half for those wanting to share one. Holding the knife out in front of himself, he warned the man to stay back. The attacker, disregarding his words, lunged at Todd and into the knife. The breakaway blade did exactly what it was designed to do: it snapped.

The police arrived. Todd was handcuffed and thrown against the wall of a nearby bar. The whole time, the crowd, including other University of Hawaii fans, kept shouting to the officers that they were arresting the wrong guy. Out of nowhere, a well-dressed man stepped forward and informed the cops that he had witnessed the entire incident. He was an attorney and was willing to represent "this innocent young man."

By now, three officers were at the scene, and within minutes, two detectives arrived. As the investigation proceeded, it became clear that the fan—not Todd—had been the aggressor. All the while, the attacker's buddies were standing nearby shouting that they were going to "kick [Todd's] ass." The officers warned them about making threats.

An ambulance made its way down the narrow, packed streets. Paramedics concluded that the blade had barely punctured the fan's skin and that no serious damage had been done. Still, they transported the man to the hospital for a second opinion. In the meantime, the police grew concerned that the man's friends might return and try to carry out their threats.

To eliminate that possibility, the cops threw Todd in the back of their squad car. Supposedly, they were taking him to jail to be booked with assault with a deadly weapon. In reality, they removed the cuffs and released him at the edge of the Quarter. He was far enough away that the officers figured he would be safe. Nevertheless, they suggested that he stay out of the Quarter for two or three days. By then, the fan and his friends would most likely have left town.

Fighting in the streets was something that Richard Moscinski, a co-worker of Todd's, also was having serious problems with in the spring of 2008. On one particular evening, Tammy, after her first money run, found Moscinski's cart abandoned on the sidewalk in front of the shop.

That was unlike Moscinski. The next morning, when he stopped by to pay the remainder of his bill, I could see that he was still shaken from whatever had occurred.

"I've got to get away," he said, sitting in my office. "I can't take the streets anymore." Four customers the previous night had apparently caused his stressed-out mental state. Each had purchased a jumbo dog, and each, after eating about two-thirds of their dogs, complained that it wasn't hot. The four customers then proceeded to surround him, get in his face, and demand their money back.

Moscinski had put his first batch of franks in the cooker when he left the shop at 5 p.m. They had been in a steamer hot enough to boil water for more than two hours. It was impossible for them not to be hot, but at sixty-two Moscinski was no match for one, much less four, younger men. Not wanting trouble, he refunded their money. Afterward, he was so upset that he stopped selling and sat on his stool, hoping that one of the guys he usually paid to push him in might stop by. After waiting an hour and a half, he pushed the cart back to the shop himself.

This was Moscinski's second physical encounter in a matter of weeks. The first one took place in the early morning hours as he walked home from work; two men grabbed him from behind and began beating him. They didn't demand his money or even bother going for his wallet. They just kept pounding him.

Then, after punching and kicking him mercilessly, his attackers suddenly stopped. One of the assailants had realized that they had jumped the wrong man.

What took place next was even more bizarre. Instead of just leaving Moscinski in the street, they picked him up and helped him down the block and into his apartment. After muttering "Sorry, bro," they walked out and pulled his door shut. That incident, followed by the four guys threatening him and demanding a refund, was more than he could mentally or physically take. Twice during the previous year, he had to be transported from his cart to the emergency room via ambulance. During his most recent visit, surgeons placed a pacemaker in his chest.

Moscinski was old enough to receive Social Security, and he wanted me to know that he was going to apply for it. I understood. However,

Best buds Tim Danner and Rick Puggini.

I wanted him to know that if he ever wanted to work again, whether full-time or part-time, all he had to do was give us a call.

Another person feeling pain was Warren, our latest cleanup man and occasional vendor. Earlier in the week, he had been hit by a car while riding his bike to work. The outcome was a few minor bruises and a crushed front rim of his bicycle. Unfortunately for Warren, the investigating officer found him to be at fault.

Sadly, his stroke of bad luck didn't end there. Later in the week, he and his roommates, fellow vendors Tim Danner and Rick Puggini, had words. As a result, Danner and Puggini threw him out. A few days later while his former roommates were at work, Warren supposedly broke into his old apartment, took his belongings, and trashed the place.

Shortly thereafter, Danner and Puggini were having a couple of cold beers over at Chuck's Sports Bar when they came up with an idea—a really bad idea. They decided to go to Jackson Square where Warren was now miming and rough him up a little as payback. Maybe they'd push him around, throw him to the ground, and then call it even.

Things did not go as planned. First Danner and Puggini shoved Warren off the milk crate that served as his stage, then they attempted to pounce on him while he was on the ground. In spite of the two-against-one odds, Warren escaped and hightailed it to a nearby restaurant, where he convinced a waiter to call the police. Whether he verbally asked or simply acted out his request isn't quite clear, but within minutes, Puggini and Danner were in the back of a squad car and on their way to jail—a place they seemed to frequent far too often.

Thirty days later, they walked out of Central Lockup free men. Unfortunately, they were free men with a strong thirst for a drink. They had one, and then another, and then a few more. They weren't out forty-eight hours before they earned the right, once again, to appear before the same judge.

Danner's blunder that earned him a ticket to court was stumbling to the shop and passing out in the doorway. Clasped firmly in his right hand was one end of a dog leash, and on the other end was a very angry pit bull hell-bent on protecting his newly acquired, unconscious master. Across the street at Chuck's, Puggini was downing a few brews, feeling no pain. Two other vendors had been matching Puggini drink for drink. Finally, his co-workers decided that it was time to head home. Puggini walked out with them and stood on the sidewalk, beer bottle in hand, watching as his two friends struggled to crawl into a cab.

Behind the taxi was an impatient driver. The woman kept blowing her horn, and eventually, Puggini became irritated. Once traffic started to move, he made certain that she was aware of his displeasure: as she drove past him, he threw his empty beer bottle right through her rear window.

Meanwhile, across the street, Danner was out cold on the sidewalk with his guard dog growling at anyone attempting to enter or leave the shop. It didn't take long for the police to show up and arrest Puggini, and as they were getting out of their car, they couldn't help but notice Danner sprawled out in front of the shop. Immediately, their stop turned into a double collar trip. Actually, it turned into a triple collar; the officers cuffed both Puggini and Danner, then had the SPCA pick up the pit bull—apparently, even animals associated with the duo ended up behind bars. Both guys were likeable, but when they drank, they were undependable and uncontrollable. Even so, after a couple of months of drying out, all would be forgiven and they would be allowed back in the fold.

While Danner and Puggini were sobering up in Central Lockup, other seasoned vendors were returning. Unemployment was up nationally, so ex-vendors were migrating back in hopes of working a cart during the 2009 Mardi Gras season. It was a great feeling, having the numbers favor us and being able to pick and choose who we wanted.

Also, seasoned managers were returning. Warren was back in the shop washing carts part-time—it seemed miming had not proved to be nearly as financially rewarding as he had expected. During Mardi Gras, he and regular cart-pusher Nick Trosclair began cleaning the carts as soon as they started rolling back into the shop. Jason had also returned and was, once again, the full-time cart washer. He was scheduled to arrive at 7 a.m., and by then, Warren and Nick were expected to have at least half of the wagons finished and the shop swept and cleaned.

George Overton, an ex-vendor, was handling the issuing of products and supplies to the vendors. George wasn't fast, but he was steady and calm. On the last weekend of Carnival, Kirk, Mark, and I helped him send out a full crew of twenty-two vendors. For the most part, everything ran smoothly. Of course, there were a few minor problems—there always are.

First, Smitty had lost more than $400. He had stuffed the bills into his red training bra, but the cash must have worked its way out and fallen to the ground. He was not a happy Lucky Dog man.

The second minor problem was that another vendor claimed to have lost more than $300 that she supposedly had stuffed into her blouse; she hadn't even been wearing a bra. She, too, figured that her cash must have fallen to the ground.

In a matter of days, Mardi Gras was over. The streets had been cleaned, the revelers had sobered up, the marching bands were back at their respective schools, and the float builders were already preparing for the next parade season. It was early March 2009, and while the madness had subsided in the Quarter, it unfortunately had not in the shop.

As usual, there was a problem. This time, it was between Nick and two fellow vendors, Becky and Gene. They were accusing Nick of stealing Gene's bicycle, and the trio was in the midst of a heated argument that was on the verge of escalating into a brawl. The four of us met in my office in an attempt to resolve the issue and reconcile their friendship.

All parties agreed that there was no indisputable proof that Nick had taken the bike. In fact, Nick was denying having done so. The accusations were based on mere suspicion. After much discussion, all three decided to put the matter behind them. They shook hands, hugged, and professed to once again be the best of friends.

It was, however, a fleeting friendship; the fighting started back up not twenty minutes after they left my office, this time outside the shop. After our meeting, Gene started pushing to his corner. Becky was walking beside him, and almost a block ahead, Nick was pushing Smitty's wagon.

Nick was almost at the corner of St. Louis and Bourbon when Becky saw him and just could not leave well enough alone. She took off running and attacked him from behind. Nick showed restraint, standing in a defensive mode to block her punches as she swung wildly. However, when Gene looked up from pushing his cart, all he saw was Becky, Nick, and arms flying. He assumed that Nick had been punching Becky, so he rushed over to "protect his woman."

With Nick's attention focused on Becky, Gene caught him with a right hook, busting open his lip. An 8th District police officer standing across the street witnessed the entire incident. It wasn't even dark yet, and he already had people brawling in the street. Needless to say, he was not a happy camper, and he handcuffed the whole bunch. Once Nick cooled down, his cuffs were removed. Becky and Gene, on the other hand, were taken into custody. Gene was released within two hours, but Becky remained in Central Lockup for several weeks. Gene called the shop the following morning wanting to talk. Obviously, his version of what transpired differed greatly from Nick's version.

I went downstairs and asked Nick if he was willing to speak with Gene and put the incident behind them. "How come I'm the only one who has to suffer?" he responded. "I got kicked out of my apartment because the manager was scared Gene and Becky might come looking for me."

"Nick," I said, "I agree what Gene did was wrong, and if you don't want him back, then I won't allow him to return. But is keeping this feud alive the sensible thing to do? What happens when you two run into each other on the street?"

Jason, who was standing nearby and had overheard our conversation, remarked, "Maybe give it a week or two and then it'll all pass over."

"Nick might feel better in a week," I responded, "but by then, Gene will have lost his apartment because he can't pay his rent, and then he'll definitely be out for revenge. If this is to be resolved, it needs to happen today, or I need to tell Gene that he should look for work elsewhere. We do not want this festering."

"Let him bring it on," Nick said. "I'm not scared."

My approach was to find mutual ground between the two guys who, only a few days before, had been the best of friends. When Nick didn't have a place to live, Gene had let him stay with him. If this pointless fighting continued, one or both would end up back in jail.

I pointed out to Nick that if the feud was over, he might be able to get his apartment back. As he pondered the situation, he began to realize that ending the hostility might be beneficial. He agreed to meet with Gene.

Just as I got back into my office, Gene called. I suggested that he come to the shop. The three of us could sit, talk, and perhaps even resolve the problem—a problem created because someone supposedly had stolen someone else's probably hot bicycle.

We met. After a few tense minutes, it turned into one big Hallmark moment. Both men apologized, and both ended up blaming everything on Becky. They determined that had she not attacked Nick, Gene would not have had to defend her. It was unanimous: It was all Becky's fault. Had she minded her own damn business, none of this would have happened. Once again, they were best buds, and they weren't about to let a woman come between them.

I figured that things would remain peaceful for at least thirty days, at which point Becky would be released. After that, all bets were off.

A few days later, I was working late at the office when the phone rang. It was Danner, and he was calling to report that his cart was out of propane. According to him, his tank was half-full when he left the shop, but it was now empty. He wanted to come back and pick up another one.

If he left with his tank half-full and it was now empty, his cart had to have a gas leak. There was the possibility that the tank wasn't as full as he originally believed, but I couldn't take that chance. His only option was to push his cart to the shop and swap it out for another one.

Danner and the cart made it to the warehouse without a problem. After transferring his supplies to a new wagon, he and a friend started pushing back down Bourbon toward his corner a little after 8 p.m. They knew better than to take that route. At night, Bourbon is a crowded pedestrian mall, and the odds of running into someone with a cart are much greater than if one pushes down a less-crowded side street. The odds held true: Danner allegedly ran into a hooker. She didn't appear to be hurt, but she claimed to have been knocked to the pavement.

Before you could say "bogus," the police were on the scene, and she was requesting an accident report. An emergency unit arrived, but she refused to be examined. Her focus seemed to be on getting an item number from the officers. Once she had that in hand, she and her friend strolled off down the block.

A friend of one of the vendors claimed to have seen the whole incident. According to him, she stepped in front of the cart and fell to the ground without ever being hit. Unfortunately, he never told his account to the investigating officers. My plan was to meet with the witness the following morning and record his story on video. Afterward, I was hoping to get him to walk over to the 8th District and give them an official version.

Before I had a chance to do so, however, the said-to-be-injured party appeared at the shop. Though I had not yet arrived, according to those present her outfit left little to the imagination. Her T-shirt read "Nashville P---y," and color-coordinated with her shirt was a pair of tight, tiny shorts. It was the same outfit that she apparently had been wearing the night before on Bourbon.

She asked for the manager. Jason explained that I was on my way and asked if she wanted to wait or come back later.

At the same time, Tommy Turner, who had spent the previous evening bar-hopping, was now commode-hugging drunk. He wandered into the shop and overheard the young lady ask for the manager.

Lucky Dogs' Tommy Turner at Jackson Square. Photo by Jesse La Plante.

The previous evening, while his brain cells were still semi-function-ing, he had heard of Danner's encounter with the streetwalkers. Dis-covering that it was the same people who were now standing right in front of him, he started shouting, "You two-bit gold-digging whores get out of the shop!" He kept repeating the words "gold diggers" as he tried to push the women out of the building and close the door. The women decided that it might be best if they left and returned later.

In Turner's own warped, inebriated way, he was showing loyalty to the company. He was still in the shop when I arrived, but I did not want him there when they came back.

After much coaxing and prodding, he staggered out of the building. On his way out, he stopped, and with a puzzled look on his face, said, "I didn't mean to disrespect anyone. I just told the truth." He looked at us for a while longer, shook his head, and stumbled on across the street. A few minutes later, he motioned for me to cross over to where he was standing. As I walked up, he whispered, "They're street whores and they're trying to jack you up for all they can get."

"Tommy, that doesn't matter. The girl claims that Tim's cart ran into her last night, and you're not helping the situation. We need to get this resolved before it gets out of hand. Please, just go on down the block and let me handle it."

His eyes opened wide, he moved closer as if we were about to share a secret, and he whispered, "I understand. I'll see you tomorrow." He then headed off toward the river to take a nap.

Within the hour, the young woman reappeared, this time more appropriately dressed and without her friend, but she came with a demand for compensation. Her boyfriend, who, she informed me, was a federal agent, had advised her not to accept less than $5,000. I offered her $100 and told her that I shouldn't even do that.

She had no proof that she was injured, she showed no sign of an injury, and we had a witness willing to testify that she had intentionally stepped in front of the cart and pretended to be hit. However, she, too, had a witness, she had filed a police report, and undoubtedly, some attorney would take her case. If that did happen, it would cost several thousand dollars to defend ourselves in court. Plus, there was always the possibility that in Orleans Parish, some sympathetic jury might side with her. Because of that, our company attorney and our insurance company both advised me that if we could settle it for a reasonable amount and avoid going to court, it would be in the company's best interest.

She called her supposed federal agent boyfriend and relayed the offer. Then she handed the phone to me. Her boyfriend strongly suggested that we pay the $5,000. I responded that I considered his statement to be extortion and that if he was a federal agent, then this had better be the last time we ever spoke or my next call would be to the FBI.

At that point, she decided to walk down the block to confer with him in person. Thirty minutes later, she returned, demanding $4,000. I offered $150. She was insulted, and started to say that she made that much . . . then she stopped mid-sentence and demanded no less than $3,000. If we didn't accept her terms, she said, we would have to deal with her attorney.

I told her fine, in six or seven years we would both get the opportunity to present our case before a judge who would then decide the outcome. I followed by saying, "I'll tell you what we'll do. If you're willing to sign a release right now, we'll give you a check for $300 and I'll cash it for you. Take it or leave it."

She and her boyfriend reconvened. They decided to accept the offer. Doug called a few minutes later and asked how the day was going. I informed him that I had just given an out-of-state hooker $300 of company money, and in my opinion, it was cash well spent.

It wasn't a week later that Turner once again staggered into the shop drunk. There had been periods when for seven or eight months, he had been a dependable vendor, but he was now slipping—and doing so at an increasingly rapid rate. He was likeable and always willing to help in any way that he could, but at the moment, he couldn't even help himself. I recommended that he get away from the Quarter for several months.

As crazy as it sounds, I hated losing him. When he was sober, he did a great job in Jackson Square. The locals, the artists, and even the police liked him, but sober days were now few and far between.

I tried helping him by calling a previous employer of his in Florida, but no one answered. Turner then figured that his best chance of finding work was in South Carolina with another ex-employer. So, I loaned him money to buy a bus ticket.

Instead of purchasing the ticket, he went on another binge. Two days later, he sobered up and hitchhiked out of town heading east. I knew that sooner or later, he too would drift back through, and depending on his state of mind, we might even give him another chance.

Turner was gone, but Nick was still here—at least some of the time. On three occasions, he failed to report for work when scheduled. Like Turner, he is as likeable as they come; when sober, he's a hard worker, humorous, easygoing, and a pleasure to be around. However, when he drinks he is unreliable and switches into an "everyone-blames-everything-on-me" mode. He becomes defensive, argumentative, and highly undependable. His downfall is the incredibly strong, sweet-tasting wine called Cisco, hence his nickname "The Cisco Kid." He preferred being called "Billy the Kid," because he claimed that when making dogs, his hands moved at lightning speed, just like those of the famed gunslinger. At the moment, I was calling him "No-Show Nick."

No-Show was scheduled to clean carts during the day on Thursday, July 9, 2009. Later that evening, he was to work a catering event for us at the House of Blues, three blocks from the shop. Usually, No-Show reported for work at 8 a.m. On this particular day, by 9 a.m., there was no Nick. At noon, there still was no Nick. At 4:30 p.m., I received a call from Central Lockup. No-Show was calling collect. He was begging me to come bail him out so he could still work the party. According to him, the judge had set his bond at "only $200." I assume that I was supposed to say, "Damn, Nick, that's a bargain."

I asked about the charges. "They got me for trespassing. My room-mate threw me out, so I went and slept in an old abandoned building and the cops caught me."

I explained that for a variety of reasons, I could not drop everything and come bail him out. I didn't tell him, but I figured he needed at least three or four days behind bars to dry out. As for the House of Blues event, we already had someone else scheduled to work it.

However, we would need someone to wash carts on Nick's three scheduled days in the shop. We either had to call in Warren the mime or have Gene fill in for those days. If Gene took over, Becky could still work the street and the mime would be in the wings, fresh and ready to take over if Gene burned out or failed to show.

Gene proved to be the logical choice, and with everything now under control, I was able to take a few days off and fly to England. The British Broadcasting Corporation was producing a five-part documentary on World War II British landing craft. Thousands of Brits had made landings in the American-made Higgins boats, and because of that, they were devoting a full segment of their series to Andrew Higgins and his thirty-six-foot ramped Landing Craft Vehicle Personnel (often abbreviated LCVP). Because of my Higgins biography, the BBC wanted me as their American amphibious landing craft expert, and they were willing to pick up my expenses if I would travel to England.

Jane and I had never been to Britain, so the decision to go was a no-brainer. We made a quick five-day trip, but it seemed much, much longer because no one asked about Smitty, Nick, Gene, or Hudson; no one came up short; no one got drunk; no one went missing in action while filming; and there was no way for the shop to contact me.

I returned home mentally relaxed. However, had I known what was about to happen, I would have stayed across the pond for another helping of fish and chips.

The day after I got back, Gene pushed his cart to the corner of Bourbon and Canal as usual, but by the end of the night, he was $619 short and nowhere to be found. That rare "mentally relaxed" feeling that I barely had time to experience suddenly vanished.

A week passed, and Gene didn't call or come by. Nick was now out of jail, and if anyone could find our missing vendor and convince him to come see me, it was The Cisco Kid.

Within hours, Gene was sitting in my office, and with him came a marvelous tale. He and Becky had been working the cart when around 10 p.m., she fell ill and decided to head home. Unfortunately, she still had more than $300 of company money in her pockets. According to Gene, instead of turning around and bringing the cash back to him, she decided to stop and buy some weed—in the middle of the night, on a dark street corner, in the middle of the hood. She reached into her pocket and out came this wad of cash. The drug dealer's eyes must have glistened as he thought, "Thank you, Jesus!" He proceeded to knock Becky upside her head and take her money.

Meanwhile, Gene had convinced a gutter punk to watch his cart while he went home to check on the love of his life. He found her on the couch, broke, weedless, and with a lump on her skull. According to his story, he, as any loving boyfriend would do, stayed to comfort her while his street buddy sold dog after dog. At the end of the night, both his one-time friend and the cash disappeared. By the time Tammy brought the cart in, Gene was short the $300 that Becky supposedly had taken, plus another $319 that walked off with the gutter punk.

Gene had a major problem. The missing company receipts now totaled more than $600. This raised it to the level of a felony, and time in the state pen was not out of the question. Gene pleaded, "Looka here boss, I'll have it all back to you by next week and I swear it ain't neva gonna happen again."

"Until the next time," I thought.

In the midst of this turmoil, ex-longtime vendor Jim Campbell returned. For the past twelve years, Campbell had been living a peaceful life on a dead-end road north of Fairbanks, Alaska. We had kept in touch via email. As he sat there relaxing in the wilderness, it wasn't the call of the wild, but rather the "call of the street" that kept beckoning him, and he just couldn't seem to get it out of his head.

After arriving back in New Orleans in November, he was shocked to discover how much Katrina had changed the city and how bad off it still was. Rents were high, a lot of his old friends had failed to return after the storm, other friends had died, and the friends who remained weren't even close to being the same. Katrina had changed them.

Jim described post-Katrina New Orleans as "a tired town without a lot of vibrancy." With the Quarter no longer feeling like home, he took off to visit a long-lost daughter that he reconnected with through MySpace.

Jim and I still keep in touch online. He's back in Alaska and back on the dead-end road north of Fairbanks, among the north woods and the moose, back home where he had grown up.

On December 5, 2009, as Jim was trying to stay warm in the cold north, Roy Gant, one of our newer vendors, was working his cart in front of Walgreens Drugs at the corner of Iberville and Royal streets. The evening started out peacefully enough. Then, around 9 p.m., a man approached him, demanding a dollar. Gant figured that if he could work, so could the beggar. He politely refused. The man threatened, "If you don't give me the dollar, I'm gonna take it."

He still refused. Some pushing and shoving ensued, and eventually, the guy walked away. Gant brushed off the incident and kept working. Just before midnight, Gant felt a knife blade pressed against his throat and heard a man's voice whisper, "Remember me?"

The street thug had returned, and now he wanted all of Gant's cash. As an ex-Marine, Gant had been well trained in hand-to-hand combat. Instinctively, he grabbed the assailant by his forearm and pushed the knife away. The two struggled, but the robber slipped. At that moment, Gant grabbed his assailant by one of his forearms and by his crotch, lifted him, and body-slammed him face down to the curb.

All the while, Gant kept screaming for someone to call the police. By the time a patrol car arrived, the thug was pinned on the sidewalk. The attacker was booked with attempted armed robbery.

The next morning, Gant's story appeared in the *Times-Picayune*. I called him to my office and explained that from now on, he needed to be extremely careful. There was always the possibly that a friend or a relative of the assailant might be looking for revenge. Or, there was the possibility that someone just might want to prove that they're tougher than Lucky Dogs' Marine.

Four days after the story became public, my prediction proved to be true. Four young men approached Gene on the corner of Canal and Bourbon, mistaking him for Gant. Gene, being streetwise, recognized what was about to go down. Luckily, before it got violent, one of the potential attackers confirmed that Gene was not their target. As soon as they left, Gene called the shop. Two hours later, the thugs returned, demanding to know what corner Gant was working. In the meantime, I had called Gant upstairs to my office and suggested that he take several nights off.

My recommendation was that he go to the 8th District headquarters and let the police know what was transpiring. Being on the front page had made him both a celebrity and a target.

Gant agreed not to work the street, but he still had to survive, and in order to do so, he needed money. He asked that I allow his girlfriend to take his cart out. My concern was whether or not the bad guys targeting him knew who she was. If they did, she might become their mark.

Gant swore they had no way of knowing because she had never worked with him. I approved his plan with two stipulations. First, she would be allowed to work only the corner of Conti and Bourbon outside the Famous Door. There, the club's doorman would be standing right behind her, and another vendor would be working just across the street outside of the Royal Sonesta. Additional benefits of that location were that the corner was well-lighted and frequented by police. It was the safest of all locations. Second, Gant had to agree to stay away from the wagon.

Gene, like Gant, had been thinking about having his girlfriend work with him on his cart. With New Year's and the Sugar Bowl game not far off, Gene wanted to bring Becky back as his helper. His reason? He needed someone he could trust. *Trust!* Hell, the last time she helped him, she donated $300 to a drug dealer and ended up with a lump on her head. In Gene's case, love wasn't just blind—it was downright dumb. But it was his decision.

9

THE PROBLEM CHILDREN

My rather quiet and pleasant morning came to an abrupt end when Raymond barged into my office wanting to borrow $60. It was a gutsy move, especially since he had failed to show for work the previous day. Of course, he had what he claimed to be a "justifiable reason."

"Mr. J, I was planning on comin', but Dee Dee wadn't feelin' too good and I had to go to the store for her first. While walking there, this young black guy pulled up in a white pickup, stopped, got out, and put a cocked pistol in my face and demanded all o' my money. After that I was too shaken to make it in."

This was coming from a man who claimed to have done hard time in the state pen earlier in his life. My theory was that he hadn't come to work because it was cold and rainy. It was the kind of weather that created miserable conditions and made sales slow. Whatever the reason, he was now standing in front of me asking for a loan. He swore that if I gave it to him, he would return and push out in a couple of hours. I knew better, but I gave him the cash anyway. Raymond and Dee Dee weren't great vendors, but they were good people and were always willing to lend a hand when needed. I figured that in this instance, I could afford to do the same.

As the sun beat down on Gravier Street the next morning, Raymond strolled into Lucky Dogs and proclaimed that he had returned the day before but was apparently too late. According to him, when he arrived at the shop at 6 p.m., no one was there to send him out. I smiled. It was one of those "gotcha" moments. Normally, no one would have still been at the warehouse at that time, but on that particular day, I stayed at the office until after 7:30 p.m., and I knew for a fact that Raymond had never returned. Since he failed to live up to his end of the agreement, I informed him that I wanted him to start repaying the loan when he checked in at the end of the night. His loan, like all the other loans that I do for vendors, came out of my pocket, not out of the company's money.

"Fine," he shot back, "And don't worry, 'cause I'm not gonna borrow any more money from you."

Even he looked puzzled after the words came out of his mouth. I knew that would never happen, so I just didn't respond—no sense in ratcheting up the tension level to where he might walk out. Raymond might not be a great vendor, but he would do all right on New Year's Eve. That, in addition to the dogs he would sell to the Sugar Bowl crowd on New Year's Day, wouldn't be a bad one-cart total for an off-corner. And, with sales still down from pre-Katrina days, we needed to sell every dog we could. To accomplish that, we needed vendors, and most of our crew, like Raymond, had not been showing up because of the cold, nasty weather.

Now, with New Year's only two days away and blue skies overhead, vendors were returning in droves, and all of them were claiming to have been deathbed-ill with the flu. A person more cynical than I might have concluded that there was a correlation between the Sugar Bowl crowds filling the hotels, the diminishing chance of rain, and the phenomenal rate of our crew's recovery, but I knew that our crew would never fake illness—not our guys. Instead, I chose to refer to the mass recuperation as "the Miracle on Gravier."

Typically, during major events, vendors are in a hurry to get their carts out on the street, wanting to capture every sale possible. In this hurried state, their brains often stop functioning, and they'll get to their corners and realize that they have only half of their buns, or that they forgot their tongs, or that they left their napkins in the shop. Nick spent several hours on New Year's Eve running forgotten items out to vendors. He also delivered a hot dog cart and supplies to the 8th District police station. Like the vendors, the officers have a tough time getting away to eat. Donating a cart and supplies during busy periods and setting it up in the station is our way of saying that we appreciate what they do.

Throughout the second half of the day and until almost midnight, Nick ran additional supplies and condiments out to the street. He was officially off, but vendors tipped him for making the special deliveries.

Around 4 a.m., after about four hours of sleep, Nick returned to work and started cleaning carts. By the time Jason arrived, half of the fleet had been washed. This is exactly why we forgive so easily. Major events require a pool of labor—guys who aren't afraid to work long hours and who are willing to do menial tasks.

The long hours, the problems created by the street hustlers, and the fact that the majority of people on Bourbon are drinking all make for a tough working environment. Bartenders at least have the ability to walk into a storeroom to get away from an aggressive or obnoxious customer. On the street, vendors have nowhere to go. They're totally exposed.

By the end of the night, the stress often makes them irritable and edgy. When fifteen to twenty irritable and edgy people are gathered together in a warehouse, you can bet that tempers will flare, problems will arise, and—once in a blue moon—fists will fly. Usually, no one ends up getting hurt, and within fifteen minutes or so, the disagreeing parties have settled their differences and are across the street downing a few beers together.

Working the long hours also creates another problem: vendors burn out both mentally and physically. The only way for them to avoid this is to pair up with another vendor and work as a team. In this arrangement, one vendor sets the cart up in the morning and pushes it out to the corner, and the partner shows up around 8 p.m., takes over, and pushes the wagon back in at the end of the night. Those who follow this example generally make it through New Year's and Mardi Gras in much better condition than those who attempt to do it alone.

The 2010 Carnival season was an especially difficult one because Super Bowl Sunday fell right in the middle of Mardi Gras. The Super Bowl wasn't in New Orleans that year, but New Orleans *was* in the Super Bowl. On game day, the early parades rolled, but those scheduled to take to the streets later in the afternoon and at night chose to reschedule for another day. The krewes knew that with the Saints in the Super Bowl, the crowds along their parade routes would be sparse. Besides, those riding on the floats were also Who Dat fans and they, too, wanted to watch their team take on the Colts.

Being a Who Dat fan myself, I also wanted to watch the game. The vendors had pushed out and the shop was quiet. I took the opportunity to go to a party being thrown by my son, Jeff, and his fiancée Jenn at her house just across the river. At the end of the third quarter I told Jane and Jenn's parents, Lyn and Randy Dickmann, that the Saints were going to win and I had best head back to the shop before "all hell broke loose." I excused myself and quickly drove back across the river.

As soon as the game—which the Saints won—was over, the French Quarter and the Central Business District became packed with fans and the roadways leading into the city were jammed by thousands upon thousands of others wanting to join in the celebration.

And celebrate they did. The fans were jubilant, excited, and nonviolent. No cars were turned over, no fires were set, and no riots had to be squashed. People came out into the streets and were cheering and hugging one another. It looked like a re-enactment of Times Square at the end of World War II. It was exactly what a mentally depressed and structurally torn-apart city needed.

Two days later, the city of New Orleans and the Saints threw the largest and most well-attended victory parade in Super Bowl history. From my vantage point atop the seventh floor of the Whitney parking garage, I could see the crowds and the street below. Hundreds of thousands of fans were lined shoulder to shoulder along the parade route. At one point, a fan in a Saints jersey running up and down the street organized a crowd cheer: he pointed to one side of St. Charles Avenue and shouted "Go," then turned and pointed to the other side and shouted "Saints!" The resulting chant was composed of thousands of fans alternately shouting "Go Saints! Go Saints!" for minutes on end.

Though the floats were not yet in view, I could tell that they weren't far away; the thunderous roar of the crowd kept getting louder and louder and closer and closer. As the floats finally rolled into view, the crowd below me went berserk.

Saints quarterback Drew Brees was standing atop a float throwing miniature Nerf footballs to the Black and Gold faithful. Players on the other floats were tossing Mardi Gras beads. It was a love fest between the fans, and the players and the coaches.

As the parade passed below and I watched the horde of screaming and waving people, for the first time I truly believed that both the city and the company were going to make it. God—the Saints had won the Super Bowl! In the words of Saints' radio play-by-play man Jim Henderson, "Pigs had flown, and hell had frozen over."

Down below, among the thousands of enthusiastic fans was Tommy Turner. The last time I had seen Tommy was at the shop, shortly before I paid the hooker who claimed to have been hit by Danner's cart. Now, Tommy was back in town and working for a company licensed to sell NFL Super Bowl pennants.

After the parade, he stopped by the warehouse to apologize for his past behavior and to repay the money that I had loaned him. He also wanted to know if he would ever be allowed to work a wagon again. I assured him that as long as he was sober, he was always welcome. He smiled, we shook hands, and then he drifted off down the block, shouting "Getcha Saints Super Bowl pennants!"

Because of the parade, streets had been blocked off, and traffic in front of our building was gridlocked. Drivers turned off their engines, got out of their cars, and struck up new friendships.

When I opened the warehouse door, a woman in a car directly in front of the shop asked if we had any hot Lucky Dogs. Though we had none at the shop, we began to talk. She was trying to make it to one of New Orleans' finest restaurants, August, located in the next block. Her husband was waiting for her there, and she was already an hour late. As we spoke, her husband walked up and insisted that she, their son, and their son's girlfriend head to dinner on foot. He would stay with the car until the traffic cleared.

After the woman's departure, the gentleman and I began to talk. We shared Super Bowl stories and Katrina stories. The woman in the car in front of him joined in, and we discovered that we had mutual friends. For more than four hours, she had been trying to get to the Hilton Hotel, which was only four blocks away, but no matter in which direction she traveled, the streets had been barricaded.

People walking by were shouting "Who Dat!" and "Go Saints!" and those with long, tubular plastic horns were attempting to play "When the Saints Go Marching In," though at times their renditions were almost unrecognizable. It was an enthusiastic yet respectful crowd. The only exception to the crowd's politeness was one brief moment when it looked as if traffic was about to begin moving.

Earlier, a woman had gotten out of her car with her children and walked off to watch the parade. When traffic in front of her abandoned vehicle started to move, everyone behind it was blocked. Four young guys got out of a Jeep with an out-of-state license plate and decided that they would eliminate the obstruction. They started rocking the woman's small car in an attempt to flip it over onto the sidewalk. At that point, several locals descended on them and forced them to back off.

This is New Orleans; when we win, we don't overturn cars, and we don't burn buildings. We party, and we party hard, but we do so within reason. As babies, we cut our teeth on Mardi Gras parades—Rex, Zulu, Bacchus, Endymion, Carrollton, and the rest of the krewes that take to the streets during the Carnival season. Some of our earliest memories are of attending St. Patrick's Day parades, St. Joseph's Day parades, parading in the Cub Scouts or Brownies, and even taking part in parades at our preschool. We grow up understanding that the four most important things in life are God, family, country, and catching beads. Four guys from some other state were not about to tarnish our record.

On Wednesday, February 11, heavy rains caused the day's Mardi Gras parades to be canceled. It was a cold and miserable day, but fifteen vendors still took to the streets. Nick pushed three carts out, but that was all that he could physically manage. This time of year, the heavily loaded wagons weigh more than 1,000 pounds, and with most of the corners being anywhere from five to thirteen blocks from the shop, a pusher can get worn out quickly. Because our licenses are for "push carts," they cannot legally be motorized or towed.

On Thursday, the weather improved. From then through Fat Tuesday, the days were eerily trouble-free. Not a single vendor got drunk, no one came up short, no one ran off with the company's money, and everyone scheduled to work showed up.

However, on Ash Wednesday, the day after Mardi Gras, only four out of what had been a crew of twenty vendors came in to take out a cart. By Saturday, everyone was still dragging, but the crew had increased to twelve. One of those reporting for duty was Smitty.

He hired Nick to push his cart to the corner of St. Ann and Bourbon. They had just pulled up to the corner when a couple in their car, which was parked just behind where Smitty's cart had stopped, began arguing with one another. As the couple continued quarreling, the man's foot accidentally hit the gas pedal, and the car shot backward, crashing into the Lucky Dog cart. The impact caused the wagon to fly into the middle of Bourbon Street, where it barely missed a passing pedestrian.

When the police arrived, they discovered that the man was drunk, had a revoked driver's license, and no insurance. They also discovered that he had a stash of marijuana and illegal pills hidden under his front seat. Hitting the cart was the least of his worries.

Smitty stood there, pipe dangling out of one side of his mouth, just staring at the officers and grinning. Over the years, he had run his wagon into at least two private cars, one police car, and a police motorcycle. He almost completed the first ever "NOPD Triple Slam" by running into an officer on horseback, but the animal was smart enough and fast enough to get out of his way. After assessing this latest incident, Smitty turned to Nick and proudly remarked, "At least this time, it's not my fault."

The following morning, another problem arose. This time, Smitty was not involved.

As I was leaving my house, I called the shop to confirm that all was well. Everything seemed fine, though a gentleman by the name of Patrick had called wanting to speak with me. He had said that it was important that I contact him.

I later discovered that Patrick was the head of the Downtown Development District. When I reached him, he informed me that one of his Public Safety Rangers had observed a beer being sold off our cart at

Canal and Bourbon. Because we were not licensed to sell alcohol, such a transaction was illegal. I said that I would take care of the matter.

"Wait," Patrick replied. "The vendor didn't sell it; one of the street guys standing next to his cart did."

The Ranger had already notified the NOPD lieutenant in charge of the Canal Street detail, and the lieutenant had already spoken with Gene, our vendor, about the incident. Patrick continued, "The reason I am calling is much more serious."

According to his Ranger, after the lieutenant left, Gene allegedly told another Ranger that "the white bitch better watch herself" or he would "have one of the street thugs get her."

My response was, "If that's the case, then you need to get the police involved and press charges."

Within the hour, Gene and I were sitting in my office, and I was explaining in detail the accusations being levied against him. He recalled the beer incident down to the specifics, recalling that the events took place on a rainy night, but he assured me that the beer was not his. It belonged to a gutter punk who, according to him, had not sold it but had given it to another street friend.

As for threatening the Ranger, he emphatically denied it, though he did admit that he and one of his friends from the Quarter, had been standing in front of the shop the next day when a Ranger rode by on her bike. She stopped and spoke with them about the previous night's incident.

In Gene's version of the events, his friend informed the Ranger on the bike that the Ranger from the night before had better watch her back or someone on the street might get her. I called Patrick at the Downtown Development District and put the call on speaker phone. Gene once again denied any knowledge of a beer being sold by anyone on or near his cart, and he denied ever threatening anyone.

The Ranger who had made the accusation happened to be in Patrick's office, and she was steadfast in her claims as to what she had seen and heard. I asked Gene to leave the room. When he left, I asked the Ranger once again if she was positive. I explained that before I took away someone's livelihood, I had to be certain about the facts. She was unwavering.

I went downstairs to speak with Gene. He was furious and again proclaimed it was his friend who had made the statement and that it was a *statement*, not a threat.

"At that moment, in front of the Ranger," I asked, "why didn't you tell your friend that you disagreed with his remarks? You would have distanced yourself from whatever it was that had been said, and the Ranger would not have had any complaint against you."

He didn't want to listen. He thought the whole thing was a ploy so that I could take him off his corner and give it to Hudson. I told him that once he cooled down, he should go to the Downtown Development District's office and speak with Patrick in person. If he was telling the truth and had never made the threat, then in person, he might be able to overcome the problem. If he was cleared, then I would allow him to come back to work.

No good would have come from simply sending him back out with a cart. The Rangers would have been like vultures waiting to pick him apart, and frankly, I would not have blamed them. In their eyes, Gene was guilty of threatening one of theirs. Additionally, if Gene had just pushed out to his corner without rectifying the problem, it would have appeared that as a company, we didn't care to work with the Downtown Development District's enforcement personnel. No good would have come from that, either. However, if he went to Patrick and calmly explained his side of the story in person, perhaps the situation could be resolved.

Gene left the shop and headed straight for the Downtown Development District's office—a fact confirmed when a DDD employee called, wanting to book a cart for a private party. She said it wasn't until our vendor walked into their headquarters that she remembered she had not contacted us. I explained why Gene was there and asked if all was well.

"No loud voices are coming from the other room," she replied, "so it doesn't sound like there's a problem. Besides, Patrick's a pretty big guy, and I feel certain that he can take care of himself."

Patrick, Gene, and the two Rangers talked. Later, as I was sitting in Commerce having lunch, Gene strolled in to let me know that "everything's good."

"Looka here, boss," he said. "Me and the Ranger shook hands and hugged, and now Patrick wants you to call him."

When I got back to the shop, Gene was telling everyone the story. I interrupted and asked if he had gotten to the part where they all joined hands and sang "Kumbaya." Gene grinned. We were back to normal—at least for the moment.

Patrick's concern was the safety of his Rangers, and he wanted to be certain that if a problem occurred on the corner of Canal and Bourbon, his Rangers could depend on Gene. Once Gene assured him and them that he would "have their backs," all was forgiven. In fact, the following night, the Ranger who had accused Gene of making the threat brought him a Subway sandwich, chips, and a drink. They hugged again. After she left, Gene called and asked if I thought it would be all right if he ate the sandwich.

"Gene, she's not trying to poison you," I responded. "She's just being friendly and saying, 'I'm glad that this incident is behind us.' That's what normal people do."

While Gene was having his cart catered, Snake was at the shop having to deal with Karl. Karl had pushed in early, drunk and short of cash. When Snake walked to the kitchen to call me, Karl took off.

I told Snake not to worry; I would handle it in the morning. Karl had been on his best behavior for weeks. The missing money was not an issue; I knew that he would pay it. The drinking, however, was a real problem.

The following day, Karl called after lunch. He tried to argue that someone "musta slipped him somethin'," but he also claimed that the only drinks he consumed that night were two Sprites, both purchased off his own cart and both with their caps sealed. The only food that he had eaten was a hamburger that a friend had bought for him, and he swore that person would never attempt to harm him. If I was to believe Karl's account, there was no logical explanation for his claim that he had been slipped something. My guess was that he had fallen off the wagon and right onto the barroom floor.

My initial thought was to no longer allow him to work a cart. However, after speaking with Jason and Nick, I discovered that Snake was afraid Karl might retaliate against him if he lost his job. I knew that Karl would never do anything of the sort, but I didn't want Snake to worry. Still, there had to be some sort of punishment. Other vendors were watching, and I couldn't make an exception and allow Karl to continue working without holding him accountable for his actions.

Later that afternoon, Karl called to say that he was coming in to pay his shortage. The moment he strolled through the door, he started proclaiming, "Cuz, I didn't get drunk because of somethin' that I had done. Had I done it, I'd tell you that I had done it. You know that. I was waylaid by somebody."

This would have been entertaining, but I had other things that needed to be taken care of and I did not have time for the unabridged version of Karl's story.

I explained to him that he could still work a cart, but there had to be some type of punishment. I figured a suspension was appropriate.

"I understand, Cuz, truly I do. How about I take off Wednesday and Thursday and get back on my corner Friday? Sound fair?"

"I'm thinking more in terms of a four-day suspension. Come back to work on Monday. That way you miss the weekend. Then Monday, I'll put you back on your corner, but remember this is a one-time reprieve. Do it again, and the next suspension will be for six months. Do we understand one another?"

"Come on, Cuz. It weren't that bad."

"Karl, this is not debatable. Also, when you go back downstairs, tell the others that you've been suspended. They're already circling like vultures and wanting your corner. They need to know that you'll be back on Monday. Do you understand?"

"Gotcha. Don't worry, I'll be here early Monday."

Karl failed to return not only on Monday, but on Tuesday, as well. On Wednesday, he strolled into the warehouse and shouted, "Cuz, I'm back!" Indeed, he was, but because he had not returned on the agreed-upon date, I suggested that he take another weekend off.

"Damn, Cuz," he responded.

A few days later, on Easter morning, Gene reported for work. The night before, Nick had been stopped by the police for violating the open container law—drinking on the street from a glass container is illegal. Were that his only offense, the officers probably would have just given him a warning, but when they ran his name through their database, they discovered that there was an attachment on him for failing

Harold Vincent working a cart in Jackson Square.

to pay a previous court fine. All things considered, I figured Nick would once again be a guest of the Civil Sheriff for at least thirty days. In the meantime, Gene would take over working all of the scheduled catering events, and another vendor, Harold Vincent, would assume Nick's part-time cart-washing duties.

Nick called from Central Lockup pleading for me to bail him out. I was not in the mood. This was tough love, tough management, or just plain being fed up with his reoccurring problem. This time, there would be no get-out-of-jail-free card.

He didn't have to go to jail; he could have paid his fines, but instead, he chose to spend his money on booze. Now, it was my turn to choose, and I, like him, chose not to spend my money on his fines. If he didn't want to pay them, why should I?

Later that afternoon, he called again, praying that I would reconsider. He learned an important lesson: not all prayers get answered.

I told Nick I was happy with the job Vincent was doing. He didn't have friends dropping by distracting him, and he wasn't pushing carts out when he was supposed to be working in the shop. He was a self-starter, and he even had a place to live other than the elevator shaft.

"I can be all that," Nick fired back. "Just give me one more chance. You'll see."

He was desperate. I told him that I would consider it, but that it might take a day or two. I figured the extra time behind bars might help serve as a deterrent.

Several days later, on April 9, I stopped by Central Lockup and posted Nick's bail. Even though Nick now was out, Vincent retained the part-time cart-cleaning position. Nick could push carts, he could work parties, and he could even help Tammy in the kitchen for a few hours on Friday and Saturday nights; but other than that, I saw no reason to reward him. I wanted him to be able to make a living, but I did not want to reward him for unacceptable behavior.

On Nick's first night back, as he was washing chili pans in the kitchen for Tammy, Hudson was having his cart pushed to the shop by one of his street friends. They left the corner of Toulouse and Bourbon around 5 a.m. Twenty minutes later, they were in front of our warehouse. As Hudson was pulling cash out of his pocket to pay his pusher, a guy came out of the alley with a broken bottle in his hand.

"Give it up, mother f—ker," he demanded.

"I ain't giving up nothing!"

"F—king give it up!"

The assailant slashed at Hudson with the bottle. The pusher took off running down the street, leaving Hudson to face his attacker alone and unarmed. The robber started jabbing at Hudson with the bottle, and Hudson was blocking each assault. The thief caught Hudson across his left forearm, ripping open his flesh. The wound was serious, but Hudson continued fighting for his life. One vendor would later describe the gash by saying, "the meat was just hanging down from the bone." The attacker also sliced James across the chest, but luckily, that cut was more superficial.

Hudson landed a solid blow, knocking his assailant to the ground, but three of the attacker's friends came out of the alley and headed straight for Hudson. Before they could reach him, Hudson made it to the shop and began pounding on the door and calling for help. The door opened, though from Hudson's perspective, it seemed to have taken forever. Once help arrived, the attackers broke and ran. Hudson took satisfaction in the fact that the "mother f—kers got nothing."

Within minutes, the police and an ambulance were on the scene. Hudson ended up with twenty-four stitches in his forearm. He was lucky to be alive—the broken bottle could just as easily have slit his throat or severed an artery.

The next day, another problem arose. As I was pulling up in front of my house around 10:30 p.m., my cell rang. It was Snake. Roy Gant had been arrested. The ex-Marine hero from a few months ago was now in the back seat of a police cruiser on his way to Central Lockup.

Gant had gotten into an argument with a street mime, and the situation had apparently escalated to the point where knives were pulled. Reportedly, the mime had made sexually explicit remarks to Gant's girlfriend. (It was another case of a talking mime. The Quarter seemed to be infested with them.) After allegedly making the remarks to Gant's girlfriend and having Gant respond angrily, the mime knocked a display of Coke bottles from atop Gant's cart. He then accused Gant of taking money out of his tip box, which led to an exchange of more heated words. The mime started to walk away, but instead he turned back, ran toward Gant, and spat in Gant's face. Then he pulled a small knife, to which Gant responded by pulling a knife of his own. We're not talking Bowie knives here—we're talking small pocketknives with three-inch blades. Nothing a respectable street fighter would ever own, much less pull out in public.

At any rate, all hell was about to break loose when the police arrived. Both parties were arrested and taken to Central Lockup. The following morning, I called the jail. The charges weren't nearly as bad as they could have been. Charge number one was disturbing the peace—a $300 bond. Charge number two was levied because, like Nick, Gant had an attachment for failing to pay a previous fine. Bond on that charge was set at $1,000. Gant, it appeared, would be placed on our "unable to report" list.

By the following afternoon, things were back to normal. I knew this because Nick, once again, wanted to borrow money. I countered by offering to let him work Canal and Bourbon—one of the busiest corners. He wasn't thrilled with the idea, but he pushed out a cart.

The next morning, as soon I walked in the shop, Nick approached me wanting a $20 draw against some future catering event he might work. I asked, "What happened to the money that you made last night?"

"I let my home girl work the cart and keep it."

"Your what?"

"My home girl Susan. She's from Mississippi, just like me."

"Nick, you were supposed to work the cart. You never said anything about any 'home girl.'"

"I know, but she really needed the money."

"I gave you the corner because *you* really needed the money."

"I'm just tryin' to help her out."

"Well if your 'home girl' worked the cart, then why don't you ask her for the twenty dollars?"

"That ain't right."

"Sure it is. I put you on a great corner and what do you do? You turn it over to some girl who hasn't even filled out an application."

The next day, Nick and Home Girl decided to partner up on a permanent basis. Besides working the cart together, they had also agreed to share an apartment and split the bills.

I had given Nick and Home Girl one of the top-selling corners. They had a chance to make good money. However, at the end of their first night, their sales were far below what they should have been. I started asking questions.

Nick, it seemed, had not stayed on his cart. Instead, he had spent the night roaming up and down Bourbon with his street friends while Susan worked the wagon. By 2 a.m., the hardcore thugs started congregating at the corner of Canal and Bourbon. She got scared, and Tammy and Thomas suggested, during their last money pickup, that she go ahead and push in. Home Girl and The Cisco Kid's partnership had survived less than twelve hours. Later, the duo would reunite and attempt a comeback.

On April 30, Gene reappeared. No one had seen or heard from him in weeks. According to his story, he had been in Oklahoma, where he had earned enough money to repay Lucky Dogs in full for all of his past shortages. With his bill now cleared, he was hoping that he could once again go back out on a cart.

At almost the same time, Gant was released from Central Lockup, and he immediately began consuming large quantities of alcohol. As he made his way from watering hole to watering hole, he stopped by and managed to irritate every vendor on the street. The next morning, he showed up at the shop, still under the influence, wanting to work a cart. That wasn't possible.

Finally, he accepted the fact that he was not going to be allowed to push out. He started to walk out of the shop, but apparently changed his mind, turned and settled in a chair by the front door. A few minutes later, he began ranting about how his old girlfriend, Susan, was now "shacking up" with Nick. Home Girl, it turned out, had been Gant's "old lady."

I had no idea, but according to him, it "didn't matter anymore." Well, it apparently had mattered the night before—when he discovered that Nick and Susan were together, he ran into them on Bourbon and supposedly "got up in Nick's face." Nick responded by putting a fist into Gant's. The fight was over in a flash, decision Nick.

Gant came back to the shop the following afternoon, sober and wanting to go out. He swore there wouldn't be any trouble. In his words, he was going to "steer clear" of anything that could send him back to jail. First, he said the guards had "worked his butt off." Second, he recalled that in prison, those who complained were not viewed with kindness. "If you complained," Gant said, "they threatened to send you upstairs with the guys sentenced from five to ten years, and those guys didn't care what they did to you." Because he was sober and because he had a reason to remain that way, I gave him another chance.

All was going fine until later that evening, when Home Girl skipped with $59 of Lucky Dogs' money. Rumor had it that she and Gant had had words on the street, and she got scared and took off.

As a result, $59 of company money was missing along with $40 of Nick's own cash. The Cisco Kid was devastated. Never, *ever*, did he believe that his home girl would steal from him—maybe from her old flame, Gant, but never from *him*!

The following afternoon, she showed up all apologetic. She offered a story, but no money. She swore that if we put her back on a cart, she would immediately start repaying what she owed. I decided not to chance it, at least for the time being.

So, for a number of reasons recently, we had eliminated Gene and Karl. Now, Home Girl was added to the list. As we moved further from Mardi Gras and into June and July, we were losing even more vendors. Most were leaving on their own to avoid the heat and humidity of the New Orleans summer. Those vendors would stay gone until cooler temperatures returned in the fall. Fewer vendors meant a smaller gross, which in turn meant reduced profits. All things considered, it seemed to be time to become more forgiving, to bring the lost sheep back into the fold, and to get the money back into the operating account.

On a more positive note, we had been doing a considerable number of catering events. Nick alone had worked three events in four days. His most recent had been the inauguration party for New Orleans' newly elected mayor, Mitch Landrieu.

The morning after that party, when I walked into the shop, Home Girl was sitting in a chair by the front door waiting for "her man." He was upstairs, sound asleep outside of my office, waiting for me to arrive. Short on cash, he was hoping that I would cut his check a few days early.

When he walked into the office, I asked if he was intending to pay off Home Girl's shortage. If he did, and if he listed the cart under his name and took full responsibility for her actions, I would allow her to work with him. As an added bonus, she could wash dishes for Tammy on Friday and Saturday nights. She could use that money to pay him back what he had paid to us on her behalf.

It was a win-win-win-win situation: the company would get reimbursed for the shortage, she could work a cart, Nick would get his money back, and the company would add another vendor to its roster. With some luck, the plan just might hold together—at least through the weekend. Anything beyond that would be lagniappe.

Nick was thrilled with the arrangement. "I'll make certain that she stays on the cart and doesn't come up short," he promised. "In my heart I don't believe that she'll ever do it again."

I wasn't entirely comfortable with the arrangement, even though it was my idea. Nick, of all people, promising to be responsible and make certain that someone else would do what they were supposed to do? The whole scenario reeked of disaster, but an extra cart on the street was always helpful. Also, by the time the partnership came to a bitter end, hopefully we would have recruited one or two new vendors. Even better, maybe a couple of old ones might have drifted back into town.

On May 5 one old vendor did reappear. It was Karl, sober, humble, and apologetic, but not clean-shaven. He was looking for forgiveness and work. We had a frank discussion—the kind you can't have in most corporations today. I brought up his last day on the job, how he was slobbering drunk and grunting like an animal about to pounce on its prey. I reminded him how he had tried to intimidate Snake and how he had made life miserable for both the day and night managers. That kind of behavior could not be tolerated. However, if he could live by the rules, we would give him one more chance. If he couldn't, then he should look for work elsewhere. In addition, if he returned and crossed the line on even one occasion, I would ask him to leave, and I expected him to respect that request and calmly comply.

He gave me his word that there would be no trouble. He even admitted that at times, he might have been a tad overly aggressive. For the moment, his tough-man persona was gone. He was broke, in need of rent money, and he had nowhere else to turn. He probably had crossed the line with his most recent employer, and as a result, they, too, had sent him packing, just as we had. Now we were his last resort.

He thrust out his hand and wanted to shake. It was more a clasp of arms than a shake. Then, he said he was heading home to shave and eat before reporting back to work. In typical Karl fashion, he didn't return for more than a week.

As Karl was walking out of the office, Nick buzzed, wanting to come up. I didn't have to be Nostradamus to know what was about to occur. So, before he got upstairs, I taped a note on the outside of my door that read: "Today is: No Draw Thursday."

When he walked up to knock, the sign was right in front of him at eye level. He stepped into the office laughing. "Is there something that I can do for you?" I asked. The note had subdued him enough that instead of asking for the customary $20, he requested only $5. I didn't mind lending it to him because he was scheduled to work a cart at a wedding reception the following evening.

As I walked into the warehouse Saturday morning, I was welcomed with a monologue. "They loved me," Nick said. "They all wanted to have their picture taken with 'the Kid.' The bride and groom, their parents, they all wanted their picture taken with me. The wedding was great. The food was fantastic. The flowers were gorgeous. The bride's dress was lovely. Everything was just perfect."

You would have thought that he was the father of the bride. Before he finished, I fully expected to hear that the newlyweds had decided to name their firstborn Nick, whether it was a boy or a girl. The Cisco Kid was back at the top of his game. I wish the same could have been said for Karl.

On May 18 around 2 a.m., Snake called. Once again, he was having trouble checking Karl in. Karl had been back for three days, and all had gone fine until tonight. Now, the old Karl had returned, and he was in rare form.

I had him come to the phone. It was obvious that he had been drinking. He kept shouting into the phone that an alligator must have bitten one of his sausages. I wasn't certain as to how he knew what an alligator's bite looked like, and frankly, at 2 a.m. I really didn't care.

I demanded that he stop rambling and allow Snake to check him in. After that was finished, I told him I wanted him to take at least three months off. He was drunk, but he had enough functioning brain cells to know that he was in deep trouble. He replied, "I'm gonna go walkin'."

I was hoping that he was making reference to something as substantial as an Australian walkabout, and as such, I replied, "I hope you're talking about a long, long walk. Might I suggest retracing the Lewis and Clark trail?"

"Yep, Cuz, I really gotta get outta here for a while."

Even Karl could see that he was spiraling out of control. The best-case scenario was for him to get away from the street. I wished him a safe trek and attempted to go back to sleep, but it was difficult. All I could think about was alligators chomping down on Lucky Dogs.

As I sat in my office finishing up some paperwork the following evening, I noticed on the monitor that Snake had arrived for the night shift and that Nick was in the kitchen. I called downstairs to let Snake know I was in the building. Upon learning of my presence, Nick got on the phone and insisted on coming upstairs.

A few minutes later, he barged into my office, demanding that I stop what I was doing and walk over to Bourbon to see how "blitzed" Tim Danner was. It was easy to tell that Danner was not the only one who had recently quenched his thirst.

"I'll have Snake check on him and he can determine whether or not Danner needs to be pushed in."

That was unacceptable. Nick demanded that *I* go, and that I do so right then.

I again said that I was going to send Snake out to assess the situation. At that point, Nick shouted, "I quit!" slammed the door, and walked out. A few minutes later, Snake headed out to check on both Danner and Nick. Danner was at least sober enough to know that he shouldn't be working, and he had already started pushing in. I was halfway proud of him.

As Danner pushed through the door, he looked at me and said, "Come on now, don't be mad. You look mad. I don't want you to be mad. *I'm* not mad. I saw Snake, and he didn't look mad. Please don't be mad. I always pay my bill. I got money, you'll see—uh, but if I don't, could you lend me $25 so I don't come up short?"

I soon discovered that Danner was $19 short. Indeed, had I loaned him $25 he would not have been short, but that didn't happen. He quickly followed with a promise that he would borrow the money from someone else and return with what he still owed within the hour. He even asked if I would still be at the shop. I assured him that I would.

"Good," he responded. As he walked past me on his way out, he put his hand on my shoulder and said, "I love you, man." He and I both knew that he wasn't going to make it back in for several days.

By the time Snake hit Bourbon Street, Nick had already pushed his cart a block up the street and abandoned it by another vendor. He, Home Girl, and exactly $141.78 were missing. I wasn't surprised. However, I knew that come tomorrow morning, he would sober up, realize that he had screwed up, and walk into my office looking for forgiveness and a cart.

Sure enough, just before noon the next day, he and Susan reappeared. According to him, the shortage was totally his fault, and Home Girl had nothing to do with it. I disagreed, pointing out that she had done nothing to stop him from taking the cash and that she had also helped him to spend it, so indeed she, too, had to be held accountable.

With what they had taken from the company and with what they had made in commissions, they had blown more than $250. Now, well rested, they were ready to go back out on a cart. However, my answer was "no."

Nick's only option was to work off the shortage, and I offered him an opportunity to do so. Friday morning, he and Gene could clean out our storage unit in Metairie. What they earned would be put toward their shortages. He went ballistic.

"Why won't you gimme a chance to work a cart and pay you back? Ya gave Gene all kinda chances. You've never helped me!"

"I am giving you a chance," I firmly replied. "And as for helping you, who took money out of his own pocket to bail you out of jail? Who took money out of his wallet the time before, when you were locked up, and brought it to you? Who has *constantly* loaned you money, even when you weren't scheduled to work? You've missed at least four parties, and either Mark or I ended up having to cover for you, yet you're still here. So don't tell me that no one ever does you any favors. Your problem is you don't appreciate what has been done for you, and I'll admit that I'm guilty of enabling your bad behavior by lending you money. But we're about to enter into a new relationship."

"What's Gene got on you? He's gotta have somethin', cause you always help him!"

"You know damn well that I haven't done any more for Gene than I've done for you."

Nick could tell from the tone of my voice and the expression on my face that I was pissed. He quickly changed the subject.

"My income tax check should come any day. I'll pay off my shortage, and I'll even pay back the $50 that I owe you."

"I believe you, but it's $75, not $50."

A moment or two later, he left the office and headed downstairs. In less than five minutes, the buzzer rang. I called down to see what they wanted. Nick answered.

"Can me and Home Girl take out a cart?"

"Jesus, Nick, I don't have Alzheimer's! Pay first, and then we'll talk."

"What? You don't trust me? You think I'm gonna take the company's money?"

"Well, let's see, just last night you took $141. Do I trust you? Hell no! And it's not because you're a thief. It's because you're weak. As soon as you get frustrated, you start guzzling Cisco."

Nick hung up the phone, and within minutes, he and Home Girl were standing in my office. In a last-ditch effort to take the heat off of himself, he tried to throw Rick Puggini under the bus by claiming that earlier in the week, his co-worker had threatened him.

Puggini, it seemed, believed that Nick had "ratted him out" to Tammy—he figured that was the only way she could have known that he had been drinking on his cart. In retaliation, Puggini threatened to bash Nick's head in with the red handle from the shop's floor jack.

Nick denied telling Tammy anything and then supposedly responded to Puggini's threat by saying, "Ya better not miss, 'cause if you do, I'll cut your throat from side to side."

Home Girl, standing by Nick's side as he told the tale, couldn't stay quiet any longer. "Puggini also kept coming over to our cart that night and throwing ice at me," she added.

"Yeah!" Nick continued. "He did that, and you're still going to put him out!"

"Nick, did you ever come and tell me about the threats? And Susan, did you ever tell me about Puggini throwing ice at you?"

"No," both replied.

"Then how can you possibly expect me to have done anything about it? However, now that I know, I'll speak with Rick. By the way, Nick, I need you and Gene here at 9 tomorrow morning."

Summers are always a tough time to hold on to vendors. Daytime temperatures reach the mid-nineties, and the humidity is just as high. The night cools down only to the eighties. Most people want to work in air-conditioned buildings, not on the street braving the heat, humidity, mosquitoes, and rain. I knew that our two problem children would repay their debts, and within a matter of days, they would be back working a cart. I knew that we needed them, but I couldn't make it seem that easy. Once their debts had been repaid, I would explain that we still needed time to consider whether or not they would be allowed to return.

They'd moan; they'd groan; they'd pester their fellow vendors to lobby on their behalf. Then, they'd try and convince Tammy and Snake to put in a good word. I would mull it over for a day or so but ultimately agree to give them one last chance.

Why? Because we had been well aware of their past failures, but we still put them in a position where they would once again fail. It was only right that we accepted part of the blame. Plus they weren't dangerous; they never harmed anyone. They always kept their carts clean, and they always repaid their debts. They were willing to work and pay their own way in society, and sometimes for months on end, they would be perfect vendors. They were, in many ways, like kids who never matured. Every now and then, they had to be put in "time out."

On May 21 Gene and Nick were at the shop by 9 a.m. Gene was rested and ready—after all, he had had more than two months to get that way. Nick was lounging in a chair by the front door. There was no sign of Home Girl.

Still, I had a two-man crew ready and—at least in Gene's case—willing to get to work. It was time to begin their trek on the road to redemption. Instead of taking them to the storage unit, I decided to send them upstairs to clean and neatly arrange everything we had stored on our third floor. By lunchtime, they were finished, and they came down to the office.

Gene sat in a chair across from me and said, "Listen here, boss, you gotta admit when I'm right—there ain't a vendor out there that can touch my sales."

"When we teamed up, we made good money," Nick chimed in.

"True," I responded, "but what about the nights that you forgot to give the company its share?"

"Come on, boss, listen here," Gene said. "You know what the problem is?"

"I know—Becky and Home Girl?"

"You got it."

"Not really. You and Nick handle the money. You're the ones that give it to the girls. If you weren't blaming Becky and Susan, you'd be blaming two other random girls."

Gene was not about to give up.

"I gotta get back to workin' and makin' money. When you gonna lemme and Nick go back out?"

"You and Nick both owe the company three days' worth of work before you're out of the financial hole. After that, I have a plan. You're both waiting for your income tax refunds. When your checks arrive, I'll cash them, and you can each leave $400 in the safe as a deposit against any future shortage."

They agreed to the plan, but I think at that point, they would have agreed to anything in order to get back out on the street. Once their debt was cleared, that could happen.

Saturday proved to be relatively normal, but early Sunday morning, our two other problem children, Tim Danner and Rick Puggini, stopped by the shop after a night out on the town. As they staggered toward the warehouse, they saw Susan and Nick standing out front having a surprisingly sober conversation.

Puggini's demeanor changed. He just could not let go of the past. As he walked up, he pulled a dollar bill out of his pocket, threw it down onto the sidewalk at Susan's feet, and spat on it. According to him, if she picked it up, then she was "the rat" who had told Tammy that he had been drinking on his cart. It was obvious that Puggini had watched one too many low-budget mafia movies.

Throwing the bill at her feet and spitting on it was pretty insulting, but it got worse. Puggini was in the middle of eating a piece of fried chicken, and when he finished the piece, he threw the bone down by her feet. He looked at her, then down at the bill, and proceeded to spit chicken on the dollar.

"At that point, Puggini and Home Girl both bowed up and got in each other's face," Nick recalled. "Susan's a country girl, and she's tough. She can take care of herself. She hits like a man." Even so, Nick did not want it accelerating into a physical confrontation. He stepped between the two to make certain that didn't happen.

Instead of backing down, Puggini cranked it up another notch. He started to unzip his pants so that he could "whiz" on the dollar as an even greater insult. Even Nick was now feeling disrespected. In his best Marlon Brando impersonation, he warned, "So help me, Puggini, if you pull it out, I'll cut it off and shove it down your throat." Puggini backed off.

When I arrived at the shop later Sunday morning, George and Jason informed me of the incident. That afternoon, when Puggini showed up for work, I called him upstairs. He walked into the office, and I slid an envelope across my desk in his direction. It contained Puggini's savings that I had been holding for him.

"When I allowed you back," I explained, "I warned you about drinking on the cart. You swore that it wouldn't happen, and it did. Since you failed to live up to your end of the bargain, here's your money. I think it's best to part ways for a while before something major happens."

"What did I do?"

"You watched too many gangster movies as a kid."

It was time to cut the cord—even Danner had to admit that his buddy had become a mean drunk. Puggini really needed a break from the mayhem.

On Monday, May 24, as I sat working at my desk, Nick flung open the office door and, with a huge grin on his face, waved a brownish gold envelope at me.

"Look what I got!"

His tax refund had arrived. "Nick," I said, "this is our lucky day."

"I told you it was comin'."

In less than five minutes, he had paid off his shortage, repaid the money that he had borrowed, and put $400 in the safe as a security deposit. The final $69 went into his pocket for food, which, in Nick-speak, meant Cisco.

As long as his money was in the safe, he could work. In his opinion, life was, at the moment, "great." He was back in the company's good graces, and admittedly, it felt good to have him back in the fold. Now, I had to focus on Gene. With a little bit of luck and some creativity, he, too, should be able to clear his debt and return to the company's active roster.

Working at Lucky Dogs is like living the movie *Groundhog Day*; it's a given that Gene, Nick, Danner, Puggini, Karl, and at least half of the rest of the crew are destined to screw up time and again. It's not that they try to, and it's not because they don't care. It's more a lack of willpower, inner demons, and the environment in which they operate. They're not bad people. They're actually pretty good people who just make bad decisions. Then, we have the other half of the crew: Lindsey, Choya, Carmen, Vincent, Porter, Burris, Hudson, Smitty, Massey, and a few others who never come up short or cause a problem.

In the late 1970s, a vendor named Bob Lucke hawked dogs for us. Lucke was an extremely good salesman, but, like Nick and Gene, he wasn't always dependable, and he wasn't always sober. Standing out in front of the shop one afternoon, I looked at Bob and said, "You need to show up on time, drink less, be neat and clean, be more personable, and miss fewer days."

"Hell, Jerry," he shot back, "if I was all of those things, I wouldn't be at Lucky Dogs—I'd be in some office knocking down six figures."

His is probably the most enlightening statement ever made by a Lucky Dog vendor. In a simple sentence, he had put everything in perspective. As we walked back into the shop, I asked, "Could we at least shoot for three out of five?"

10

GOODBYE, GENE

On Friday, May 28, 2010, I spent the evening serving Lucky Dogs at a bachelor party in New Orleans' Garden District. It was a special occasion in more than one sense.

On December 19, 2009, an incredibly well-written article appeared on ESPN.com titled "Saints the Soul of America's City." I was impressed by the piece—so impressed that I did something totally out of character; for the first time in my life, I responded to an email address at the bottom of an article.

"Thank you for your brilliantly written article about New Orleans," began my message to Wright Thompson, the story's author. "It wasn't simply that the words flowed, but as a New Orleanian who has been back in the city since September 4, 2005, I feel that you truly understand and appreciate the city and what it's been through. We are a Mediterranean city that, by the grace of God, ended up on the shores of the Gulf of Mexico. We're not totally back, but we have come a long, long way, and we have the love, drive, and the dedication to finish the task."

I typed my name at the letter's closing, and then, out of habit, I typed "Manager, Lucky Dogs, Inc." In response, this gifted writer—this incredible master of the English language—emailed back, "Dude . . . this is literally the greatest moment of my life: i got mail from the manager of lucky dogs! thanks for taking the time to write. i happen to adore your product and am attaching photos of myself in an impromptu lucky dog eating contest while in new orleans for a bachelor party several years ago."

I read his response and smiled. He was an extremely talented writer with a down-to-earth ego. I liked him even more. Later, I received a second email from Thompson, this time informing me that in the spring, he and a group of fellow sportswriters were coming to town for another bachelor party. On their first day in New Orleans, they were to have lunch at Galatoire's, one of the city's oldest and most famous restaurants. That evening, he wanted to know if it would be possible to have a Lucky Dog cart serve about fifteen people at a private residence in the Garden District.

Our minimum catering package is 300 hot dogs and costs about $740. He insisted on paying the total amount. I insisted on a greatly reduced fee, but truth be told, I had no intention of charging him at all.

In a time when all we were hearing were negative remarks about the city and why it should not be rebuilt, Thompson had written a marvelous exposé on New Orleans, its soul, its uniqueness, and its importance to the nation. I figured the least our company could do in return was help see to it that he and his friends had an enjoyable time in the Big Easy.

I even decided to serve as the vendor. On the night of Thompson's party, I stood behind the cart wearing the traditional red-and-white-striped Lucky Dog shirt as I dished out dogs and listened to some of America's top sportswriters talk off the record about the events and athletes they covered. At the end of the evening, as I was loading the cart into my truck, a couple of the attendees walked over to offer their assistance. Again, they tried to pay. I refused. I was thinking, "Hell, I should have paid them for allowing me to hear their stories!"

The following morning, things were still looking up. Gene and Nick had been helping out in the shop, and the building was in the best shape it had been in for months. Nick had completely repaid his debt, and Gene was only $34 away from clearing his.

As we worked together, we joked and kidded. Gene turned to Nick and said, "If you get called to the office and Jerry takes his glasses off and puts them down on his desk, get ready—you're about to get a full-blown ass chewing. If he leaves his glasses on, then it's not gonna be too bad." In turn, I ragged them about Home Girl and Becky. Both guys had likeable personalities. I could get mad and upset with them, but I could never dislike them.

Later that afternoon, Roy Gant came to the office to ask for a few days off. He wanted to visit his ailing father in St. Louis.

His dad's prognosis didn't sound good, so I suggested that he leave as soon as possible and take as long as he needed—a week, a month, whatever. His job and corner would be waiting for him when he returned. However, instead of leaving immediately, he chose to work Friday and Saturday and head for St. Louis on Sunday. That way, he would have money in his pockets when he arrived home.

Unfortunately, God was following a different schedule. Gant received a call Saturday night; his father had died. By the following weekend, he had attended the funeral and was back in the shop loading his cart. As he saw it, with his father gone there was no reason to stay in Missouri.

That same weekend, Nick was riding his (probably stolen) bicycle that he had purchased from a shady character in the Quarter when a car ran a stop sign on Royal Street and plowed into him. He landed on the hood of the vehicle, and when the car slammed on its brakes, he went sliding off onto the pavement. Paramedics arrived and transported him to the hospital; yet the following day, he showed up at the shop. He was sore and bruised but willing to fill in for Jason.

"Did the other guy get a ticket?" I asked.

"I don't know, but I'm gonna find out, 'cause the cop gave me one and I'm the one that got hit. I don't deserve no ticket. I'm gonna call the major over at the 8th district. If he won't help, somebody else might. They all like me over at the station."

Four days later, Nick was scheduled to go to court.

On Tuesday, June 29, Gene called my office wanting to know if he could come in and see me. I assumed his income tax refund had arrived and he wanted to pay off the last $34 of his shortage and put up his deposit, but I was wrong. What he actually wanted was to borrow $33. Becky's mom had died, and she was $33 short of the bus fare home to Colorado.

Over the years, Becky had wreaked havoc in the shop and on the street. Though I had banned her from the warehouse on more than one occasion, $33 was a small price to pay in order for her to be able to attend her mother's funeral. There was no question—I would lend Gene the money. However, I did not want it to appear that Gene had been forgiven for all of his shortages, nor that Becky had been pardoned from all of the problems she had caused. Thus, I told Gene that I would give George a $40 draw against his paycheck and that George could then lend him the $40. The company would get its money back when I deducted the draw from George's check on Friday. Since Gene rented a house and sublet a bedroom to George, George would deduct $40 from his portion of the rent. That way, Becky got her bus ticket, the company was certain to be repaid, and George got his money back by deducting it from his rent.

Sitting on the other side of my desk, Gene grinned and shook his head. "You know, boss," he said, "you somethin' else."

"I'll take that as a compliment. When you go downstairs, send George up, and I'll give him the money."

Just before leaving the building, Gene stopped to talk with Nick and Home Girl as they were about to push out to their corner. The Cisco Kid and Susan had been doing well lately. This good behavior would continue for a few more days, even through the 4th of July, but the following morning the fireworks started.

On the 5th, Nick came upstairs demanding all of his cash. According to him, he was through with the Quarter; he was heading home to the country. I knew that he wasn't going anywhere—this was just his excuse to ask for his savings. About an hour after I gave it to him, Gene called. Nick had stopped by his house.

"Boss, looka here," Gene began. "You and I both know Nick ain't going home."

"I know. By the way, we have a two-cart party next week. If you want, I'll let you work one of the carts, but there's a catch: you have to put 50 percent of what you make in the safe as part of your $400 deposit. In fact, we have enough catering events on the books that within two weeks, you can put the whole $400 deposit in the safe. Once that's done, you're back on a cart."

"Sign me up."

Gene, like Nick, was weak. Odds were he had already spent his tax refund.

On the afternoon of Tuesday, July 6, Nick strolled into the office and plopped down in a chair with a huge grin on his face. "I feel great!"

he announced. "After sleeping sixteen hours, I'm ready to get back in the game."

I reminded him that for the moment, he was benched until he replaced the money that he had withdrawn from the safe. Like with Gene, I explained that we might be able to use him to work a party on Saturday. He walked out of the office disappointed about not being able to work the street, but happy that he could at least work a party.

The following morning as I sat at my desk, Nick buzzed and wanted to come up. As usual, he needed a draw—but not the standard $20. Because he was now supporting not only himself, but also Home Girl, he needed twice the cash. The other bit of news he wanted to share with me was that the insurance company representing the car that struck him was eager to settle. They had agreed to pay his doctor bills, his ambulance charge, plus $2,000; all he had to do was sign on the dotted line. To him, it was a dream come true. I suppose that in life, there are those who grow up wanting to own a Porsche, and those who grow up just hoping to get hit by one.

Nick was figuring that once his settlement arrived, he could kick back and take it easy for a while. That would have been fine with me, because for some unusual reason, we had an abundance of vendors on weekends during the summer of 2010. Normally, as the temperature and humidity rise, the vendors go scurrying north, but this year was different. Instead of having eight to ten carts hitting the streets each day, we were putting out seventeen. There have been Mardi Gras days when we couldn't amass that many bodies.

On July 16, Nick rolled into the shop on his bike smiling from ear to ear, settlement form in hand. All he had to do was sign it and mail it back. From his look, you would have thought that he had won the lottery, and I guess in his mind, he had.

However, the original $2,000 offer had been reduced to $1,500, and the amount that he was to receive for his bike had been lowered from $150 to $40. The good news was that the insurance company's compassionate legal representative was still willing to pay Nick's $1,300 worth of medical bills. Still, The Cisco Kid was ecstatic, and the insurance company was probably giving their representative the company's "Negotiator of the Month" award.

All in all, Nick was probably receiving more than he actually deserved, but a lot less than some unscrupulous attorney and unethical physician could have gotten for him. The insurance company got off with a bargain in today's litigious society.

Since his settlement was coming but had not yet arrived, Nick was in the "can I get an advance?" mode. I happened to be working late, and he buzzed at 11 p.m., needing the standard $20. This time, the money was not for himself, but so that he could buy Home Girl a bus ticket to Mississippi. According to him, their relationship was over and he wanted her "out of his life" and "out of his sight" as quickly as possible.

Nick knew it and so did I: Susan wasn't going anywhere. It was all a ruse. So, I figured that if I was going to lend him the money, I should at least get something in return. What I got was an award-winning, one-act impromptu play with Nick starring as the boyfriend calling off their relationship, and Susan playing the part of the jilted girlfriend. She was sitting in the chair by the front door, looking dejected with her head hung low. I, of course, was playing the part of the wealthy financier. Having the opportunity to watch them ad lib their lines and develop the story was worth well more than the $20 loan.

When I walked into the shop the following morning, I noticed that neither the leading man nor the leading lady had yet taken their final curtain call. Of course, Nick needed to borrow $5 "for smokes."

"Is that not Susan sitting right there in front of us?" I asked.

"Yes," he replied.

"She never took the bus to Mississippi?"

"Right."

"Then if she didn't take the bus, you should still have the $20 that I loaned you last night to buy her a bus ticket."

"But I don't have it."

"So you did buy the ticket?"

"Not exactly, but if you lend me another five, I'll repay everything that I owe when the insurance money comes today. You'll see. I'm gonna pay off both you and Liz."

"Liz from the street? Why do you owe Liz money?"

"Well, she made some calls to the insurance company for me, so I told her I'd give her $200 for helping."

"You're paying her because she represented you in negotiations with the insurance company?"

"Yep."

"Nick, you must've lost your mind. Though admittedly, she did a helluva job. Right off the bat, she got the insurance company to reduce the agreed-upon $2,000 settlement down to $1,500—Home Girl, are you catching this?—and then she got a $150 offer for the bike reduced to $40. By the way, I'll lend you the $5. You definitely need a break, and for God's sake, don't let Liz talk to the insurance company again, or you'll end up owing them money!"

The next day as I walked down Camp Street and rounded the corner onto Gravier, I could see George, Home Girl, and Nick standing in front of Lucky Dogs. Nick was easy to spot because of his white Reggie Bush Saints jersey. He was all smiles—the picture of happiness. From half a block away, I could tell he had money in his pockets.

As I got closer, he started to say something, but before he could, I said, "I already know. Give me a minute, then come upstairs." I headed to my office and took the time to print out and cash George and Jason's payroll checks.

Before Nick came up, Mark shouted from his office, "He'll be broke by Wednesday!" That meant he figured Nick would be able to make the money last only a week. Kirk wanted odds on Friday—just two days away. Jason figured that the funds would be gone by Monday. I picked Sunday, and George wanted Tuesday. The pool was on.

When Nick walked into the office, he was laughing. "I heard y'all got a bet going on."

I confirmed it, but I also said that I hoped we were all wrong. I then took the previous night's receipts and cashed his check. As agreed, he put $400 in the safe. He was now cleared to go back to working a cart. He even decided to do so that same day. No partying? Could this be a new Nick? Out of the $1,540, he had $1,140 left. He then used $80 to pay off a few debts, and he paid Liz $200 for her outstanding legal representation. That left him $860. He decided to leave it all in the safe.

Later that afternoon, he found a room for $185 a week and the next day, he figured he'd pay two weeks rent on the place. I was impressed. Nick was making rational decisions. Plus, he hadn't even mentioned buying a Cisco.

Nick pushed his cart out at 5 p.m. At 5:45, Home Girl called. Nick wanted her to come get $90 out of the safe and go buy a few household items at Wal-Mart. That seemed reasonable, but Nick was now down to $400. My guess of Sunday was looking really good, though I was hoping I would be wrong.

While all of that was taking place, a slight problem developed just outside the shop. The police chased down and took in for questioning a young man wearing a ski mask. Despite the fact that it was mid-July in New Orleans, ninety-six degrees outside with humidity of more than 90 percent, it apparently never dawned on the man that wearing a ski mask in such conditions might attract attention.

Earlier, he had walked into the shop, but before saying anything, he headed right back out. He then went next door to the hotel, but also left there rather quickly.

I'm not certain what was happening. Maybe he wanted to rob a vendor, but with it being so hot in the shop, he had to retreat into the air-conditioned hotel to get a little relief. Or maybe once he saw our crew, he realized that he needed to find an easier mark. Whatever the reason, he should have scoped out the neighborhood a little better; perhaps he would have noticed that almost every day, New Orleans police officers eat lunch at Commerce. In fact, one happened to be walking back to his patrol car when the lost skier wandered out of the hotel and headed across the street.

The officer probably thought he was having a flashback to an elementary school IQ test: Can you pick out the item that doesn't belong in this picture? Hmm . . . Maybe the guy in the ski mask?

I don't know if he was ever charged with anything, but I do know that he got to ride in the back seat of a police car.

Later that afternoon, Gene showed up at the shop. "Looka here, boss," he said, "I'm starvin'. Ain't there no way I can go back out? I just turned 55, and I ain't gonna do that stupid shit no more."

"I've always wondered why the speed limit on the interstate was 55. Now I know. It's a magical number."

"Come on, boss, gimme me a break. When I walk the street at night, I know I can outsell anybody you got on a cart. It burns me up that I can't be out there."

"Sure you can outsell them, but you're the one that came up short three times."

"Looka here. I know it's my fault. I screwed up. Just give me one more shot. That's all I want. Looka here. Even Lieutenant Frick came up to me on the street and asked, 'Gene, where you been?' I told him Jerry won't put me out. I'm in his doghouse. Then the lieutenant said, 'So, Jerry's on your ass because you screwed up.' 'Yeah, but I deserved it. It ain't his fault.' Then the lieutenant told me, 'Do I need to send one of my officers to stand by you all night so you don't screw up?' Jerry, if you give me one more chance, I promise I won't screw up. Becky won't come by the cart. The first two years I worked, I never came up short. Never! I can be like that again."

"I'll tell you what I will agree to. Every night that you work, you drop 50 percent of your take-home percentage in the safe until the amount totals $500."

"Boss, I thought it was $400."

"It was, but it's now $500, and it's no longer a deposit. You can withdraw a deposit. That was Nick's problem. He'd drop money in the safe and then ask for it back the next day. We're not going to play that game. The money that you drop in the safe will be a gift from you to me for all of the mental anguish and suffering that you've caused. Now, at some point in the future, when we both agree that you'll never work here again, the odds are astronomical that I'll be giving you $500 as a going-away present. If you agree to it, then you can start back to work today."

Truthfully, his savings would be in the safe to cover any future shortages and it would also be there in case he ever ran short of rent money.

"I'd rather start on a weekend," he responded.

"For a guy asking for a favor, you're pretty damn picky."

If Gene was coming back, he was going to do so on terms set by the company, not on terms dictated by him. There were reasons to bring him back. For one, the vendor that had taken over his corner was leaving in a few weeks to go to San Diego. Gene was the best possible choice to assign to Canal and Bourbon. When he was focused, his sales led the pack, and when he did well, he pushed Hudson, Puggini, Gant, and everyone else to do better. He and I both knew that he would take over his spot again; he just had to get himself back under control. At 4 p.m., he showed back up, ready and eager to work.

Gene had barely made it downstairs when George buzzed to let me know that Karl wanted to see me. The last time he was here, I had suggested that he take an extended leave of absence. Now, apparently fresh off the Lewis and Clark Trail, he was back and wanting to work. Neither George nor Jason was thrilled about his returning. Tammy definitely did not want him back; Karl often refused to turn in money when she made the runs. When he pushed in, it was usually very late, and after procrastinating, he would finally unload his cart. Then, he would want to sit in the kitchen and slowly, painstakingly straighten his money. The process took forever because he wadded his bills into small balls and stuffed them in his pockets.

Then there were the nights that he drank. The alcohol changed his personality. The nice, friendly Karl disappeared, and Karl the bully materialized.

I liked Karl, but I didn't have to check him in at 4:30 in the morning. I called him upstairs and explained why I didn't want him back. I told him the truth—that he was his own worst enemy, and that I could not allow him to treat me one way and treat George, Jason, and Tammy another. I recommended that he go back to the tugboat where his behavior might be acceptable and that we talk again in a few months. He got up and walked out. He hung around downstairs complaining for a few minutes, then left.

The following Wednesday, I received a call at the office. The voice on the other end said, "Hey, boss, looka here, I think I've reached the $500 mark."

"You're right, Gene. In fact, you're a dollar over. You don't have to drop anymore."

"But boss, I wanna drop. I wanna keep droppin'. I'll leave money with Tammy every night. Just hold it in the safe for me. Hey, how many dogs you sendin' me out with tomorrow? If the Saints win, all hell's gonna break loose."

Gene was inspired. After hitting $500, he could pocket everything he made, but he now wanted to leave his money in the safe. As long as it was there, neither he nor Becky could impulsively spend it. I tried to convince him to open a bank account, but he refused. He didn't trust banks, he said, but he was totally comfortable leaving his cash in the company's safe.

He was right about one thing: once the Saints beat the Vikings, the Who Dats headed to the Quarter in droves. Sales ended up five times greater than that of the previous Thursday. The victory had put the fans in a partying mood.

The following weekend, the partying continued—at least for Lucky Dogs. We had three catering events scheduled. Because of their staggered times, Nick was able to work all three.

The Saturday evening event was a fundraiser for an 8th District police officer injured in the line of duty. We donated a cart, vendor, and product. I informed Nick that he was the perfect person to work it.

"Why?" he asked.

"Because you'll know just about everyone there; they've all arrested you at one time or another."

He grinned and then corrected me.

"No 8th District officer ain't ever arrested me. It's always the cops they bring in from the other districts for New Year's or Mardi Gras. Those are the ones you gotta watch out for. They get mad if you just stand in one place too long.

"Ya know, this might not be so bad," he added. "It might help out me in the future."

At the end of the party when I arrived to pick him up, he and one of the lieutenants were talking and laughing. When she walked away, he made a point to tell me, "They loved me. They tipped well and they wanted to know when you're gonna let me go back out on the street."

As we were rolling the cart up a set of ramps and into my pickup truck, another officer, pulling out of the parking lot, lowered the window in his squad car and shouted, "See you later, Nick!" Another blew his horn and waved. It appeared that at least on this night, Billy the Kid had been a hit with the law.

On Sunday, when I walked out of the shop to head home, Little Mike rounded the corner from Camp Street heading straight in my direction. It had been more than three years since I had seen him. I missed Mike; we had grown close during those days we spent together repairing the shop after Katrina.

As he walked up he said, "Hey, boss, you doin' okay?" Then he gave me a hug and a pat on the back.

"I'm doing fine, Mike. You know, you were the best maintenance man we've ever had. No one has ever cleaned the shop as good as you. I'm sorry that it ended the way it did, but you came within inches of killing Hudson."

"I know, boss. It wadn't your fault. You had to do whatcha did—I woulda killed him. He made me so mad 'cause he was out there on his cart disrespecting you. You'd tell 'em to do one thing, and when you wadn't there, he'd do something else. That wadn't right."

"Even so, you just can't throw metal rebar at a person's head. Anyway, that's in the past. How've you been? Are you working?"

"Boss, I learned to do roofin'. I work for a man and I do a little on the side. I don't drink no more—can't do that. Tryin' to do better. I still live over by the river. My wife's still workin' for the Indian. I was gonna stop by and see you, but I didn't know if I should."

"You're always welcome at the shop."

"Boss, I'm gonna stop by sometime. Okay?"

"I'd like that."

Mike was hoping that he could come back to work, and I would have loved to have been able to rehire him. When he worked, he was like a robot; the shop never looked better. But once he started drinking, he became uncontrollable.

The vendors, in trying to be his friend, ended up doing him in; they were mostly responsible for his irrational behavior. They'd sneak across to Chuck's Sports Bar, buy a drink, and slip it to Mike, hoping to get him to clean their cart next. The problem was that he could not handle alcohol, and after one or two drinks, his personality changed. When that happened, I was the only one he would listen to. And that was only because of the relationship that we had developed during that early post-Katrina period when it was only him and me in the shop. Had I been absolutely certain that he could stay away from alcohol, I would have taken him back in a heartbeat.

The next morning, I was hoping for a calm day, but Becky showed up wanting to take out a cart. That would not be possible. She could help Gene on his wagon, but that was as far as I would go. Her record had not exactly been unblemished.

On Friday, November 5, as I was coming back from lunch at Commerce, I ran into Karl, another vendor with a less than flawless record. He'd been drinking, but he walked up to shake hands.

"Cuz, I heard ya only had a few carts out the other night," he said. "That sucks. I'm ready to push out to the street right now."

"Karl, you can't. You've been drinking."

"But I only had one at the casino."

"It must have been a really big one."

"Cuz, I'm fine."

"No, you're not."

"I can do this."

"I can't let you."

"Why?"

"Because you're not sober."

"That sucks, cuz."

"You're right, it sucks, but that's the rule."

Once again, he insisted that we shake hands. Afterwards, he headed back in the direction of the casino, and I turned and headed back to my office.

Unfortunately, bad news was waiting: Richard Moscinski had passed away. The probable cause was heart failure. He had retired so that he could finally enjoy life; he never got the chance.

Several weeks later, on December 22, 2010, Hudson called to inform me that he was ready to start working again. It had been months since he had pushed out a cart.

"It's all I know," he told me. "You won't have no shit out of me, I give you my word. You didn't have any trouble out of me the last time, and you won't have any this time."

Within twenty-four hours of Hudson's call, Gene and Roy Gant also returned. New Year's Eve was a week away, and they all wanted to be on a cart for the "money days." After New Year's, it was only six or so weeks before the Mardi Gras parades would start rolling. Those returning needed money, and we needed vendors. All of them had been a problem at one time or another, but at least I knew their tendencies.

Karl even stopped by to wish me a belated Merry Christmas and a Happy New Year. He also wanted me to know that he was back working on the river. I was happy for him. Maybe it would help him stay straight.

As the end of 2010 approached, I had only one last concern. An ex-vendor approached Tammy's cart with an unsavory-looking character and remarked, "This is the lady that picks up the money. If she doesn't do it, then her husband or Snake will." With that, they turned and walked away. From that moment on, Tammy, Thomas, and Snake would have to be extremely careful.

Because of the unsettling statement, Tammy requested that Donald Plunkett be allowed to walk with her when she made the money runs during New Year's. Plunkett hadn't worked as a vendor for several years; rumor had it that he had moved up north. But, he was now back and looking for work.

At first, Tammy wanted Home Girl to accompany her, but the same ex-vendor who had made the comments about her being the one who picked up the money later got drunk and stopped by Gene's cart, telling him that he was "gonna get [his] lady manager." I informed the 8th District of the threat, and Plunkett was chosen to accompany Tammy on her nightly runs. There was no trouble.

On January 1, Gene came to the shop at 10 a.m. to push out, but he was pale and complained of not feeling well. George recommended that he take the day off and go to the doctor. Instead, Gene decided to lie down on a piece of cardboard beside one of the carts and rest for a while. A few minutes later, he got up and sat in a chair near the front entrance.

Susan, Snake, Jason, Porter, and George were hanging around nearby, engaged in conversation. Snake noticed that Gene looked even paler than before, and that he was now propping himself up by leaning against the cart next to where he was sitting. Suddenly, Gene began falling forward. Another vendor who happened to be walking into the shop at the time reached out and caught him before he crashed to the concrete floor. With help, he eased Gene down and back onto the cardboard. Jason quickly called 911, and George rushed upstairs to get me.

By the time I got downstairs, Gene could barely speak; his voice was soft, and his words were incoherent. The ambulance arrived within minutes. As the paramedic took his vital signs, Susan held his hand and tried to comfort him.

Once Gene's vitals were stable, the EMTs placed him on a gurney, put him in an ambulance, and took off with sirens blaring. Half an hour later, a nurse called. She had a patient in critical condition and desperately needed help. He had no identification, and the only thing she knew was that the ambulance had picked him up at Lucky Dogs. She asked if I knew his name and, if so, could I contact his family and have them come to the hospital as quickly as possible.

While I pulled up Gene's personnel records on the computer, Susan jumped on her bike and rode as fast as she could to Gene and Becky's apartment to let Becky know what happened.

As I was giving the nurse Gene's Social Security number and his family's out-of-state contact information, she received updated information: Gene had died. Less than an hour before, he was in the shop wanting to push out. Now he was gone.

When Susan returned, I called her, Jason, and George upstairs and broke the terrible news. As we were speaking, the nurse from University Hospital called again. Becky was there, and understandably, she was very emotional. The nurse explained that Becky wanted to personally tell me about Gene's death and asked if I could act as if I didn't yet know.

When she put me on the phone with Becky, Becky broke down crying and asked if I would come to the hospital. She had no one else to turn to. Over the years, we had butted heads; there had been times when I had refused to allow her to work a cart, and on more than one occasion, I had banished her from the shop. But none of that mattered under the present circumstances. I locked the office and headed for the medical center.

I sat with Becky at the hospital for more than two hours while the staff cut through the red tape so Gene's belongings could be released to her. The problem was that she and Gene had never married, and other than our word, the hospital had no proof that she even knew him.

All the while, Becky kept crying and repeating that she didn't know if she could go on without him. She was devoted to Gene. Her pain was unimaginable. Gene's personal items were finally released, but only because of the remarkable nurse with whom I had spoken over the phone. She handled the tragedy in an extremely caring and professional manner.

When Gene and I had spoken on New Year's Eve, he had said, "Boss, this here cold is kicking my ass, but I'll be fine." I went upstairs, and he loaded his cart and headed out. Now, less than twenty-four hours later, he was dead.

When I called the shop at 6 the following morning, Tammy informed me that she heard that another ex-vendor, Barbara Huggins, had died on New Year's Eve. In Huggins's case, diabetes had taken its toll. Huggins was responsible for several memorable stories. Once, while she was working her cart, she called the shop to inform us that a drunk had tossed a beer bottle into the air and it had landed on her helper's head. He dropped to his knees and appeared dazed. As she was talking with me from a pay phone next to her cart, she held up six fingers and asked her helper how many he saw.

"Nine," he replied.

"Lord! Lord!" she screamed. "Somebody get an ambulance—I think he's brain damaged!" Minutes later she called back to inform us that he wasn't hurt. He just couldn't count very well.

Now, Huggins had passed away, as had Big Alice, Lamar, Gene, Mayfield, and several other vendors from the 1970s and 1980s. Age was catching up with our crew. Others, such as Huggins and Gene, were dying far before their time.

Susan stayed with Becky through her initial period of grief. On January 3, Becky showed up at the shop with Home Girl. She wanted to help in the kitchen and give Jason a hand cleaning carts. Though we didn't need the help, she needed to be with people, so we created work for her.

Another person having a tough time accepting Gene's loss was Nick. The fact that his best friend was gone was hard on him, but his attempt to drown his sorrow in Cisco was not the answer. I knew that eventually, he would run out of money—and out of Cisco—and have to face reality. I figured we could talk then.

On Wednesday, January 12, Becky showed up at the shop again, though it was not to work. She wanted to borrow money so she could buy a bus ticket to Gene's hometown. A memorial service was to be held there in two days.

I thought about it, but Home Girl claimed that when she was on the phone speaking with Gene's relatives, she thought someone in the background made reference to Becky by saying, "That bitch better not show up." If Susan was correct, Becky was better off not going. She had hugged Gene's body and said her goodbyes at the hospital. To go to a family memorial service and perhaps not even arrive in time would be a problem, but to arrive and not be welcome would be an even greater one.

As an alternative, I suggested that she select a time for Gene's friends to gather at the Moonwalk overlooking the Mississippi River at Jackson Square. She could place a bouquet of flowers in the river, and there, among friends, she could say her final goodbyes. In my opinion, the outcome and the memories would be better. Obviously, the choice was hers.

I also suggested that she call Gene's family and ask if they minded her coming. It was highly possible that Susan had been mistaken in what she thought she heard. Becky considered calling but decided that going might not be such a great idea. In the end, she chose not to have a ceremony.

With the holidays behind us, my focus turned to selecting a contractor to structurally repair our building and restore its façade. The warehouse had been built in the 1840s and still had the original massive heart of pine floor joists. Most likely, they had been cut and installed by slaves. Now, because of termite damage, a few needed to be replaced.

As the renovations got under way, I was at my desk figuring out what supplies to order for the upcoming Carnival season when Jason walked into the office and announced, "I've got a problem. I need $760 by tomorrow or I'm going to jail. Can you lend it to me?"

Twenty or so years earlier, I would have been shocked by such a request. After all these years on the job, almost nothing shocked me anymore.

"What happened?" I asked.

"I don't want to say. I'm too embarrassed."

"If you want me to lend you that much money, I need to know."

"I just feel so dumb."

"What happened?"

"I went out and celebrated on my birthday, and later that night, I was at home alone watching TV. One of those hotline numbers flashed across the screen. I had gotten a $25 MasterCard gift card as a present, so I thought why not? I figured the call would end when the money ran out. But a guy called today saying if I don't pay an extra $760 by noon Pacific Time tomorrow, they're filing charges against me for credit card fraud. He said I could get up to four years in prison."

"Have they sent you a bill?"

"No, that was the first time they contacted me. I was so shook up, I didn't know what to ask."

"Did you make the call?"

"I remember making it, but I don't know how long I talked. I guess I owe it. I just don't want any trouble."

He was right. What he did was dumb, but he wasn't the first male to get blitzed on his birthday and regret something the next morning. At least he didn't have a girl's name tattooed across his chest and a ring on his left hand. Still, the whole thing seemed extremely shady, especially since no one ever sent him an invoice. Then there was the fact that they would not accept a check, and term payments were not a possibility. The caller had demanded that the money be wired by Western Union no later than noon the following day.

I went online and researched the company. There were numerous hits, and, like Jason, most respondents reported that they had called the hotline for only a few minutes but had been charged for hours. Others said that they had paid the extra money and shortly thereafter received a new demand for additional money—most of the time in excess of $1,000. Everyone wrote of being threatened with jail.

Those demanding the payoff were scum. However, I reminded Jason of the old adage: If you play with fire, you're going to get burned. In his case, he had just been torched. He swore if he ever got out of the mess, he would never ever call another hotline as long as he lived. I believed him.

He obviously needed much more help than I could offer, so I called Steve Lozes, our company attorney. Lozes has represented us on various occasions: sometimes when we opened a new business; other times, because someone had hit a cart with their car; and, of course, there were those instances when people claimed to have been run over by a Lucky Dog cart, resulting in physical injury, severe mental anguish, and a continuing fear of mobile food vehicles. If nothing else, I figured Lozes could advise Jason as to how he should proceed.

The company hounding him specialized in entrapping lonely people, and what they had done to Jason was what they had done to countless other unsuspecting callers. Had the charges stopped when the card limit had been reached, there would not have been a problem, but there were $760 in additional charges.

If need be, I would lend Jason the money to pay the California-based crooks. He could then repay me out of his Mardi Gras bonus. My problem was that I knew how hard he was going to have to work to make his bonus, and this sleazebag operation wanted to take it.

Lozes was aware that I volunteered on Saturdays at the National World War II Museum helping to restore PT-305. Jim Letten, the federal prosecutor for the Eastern District of Louisiana, also worked on the boat. Lozes suggested that I speak with Letten since the transaction crossed state lines.

I planned on doing so, but for the moment, I needed advice on what we should immediately do. Lozes recommended that I call the New Orleans district attorney's office and speak with the assistant DA, who held the position of "duty prosecutor." Should charges be brought against Jason, the duty prosecutor would be the individual responsible for having him arrested.

The duty prosecutor agreed that it sounded like a scam, but he needed additional information. One of the things that he asked was exactly how long Jason and the friendly lady had spoken.

AT&T had a store two blocks from the shop, and Jason went over to try and get a copy of his call history from the previous two months. With that information, we should have been able to determine how much he actually owed. Unfortunately, his phone had prepaid minutes, and according to AT&T, records are not kept for those models.

The following day, I spoke with Letten. He suggested that we bring the matter to the attention of the Secret Service because it was possible that they were already investigating the company.

After speaking with Letten, I spoke with Harold Buechler, another fellow PT-305 volunteer. Like Lozes and Letten, Buechler also is an attorney. He said that if the company kept offering the service after the debit card ran out, then it was "their problem." He recommended that Jason not send any money, stating that if it were him, he would take his chances in court—assuming it ever came to that.

I passed all of the information—both the pros and cons—on to Jason. It was up to him to decide what to do, but either way, it was a gamble. He could send the money, but it was more than likely that they would demand more.

I suggested that Jason demand a printed bill, so he did. They refused. What they sent instead was a list of supposed charges and with it, a disclaimer that the document was a call list, not a bill. They didn't seem to be willing to put in writing that he specifically owed the extra amount.

Jason happened to be in my office the next time he received a threatening call on his cell. After listening to the threats for a few minutes, he handed me the phone. I explained that I was Jason's boss, and I was considering lending him the $768 being demanded. The voice on the other end said that the amount owed was now more than $1,200. I informed him that according to their own call list, their last four charges to Jason's credit card had been denied. I wanted to know why, under those circumstances, the call had not been terminated.

"The best thing you can do is hire your guy a good attorney," the man shot back. Then the line went dead.

Jason decided to call their bluff and send nothing. If they wanted him, they would have to come to New Orleans to get him. To this day, he has never heard from them.

11

THE WINN-DIXIE BANDIT

All seemed calm, but the following Monday, I discovered that Susan, not Jason, was now the one needing legal representation; Home Girl had been arrested. She and Nick had let another couple stay with them, and Susan had gotten into an argument with their male guest and punched him. He called the police.

Susan was taken into custody not because of the fight but because of a 2002 attachment issued by the state of Mississippi for a probation violation. Home Girl called the shop wanting Nick to bring money and deposit it into her newly opened Central Lockup account. Unfortunately, Nick had failed to show for work.

When he finally did arrive, he looked haggard. After an hour of moving at half-speed, he announced that he was going home.

He grabbed his bike and rode out of the shop. Everyone knew he'd return in a couple of days, but the problem was that he became the most undependable when we needed him the most. He could not handle pressure, and Home Girl being arrested had pushed him over the edge.

George cleaned the few remaining carts and sent out the vendors. As a reward, I paid him the day's salary for both jobs, even though their times coincided. In addition, I gave him a ride home at the end of the day so he wouldn't have to wait for a bus.

There was another reason to drop him off: George and Nick lived in the same rooming house. I asked George to knock on Nick's door and tell him that I wanted to speak with him. A few minutes later, a shoe-less, T-shirt-clad Nick emerged from the building, walked to my truck, opened the door, and climbed into the passenger seat to escape the cold.

"Have you gotten it all out of your system?"

"I'm OK now. I'll be there in the morning."

"Are you sure?"

"I'll be there."

"Don't forget to apologize to George."

"I won't. I promise."

The following morning, Susan called. She was expecting to be extradited to Mississippi any day. If all went well, she figured she would be released a day or two after that. According to her, all charges had been dropped, but for some reason, the attachment had never been canceled.

Nick showed up the following morning as promised. After work, he planned to head to Central Lockup and deposit money in Home Girl's prison account.

While she was nervously waiting to be released, the number of vendors pushing out dramatically increased. By early February, guys were racking up perfect attendance records. No one wanted to lose his corner with Carnival only weeks away. During the week as many as fifteen vendors a day were showing up, and on weekends seventeen became the norm. By the time the Mardi Gras regulars drifted back into town, we would easily reach our twenty-two-permit limit—which was definitely a good thing.

Another good thing happened. On February 19, 2011, an article appeared in the *Wall Street Journal* titled, "America's Unsung War Heroes." The article by Robert Coram listed what he considered to be the five best books ever written about America's unsung war heroes. The time frame ranged from the American Revolution to the present, and the books' publication dates stretched from the mid-1920s through 2009. My book, *Andrew Jackson Higgins and the Boats that Won World War II* was listed as number one! I felt honored that it had been chosen and thankful that the article helped spread light on Higgins's critically important accomplishments. I could only allow the euphoria to last a few seconds; I had to get back to concentrating on the task at hand—preparing for Mardi Gras.

Carnival started off smoothly, but on the first Sunday of the parade season, things took a turn for the worse. Our carts need to be out of the shop before the parades start rolling. On Sunday, the first floats take to the streets at noon. The plan was that Nick would begin washing carts at 4 a.m. Jason would arrive at 7 a.m., and together they would finish the task. That was the plan, but it never became a reality.

Nick strolled in at 10 a.m., a full six hours late. When he finally arrived, I suggested that he take the day off. He objected rather profusely. At that point, I recommended that he also take off the following Monday through Thursday. That way, he would be fully rested for the next weekend. He was dumbstruck. He wasn't sure what to do.

"I need to work," he responded. "I really need the money."

"We really need someone in the shop that we can depend on, and this morning, I hired a new guy that seems to fit that description."

"You can depend on me."

"You can't be serious."

"Come on, you know you can depend on me."

"You were six hours late today. Go back home and get some rest. We'll talk tomorrow. Do *not* run the streets all night."

As he walked away, I called to the front of the shop for George to come to the kitchen. Nick mistakenly thought that I had called his name and came back to see what I wanted. I explained that I had called George, not him. I didn't need him.

As he neared the front entrance on his way out I could hear him telling the other vendors standing near the door, "Jerry doesn't need me."

"You've got that right," I responded. Jason chuckled.

"Aw, come on!" Nick yelled back as he walked out of the shop. "You know I'm like a son to you!"

On Wednesday, I let him work a cart at a catering event for Tulane University. That way, I was certain that he would at least have grocery money. Jason and the new recruit cleaned the carts.

Thus far, Tammy, George, and Jason had been holding up fine. George was getting the vendors out and Jason was focusing on supervising the new recruit. By Friday, Nick had been reinstated.

One of his duties would be to resupply our wagon at the 8th District police station. He transported the supplies in an old, rusted Winn-Dixie grocery basket that someone had found on the street and brought to the shop.

Most of the officers in the 8th knew Nick—some because of his days working a cart, and others because he had served them a hot dog at the benefit for the fallen officer several months earlier. Now, at Mardi Gras and with stress levels far above the norm, a few of them decided to have a little fun. One of the officers saw the basket and arrested Nick for supposedly being "the notorious Winn-Dixie Bandit."

The officer informed him that the cops had been on his trail for years and now that they had him in their grasp, he was not going to escape. To make certain of it, they handcuffed him to a bench in the station with two sets of cuffs. The arresting officer delivered his dialogue without a trace of a smile. Nick was worried. He figured that like Susan, he, too, would soon be behind bars. The ruse was going well. Even the major came out of his office and asked, "Nick, what did you do?"

"Major, they think I'm the Winn-Dixie Bandit. You gotta help me. Please!"

At that point the major broke out laughing. A few minutes later, the infamous Winn-Dixie Bandit was back at the shop grinning and saying, "They were just screwing with me. I thought I was in real trouble, but they were just havin' fun."

Later that evening, after Snake arrived to help Tammy on the night shift, I decided to head home. As I was about to leave, Snake remarked, "You know, I miss the old Jerry. You've gone soft. In the '80s, you would've kicked serious ass. These losers would have been taken off their corners and put on lesser spots when they showed up late or pushed in early. You would've fired just about everybody in the shop and replaced them by now."

"Snake, the '80s are gone. The times and the people have changed. Other than Hudson, Mitch, Burris, and Anderson, none of the vendors are willing to put in the extra hours. Those guys still compete to see who can sell the most dogs each night. The others don't care. They're not driven. They complain when they end up on a lesser corner, but they won't do what it takes to hold down a better one.

"The younger guys lack a strong work ethic and they lack a sense of pride. They're more interested in sitting at home, surfing the web and playing video games. To keep a crew, we've had to adapt. The old days are gone, and so am I, at least for today. I'll check back with you in a couple of hours."

Early the following morning—Fat Tuesday—when I arrived at the shop, Nick and Jason had most of the carts cleaned.

"I made your day, didn't I?" Nick said. "I bet you didn't think I'd be here."

"What in the world would make me think that? Probably the fact that this is the first day of Mardi Gras that you've actually made it to work on time?"

Mardi Gras Day actually was going surprisingly well, until around noon. Then Nick suddenly disappeared. Unbeknownst to us, he was out on the St. Charles Avenue parade route at a family reunion. He was eating fried chicken, downing cold beers, and relaxing in a lawn chair as he watched the floats roll by. All in all, he was having a marvelous time with all of the relatives. Then someone at the reunion remarked that they couldn't ever recall hearing of a cousin Nick. In fact, no one at the reunion could recall a cousin Nick.

Within minutes, more than the chicken got hot. Nick took off with a beer in hand and two counterfeit cousins in full pursuit. Later at the shop, he reminisced, "Aunt Bessie sure knows how to fry chicken, and I've got to give it to the family—they laid out a great spread."

It was a classic Nick move. Now, with a full stomach, he was back at the shop and ready to pitch in wherever needed.

At the stroke of midnight, Mardi Gras was over. The end of Carnival also meant that it was now time to make adjustments in our shop personnel. Vincent would permanently replace Nick, taking over as the part-time maintenance man in the shop three days a week. On the weekends, he would continue selling dogs in Jackson Square. Danner would take over working the catering events.

I had been hesitant to release Nick because I knew that when I did, he would lose his apartment and more than likely end up living back under a Superdome stairwell or under a bridge. It was not a decision that I took lightly.

But Lucky Dogs is a business, not a mission. My job is to keep the carts rolling and do what's in the best interest of the company. Nick had become totally undependable. George and Jason also liked Nick, but they had been carrying his weight and had grown tired of doing so. It was time for Nick to take a sabbatical.

When he came to the shop on Tuesday to pick up his check, he tried to negotiate one last time.

"Jerry," he said, "please don't do this to me. I promise I'll change. I've been under a lot of stress lately."

"Nick, two weeks ago I was about to make a change and bring Vincent into the shop. You swore then that you would change. You did— you got worse. I don't want you to lose your apartment. I'll tell you what I'll do. I'll put you on a cart on a great corner. If you don't show, then no one else will be affected. You'll make more than enough money to keep your apartment and to cover your expenses."

"I don't want to work no damn cart," he replied, and he turned and stormed out.

Without Susan, there was no one to take care of him. She had helped him clean the carts, made certain that their rent was paid, and put food on the table. She had been covering for him for months. Without her to pick up the slack, he was doomed. There was only so much that we could do. I didn't mind helping, but I had an obligation to the business.

The following day, I officially offered the part-time position to Vincent. He didn't have Nick's personality, but he also didn't have Nick's vices.

That afternoon, Nick showed up. He wanted to push carts, but he wasn't sober enough to push anything anywhere. Making matters worse, he admitted that he had not paid his rent and that his landlord had given him until 6 that evening to vacate his apartment. If he didn't, his possessions would be put on the sidewalk or thrown in the trash. Out of pride, he responded, "I don't care."

"I'll tell you what I'll do," I said. "You go home and pack your belongings, and I'll pick you and them up at exactly 5 p.m. For the time being, you can store everything at the shop. Once we get that done, then we'll figure out what your next move needs to be. Is that a deal?"

"That's a deal."

It might have been a deal, but only one of us ended up holding up his end of the bargain, and it wasn't the Cisco Kid. When I showed up at his apartment, he wasn't there. The manager hadn't seen him for hours. I headed back to the shop, parked, and was walking into the building when his landlord called. The Kid had returned and was now packing his belongings. He was an hour late because he had been out drinking. I wasn't happy, but I drove back to pick him up.

Nick now had the look of a crack addict. Even he had to admit that he was out of control and needed help. Ironically, though I had just fired him, he looked at me and said, "You're the only friend I have. You're like a father to me."

"Nick," I responded, "you're the son I'm glad I never had."

He smiled. He understood that letting him go was a business decision, not a personal one. I had to replace him because he failed to do his job. On the flip side, he also understood that I was not just going to throw him to the wolves. As I drove, we talked about options. By the time we got to the shop, I knew what needed to be done.

His belongings could temporarily be stored in the elevator shaft. The seven-by-ten-foot piece of real estate is the most versatile square footage the business owns. Through the years, it has served as an apartment, a catering cart storage facility, a Coke product storeroom, a tool shed, an excess hot dog bun warehouse, and, on rare occasions, an actual elevator shaft.

Now that Nick's personal belongings had been taken care of, it was time to take care of him. He had to get away from the street, and his best option was to visit his sister in Mississippi. She still lived on the family farm, and on a farm, there's always work that needs to be done. Nick loves the outdoors. When he was straight, he wasn't afraid of work. He needed to go home and get red Mississippi dirt on his hands. He needed to feel the sweat from working on fences and bush-hogging fields. He needed to get back to his roots. Maybe he would dry out and come back. Or, maybe he would dry out and discover that what he once left behind was truly where he needed to be.

I called Amtrak. The next train heading his sister's way would leave at 7:05 Sunday morning and arrive at her hometown a few hours later. The cost of the ticket was $49. The price sounded about right, but there was another problem: in order to purchase a ticket, you had to present an ID, and Nick no longer had one. It, along with his wallet, had been a casualty of his last four-day binge.

Option number two: Greyhound. It didn't stop in his sister's hometown, but it did stop thirty miles up the road. No ID was required to buy a ticket. It was cash-and-carry. If you want to travel under the radar and off the grid, my suggestion is to "Go Greyhound"—and that was exactly what Nick was about to do.

He gave me his sister's telephone number. Before I bought the ticket, I had to find out if she was willing to welcome him home. After all, they hadn't spoken in years. I called and explained the situation. Once I finished, Nick spoke with her. A few minutes later, we were on our way to the station.

For six days, I heard nothing. Then one afternoon, I got a call. Nick was relaxing on his sister's back porch watching squirrels play. During the past several days, he had been cutting fields, doing minor fence repairs, riding motorcycles, and had even renewed his driver's license. He sounded better. He ended with, "I'll keep in touch."

I figured in two or three weeks, he'd return with a renewed spirit and maybe even a better work ethic. The new Nick would last for three to four weeks, after which he would start running the streets at night again, and the downward spiral would start all over. My hope was that he would stay where he was.

In the meantime, I had other problems. While Nick was away at camp, a new vendor, Conrad Wyman, sprayed Hudson with mace. On Friday night, April 1, I got a call from a very upset Hudson. He kept repeating that his eyes were on fire and that his arms and hands were burning. He also kept exclaiming, "I didn't deserve this!"

I calmed him down and asked for details. He told me that earlier that evening, a fellow vendor had stopped on the corner of St. Peter and Bourbon and taken the stool that Hudson's helper was using, claiming that it was his.

When Hudson showed up and discovered his stool was gone, he took off down the street in search of it. As he approached the wagon on the corner of St. Louis and Bourbon he noticed that the vendor wasn't there. Instead, a twenty-something-year-old girl was watching the cart. Hudson politely asked if he could see her stool.

"Sure," she replied. As he picked it up, Wyman, who had been away on a break, suddenly appeared out of the crowd and began spraying Hudson in the face with mace.

The man working the cart on the opposite side of Bourbon Street ran over and began screaming at Wyman, "What in the hell are you doing?"

A few minutes later, Hudson called me. After gathering the facts, I told Tammy to have Wyman push back to the shop.

When I finally spoke with the mace-happy vendor, he claimed that Hudson had pulled the stool out from under him and threatened to hit him with it. According to him, he had used the mace solely as a defensive measure.

The following day, Jason discovered Hudson's stool on cart number fourteen. Fourteen had been used the previous night by the vendor working the corner of St. Ann and Bourbon. This was the guy who had actually taken Hudson's stool and set the whole chain of events in motion.

When that vendor showed up for work, George sent him to my office. The vendor unapologetically admitted to taking a stool that didn't belong to him. His excuse? Someone had used his stool when he was off and had broken it. So, he decided to take someone else's.

By the time our conversation ended, he understood that negative acts have repercussions. Because of his action, one vendor ended up getting maced and another lost his job—all because he knowingly took something that didn't belong to him. We came to a meeting of the minds. For the next several days, he would work what I considered to be an "off" corner. Sales there tended to be less than on more tourist-attractive locations. Additionally, we agreed that he would apologize to those affected.

Within minutes of the real perpetrator leaving my office, Wyman appeared pleading for his job back. He admitted that Hudson had asked his daughter if he could look at the stool, but he still insisted that Hudson had pulled it out from under him. The fact that Wyman was still refusing to tell the truth bothered Hudson more than being maced.

It took a while, but Wyman finally admitted lying. With the truth now out, he wanted to go to Hudson's cart and apologize. I nixed that idea. Thus far, Hudson had remained fairly calm; I didn't want the old Hudson resurfacing. If that happened, the doorman at the 544 Club behind Hudson's cart would be holding up Hudson's right arm and declaring him the winner by a knockout before Wyman even got the word "apologize" out of his mouth. I suggested to Wyman that he let me speak with Hudson first.

I called Hudson on his cell and related everything that I had discovered, including the fact that the vendor who worked the corner of St. Ann and Bourbon was the one who had actually taken his stool while it was still in the shop.

I asked Hudson what he wanted done with Wyman.

"I've done some stupid things in my life. I don't want the dude to get fired. All I ever wanted was for you to know that I was telling the truth. Let him work if you want."

"No, you make the call. You were the one maced."

"I'm not God."

"No, but I want the decision to be your decision."

"Let him work."

"No problems?"

"Not from me."

I mentioned that Wyman wanted to stop by his cart and apologize.

"He doesn't have the mace with him, does he?" He chuckled. At that point, I knew that everything would be fine.

I called Wyman back upstairs and informed him of Hudson's decision.

Then, as if on cue, Nick rode into the shop on his bike the next morning. After two weeks of R&R in Mississippi, he was back in New Orleans for several days. His sister didn't mind him visiting, but she wanted to make certain that it was not going to be a permanent arrangement. According to Nick, he could come to New Orleans, but it was like working on an oil rig: two weeks on, two weeks off. I had to admit that it was good to see him clean and rested. We sat in the office and talked. My hope was that he would stay straight, but I knew that was wishful thinking. He was coming back to the Quarter. If he went back to running with the same old crowd, he would soon be back to his same old habits.

Later that evening, as I was about to leave the shop, Susan called to tell me that she was being released from jail. She was going to be put back on probation. However, if she left the state of Mississippi without permission, her parole would be revoked.

The following morning, she called collect from the county jail. I accepted the charges.

"I thought you had been released."

"Officially, I have, but my probation officer still has to come and sign some papers. Then my mom can come pick me up. I don't think that's gonna happen until morning. Once the papers are signed, I can even come to New Orleans and work. It's only $12 by train."

She sounded good. Her system was clean and her mind was relaxed. She offered to come back and work anytime we needed her. Suddenly, Lucky Dogs was about to become a stimulus package for Amtrak. Nick wanted to commute from his sister's hometown; Susan wanted to board the train when it reached southern Mississippi. I wasn't certain that such a plan was good for either of them. Temptations in the Quarter are everywhere. If they wanted to stay straight, they needed to stay away from their old street friends.

Susan wanted to speak with Nick, so I called him upstairs. When he hung up, he said, "It's all Gucci."

"It's what?"

"It's Gucci. Everything's all right."

"Make sure it stays Gucci."

"I promise you this time I won't let you down. I got your back."

"What? I need to watch my back?"

"Come on, now, that's not right. You know what I said."

Nick was scheduled to work a party the following morning, and I had nothing but the word of a man who, in the past, had trouble keeping it. The Kid might get weak, put on his Gucci shoes, and sashay down the street for a couple of Ciscos. If that happened, he would be useless the next day.

The obvious question, then, was why assign him to the event? The answer was because if Nick worked the event, we didn't have to pull someone off the street or from our casino or airport crew to work it. If we had to do that, we were simply swapping regular sales for catering dollars. Besides, when Nick was right, there was no one better. He was personable; he smiled, he joked, and he kept the line at the hot dog cart moving at a brisk pace. Everyone loved him, but you always had to be prepared in case he wasn't right. On days we had catering events, I often carried a change of clothes in my truck in case *I* ended up having to be the server. However, true to his word, Nick showed up on time to work the event.

The following Saturday, he was scheduled to work another party. The same day word came that the charges against Susan might not be dropped. Nick responded by falling off the wagon. I ended up working the cart.

The event was a wedding reception held at the New Orleans Country Club. It was the end of the evening, and my line had dwindled when three couples walked up wanting dogs. After being served, they sat their drinks down on the cart and continued their conversation. The topic apparently was favorite places that they had visited. The first couple began talking about their trip to Nova Scotia and the gorgeous drive they had taken in the northern part of the country. Unfortunately, they could not remember the name of the road. After a few minutes of listening to them trying to figure it out, I spoke up.

"I don't mean to interrupt, but I believe you're referring to Cabot Trail."

"That's it!" the storyteller remarked.

The second couple spoke of driving north of Banff, Canada, visiting a glacier, and then continuing north to a small, quaint town. They, too, were suffering from alcohol-induced dementia.

"Jasper?" I offered.

"You're right!" the woman exclaimed.

Finally, the third couple began talking about their trip to China. The Great Wall came up, and they were raving about it and its majestic views. Like their friends, they, too, were having difficulty recalling the name of the specific site.

"Badaling?" I suggested.

"It *was* Badaling!"

By now, all three couples were damn curious as to how a hot dog vendor knew all of the answers to their exotic travel riddles. I explained that it was because I had been to all of the locations they were describing.

"But you're a hot dog vendor," one of the group replied, in a slightly derogatory manner.

I probably should have mentioned that Lucky Dogs had operated in Beijing. I also should have explained that my sons are commercial airline pilots, and because of that, Jane and I have incredible flight privileges. Instead, I leaned over the cart and whispered, "Most people don't know this, but Lucky Dog vendors make phenomenal tips."

They looked bewildered. Each couple had been to one of the locations, but their weenie man had been to all three. They didn't know what to say. As they walked away, one gentleman turned to take one last look over his shoulder. He still looked perplexed.

The following morning, I determined that Nick needed more time back on the farm. When he was in town, he would run the streets all night. He couldn't seem to let go of his old habits.

He agreed that going back to his sister's might be his best move. That's what he said, but I wasn't certain that he really believed it. So, I drove him to the train station and waited for him to buy a ticket— something he could now do because he had a driver's license. Departure time was 7:30 the next morning. Until then, I agreed that he could stay in the shop.

I set my alarm for 5 a.m., and when I woke, I called the warehouse to make certain that Snake woke him up. Nick had to be at the depot no later than 7.

It was a pleasant morning on April 23, 2011. Everything was going well; Nick was on board and homeward bound as planned. However, that pleasant morning came to an abrupt end about three hours later, when Nick called to inform me that an hour or so after they pulled out of the station, a tractor-trailer carrying military vehicles tried to hurry across the tracks ahead of the train. The truck lost the race, and five train cars derailed. There were no deaths, but several passengers, including him, had suffered minor injuries. Amtrak was busing everyone back to New Orleans to be checked out at a local medical facility.

I was depressed. I had made certain that he had a ticket; that he woke up on time, and that he made it to the station on time, only to have a tractor-trailer driver derail both my plan and the train. The only positive thing out of the whole disaster was that no one had been seriously injured.

Nick showed up at the shop with a one-night voucher for the Holiday Inn. The following morning, he was to undergo a medical evaluation. According to his account, he had been thrown from his seat and into the aisle, hurting his back and neck. The doctor representing Amtrak supposedly confirmed the injuries.

Once his examination was over, we rescheduled Nick's trip. He was to take the train out of town at 7:05 on Wednesday morning, April 26, but that didn't occur; Tuesday night, he went out drinking with his street buddies, and Wednesday morning, he was, to put it kindly, under the weather.

That afternoon, I rescheduled Nick's trip yet again. He was to now leave the following morning. I called Tammy at 10 on Wednesday night and explained that she had best make certain Nick was sober, awake, and at the station on time, or she and Thomas would have a new houseguest.

"Don't worry, his butt will be on that train," she responded.

I set my alarm for 5:30 a.m. so I could call and remind her. When I called, Nick was up, but he didn't want to leave until 6:30.

"Tammy, the train leaves at 7:05. If he waits until 6:30, he might not make it. If that's the case, then he's your problem."

"He'll be out the door in five minutes," she promised.

When I arrived at 7 a.m., the shop was quiet and peaceful. The day was gorgeous; the sky was clear, the temperature was in the mid-sixties, humidity was low, and a gentle breeze was blowing from the north. Life on Gravier Street was good. Then at 11 a.m., a taxi stopped in front of the shop, and out crawled Nick. This time, the train allegedly had "mechanical problems." He swore that he had boarded it and was asleep in his seat when a conductor woke him up and informed him that he had to exit the car. I had my doubts.

As we stood on the sidewalk, I had him empty his pockets and hand me all of his cash. I wanted to make certain that he and his Guccis would not be partaking in another all-night binge. Also, before I let him stay in the shop, I wanted verification that the train had not left without him. I called the 1-800 reservation number, and, to my astonishment, the agent confirmed that the Crescent City Limited indeed had not left the station. However, it was not because of mechanical failure; it was because a massive tornado had ripped through Alabama, devastating everything in its path, including the city of Tuscaloosa. The train couldn't roll because of debris on the tracks.

Nick slept in the shop one more night. Come morning, once again, Tammy put him in a cab, and once again, he headed back to the station. This time, the train did make it out of town, but two weeks later, Nick was back in the Quarter and back running with his street friends. By now, Home Girl had been released from jail and was living with her mom. If she couldn't leave the state to be with her man, she decided she would have him come to her.

After two or three failed attempts, she finally got Nick out of the Big Easy, away from the element that he had been hanging with, and to Mississippi where her folks lived. In late July, when he came to town to see the lawyer representing him in the accident, he stopped by the shop. He looked good; he was clean and neat, but most importantly, he was happy. He and Susan were living together and they were planning on getting married. Nick was also now the proud owner of a truck and a motorcycle. Maybe—just maybe—he was turning his life around. The only question I had was whether he had a real attorney handling his case with Amtrak or if Liz was once again representing him.

Outside, the summer temperatures were brutal, and sales on the street were slow. At least the shop was peaceful. Or so I thought.

In early September, Jane and I headed to North Carolina for a wedding. The Saturday morning of the nuptials, I got a call from George informing me that a note on the nightly recap sheet stated that Tammy had left for Tennessee and that Snake had headed to Yuma, Arizona.

The timing could not have been worse. I was out of town, and suddenly both the night manager and the relief night manager had quit and moved out of state. My first concern was making certain that all of the shifts were covered. George took over the nighttime slot while Jason and Vincent filled the daytime positions. Carts would roll as normal. Tim Danner had been sober for several weeks, and since the pit bull was no longer around, I hired him as the fill-in day manager and part-time cart washer. Our backup cart washer would be Rick Puggini, as long as he could refrain from throwing dollar bills on the ground and spitting on them. Our backup night manager would be Hudson.

I had been through this situation more times than I cared to remember. Occasions like this were exactly why we recycled guys like Danner and Puggini, and cross-trained employees.

Surprisingly, that afternoon, I received a call from Tammy. She wanted to apologize for leaving as she had. Her daughter-in-law was having a difficult pregnancy and the doctors wanted her immediately bedridden. Tammy's son had to work, so they were in desperate need of someone to care for their children. Grandma was their first choice.

Snake's reason for his sudden departure was that he lived with Tammy. When Tammy and her longtime companion, Thomas Porter, took off, he no longer had a place to stay. He, too, later called and apologized.

"Why didn't you at least wait until I got back into town?" I asked.

"I don't know," he said. "I had to pack everything, so once I got into the cab, I just headed to the bus station."

Most of the people who work for Lucky Dogs are impulsive and not materialistic. Snake was included in that group. He, like the rest of them, could pack a bag and be on the road in a matter of minutes. As a company, it is something that we have learned to live with.

In Snake's case, it was time to retire. He was mentally worn down and physically worn out—working long hours and running the streets had taken its toll. Now, all he was interested in was peace and quiet.

In all his years of working for Lucky Dogs, Snake had been there when we needed him. I wasn't going to hold this last act against him. His time had come; age had caught up with him, and he finally burned out. I understood, and I wished him well. No longer would he be a part of the Great Vendor Migration.

Tammy and Thomas Porter, however, were still in the loop. They returned to the Quarter to work a cart in time for Halloween. After only two months in Tennessee, they missed the excitement of the street. They missed their friends, and they missed the money.

Still, Tammy was torn between staying with family and returning to the Big Easy. Life in the Quarter was far more exhilarating, but the strong maternal bonds of a grandmother remained. Once Halloween was over, she and Porter headed back to the hills. Truthfully, like Snake they were mentally and physically drained, and though they loved it, their Quarter days were over.

Now that I knew Tammy would never be returning on a full-time basis, we needed to find a replacement. I moved George to nights permanently. Danner was sober and willing, so I promoted him to full-time day manager. The odds of his succeeding were slim, but in my favor was the fact that he would be working days, not nights. He could party within reason after the sun went down, and I would be there during the day to monitor his every move.

With Danner in the shop and Nick back in Mississippi, Harold Vincent became our special event guy. One such occasion that required his services occurred in early December 2012.

I was on my cell speaking with one of my sons when a call came in on the office phone. Mark answered. On the other line was none other than Sean Payton, head coach of the New Orleans Saints, and he wanted to speak with me. Mark informed him that I was currently in the middle of another call and would have to call him back. Now how often do you think a Super Bowl–winning coach hears that?

When I called, Payton was in the training room icing down his leg, which had been injured during a recent game's sideline accident. I spoke with Greg Bensel, Saints vice president of communications. Bensel explained that Payton would like us to meet Fred Gaudelli, producer of NBC Sports' *Sunday Night Football*, as he stepped off his flight at the New Orleans International Airport and present him with a box of steaming hot Lucky Dogs.

Apparently, during the broadcast of an earlier Sunday night Saints game, NBC's cameras had caught the injured coach in the team's upper-level coaching box eating a hot dog. On-air comments were made that Payton considered offensive. I was told that for a short period, NBC personnel had been banned from the Saints' training facilities. Now, all differences had been reconciled, and our delivering of the dogs was

FRED GAUDELLI
NBC SPORTS

Harold Vincent holding a box of Lucky Dogs while
he waits for Fred Gaudelli to deplane.

meant as a humorous gesture to welcome Gaudelli back to town for
the Saints vs. Lions Sunday night game.

Jane wrapped a box with black and gold Saints wrapping paper and
placed a fancy gold bow on top. The next morning, Vincent, Kirk, and
I headed to the airport. Using our kiosk on Concourse C, we steamed
fifty dogs and buns and packed them into the box. Vincent, dressed
in black slacks and a new red-and-white-striped vendor jacket, stood
just beyond where the passengers exit the jetway. In one hand was the
decorated box, and in the other was a two-foot-long sign that read,
"Fred Gaudelli—NBC Sports."

Fred Gaudelli, Dick Ebersol, and Drew Esocoff, all of NBC, were
traveling together. As they deplaned, they walked toward Vincent,

with Gaudelli bringing up the rear. As Gaudelli approached, Vincent welcomed him to the city of New Orleans on behalf of Coach Payton and handed him the box.

Gaudelli graciously accepted the gift and wondered aloud what was inside. As I lifted the lid, he asked, "What is it?"

Ebersol smiled and responded, "It's hot dogs." He immediately followed with, "Are they hot?"

At that point, Gaudelli made the connection between the box and the on-air remarks. In a low monotone voice, he said, "Tell Coach Payton thank you." Then he placed the box on his luggage and rolled down the concourse toward the exit.

However, that was not the end of it. The following day, we pushed a Lucky Dog cart to the Superdome and placed it inside the stadium next to NBC's broadcast truck. On the wall behind Vincent, we hung a five-foot-long sign that read, "Hot Dogs Compliments of Head Coach Sean Payton." Ebersol, Gaudelli, and Esocoff all stopped by the cart for a dog. A smiling Gaudelli even had his picture taken next to the cart with Vincent.

A few weeks later, Christmas had passed, and Tammy was back in town working a cart during the New Year's holiday season and the 2012 BCS National Championship game. After pushing her cart in, she helped George check in the other vendors. She returned home to Tennessee after the holidays, but was back a month later to help with Mardi Gras.

We certainly needed her help. With the city hosting Super Bowl XLVII right in the middle of Carnival, there would be three weeks of festivities instead of two.

The only memorable incident during Carnival 2013 was a problem over which we had no control. A Jefferson Parish detective called to inform me that a caller to the CrimeStoppers hotline was claiming that a former Lucky Dog salesman and an accomplice were planning to rob and murder a Canal Street businessman. I sent the detective all of our information relating to their primary suspect.

Because of this particular ex-vendor's military training, they contended that he was capable of planning and executing such an operation. Later, more facts were requested on a second suspect. Because it was an active investigation, I was instructed to not mention it to anyone.

That was our major problem. A minor problem that also occurred during the middle of Mardi Gras was Choya declaring an end to his vending career. No longer could he take the constant in-your-face drunken revelers, or the people butting in to ask for the location of a certain bar or club while he was trying to take an order, or the drunken tourists on balconies trying to pour beer on his head.

There was also the added frustration of people complaining about the posted price and wanting to haggle for something lower. Then there were always those who bitched because we don't carry forty-five different kinds of condiments. I once told a New Yorker who was berating me at a catering event because we didn't have sauerkraut that, "Just because we lost the war doesn't mean we have to eat your food."

Choya had reached his limit. He could no longer mentally deal with the chaos on the street. He had thought he could, but right in the middle of Mardi Gras, he discovered that he couldn't. He pushed his cart in one last time.

On Thursday, February 23, two days after Fat Tuesday, the Jefferson Parish detective called with an update. Our ex-vendor had been arrested on Lundi Gras, the night before Fat Tuesday. He was booked with planning the robbery and murder of a New Orleans businessman.

The detective also informed me that after our ex-vendor's accomplice had deserted him, the ex-vendor started shifting his focus away from the Canal Street merchant and more toward Lucky Dogs, which he considered to be less profitable but an easier mark.

Strangely enough, forty-three years ago my predecessor Bob Alexander, a man whom I had met on several occasions, was shot and killed in our warehouse after being forced to open the safe. Bob was murdered by an ex-vendor. I have never forgotten Bob or the circumstances surrounding his death. History could very well have repeated itself that year. However, thanks to great police work by the NOPD and the Jefferson Parish Sheriff's office, the culprit was apprehended before he could put his plan in motion.

As for the ex-vendor and potential murderer, he wasn't just an ex–Lucky Dog employee as the press reported; he was also an ex-employee of numerous companies as well as a former member of the US military. Our company's name was probably used because it would attract the most attention.

It's important to note that the vast majority of Lucky Dog vendors are trustworthy, slightly eccentric, not motivated by materialistic possessions, hard-working, free-spirited, self-supportive, and just want to be left alone. Sometimes they might party too much, and sometimes they might work too little, but all in all they're good people. I have to admit that in the pages of this book, I have focused on the more colorful characters because those are the ones with the most interesting stories, but our workforce is not limited to those mentioned.

As for longevity, James Hudson, Bruce Briant, Smitty, and Snake have all worked for Lucky Dogs off and on for more than thirty years. Choya, John Burris, DeeDee, and Raymond have all been drifting in and out for more than fifteen years. Tammy, Thomas Porter, Lance, and Jason have been here for more than ten years. George, Vincent, Roy Gant, Tim Danner, and Rick Puggini have worked for us for more than eight years. Though parts of our crew come and go, we're lucky to have a solid base of year-round workers. They're all long-term friends and part of the shop's dysfunctional family. Do we always get along? Absolutely not. But like family, wrongs are forgiven, and hurt feelings heal.

In some cases, we've grown old together. When I started managing the company forty years ago, one of the vendors looking for me asked another, "Where the hell did the young pissant go?" The other day I heard one vendor ask another, "Where the hell did the old man go?" By the time I retire, it'll probably be, "Anybody seen Pops?" But that's a ways off. I still have a few more Carnivals to weather.

Thank God the last one is over and we all survived. Another reason for us to be thankful was that by late summer of 2013, the construction at the shop was finally finished. The building once again was structurally sound and the facade had been restored to its original 1840s appearance. Along with the exterior, the interior had been renovated to its pre–Civil War appearance. The results were impressive.

Vendors were ecstatic. No longer did they have to contend with sawdust or construction workers. One of them went so far as to suggest that we celebrate the occasion. And to our guys, nothing screams "corporate pride" louder than ice-cold pitchers of free draft beer—free, because they expected the company to pick up the tab. I squashed the idea. Vendors sighed, and morale tanked.

It was obvious; I would not be hailed as the greatest boss who ever lived. There would be no "hip-hip-hoorays," nor would I be hoisted on the shoulders of a grateful crew. I had been at this job long enough to know that the euphoria, had it come, would have ended within minutes after I paid the bar tab. Someone would have suddenly become upset because they hadn't gotten the corner that they wanted, and once again I would be a "no-good bastard" and "a rotten mother f—r." Come to think of it, life at Lucky Dogs was moving closer and closer to pre-storm normal.

As for New Orleans, flood protection has gotten better, convention bookings are up, and tourists are returning in ever-increasing numbers. Life between the levees for the majority of us now seems pretty normal.

As the Cajuns down the bayou say, "Laissez les bon temps rouler," which means "let the good times roll." For those of us who returned to a devastated city and struggled through its rebirth, I say, "It's about damn time."

12

THE SANDS OF TIME

M uch has changed at Lucky Dogs since I started managing the company. Then again, much has remained the same. In the 1970s, after a vendor rolled his wagon out of the shop, we had only two ways to communicate with him: we could walk out to his corner and speak with him face-to-face, or we could call the business behind where he was operating and hope they'd allow him to use their phone. Today, we simply contact him on his cell.

As for the carts, they've pretty much remained unchanged. They still look like a hot dog, they still have to be physically pushed to the corner, and they still use steam to heat the franks, just as they did in the 1940s. However, today's steamers are heated by propane burners instead of the old hand-pumped kerosene stoves used from the 1940s though the mid-1970s. In addition, each cart now has a pressurized hand wash system and a three-compartment sink. As a result, a cart's length has increased from 7 feet to 10 feet, and its weight has escalated from 150 pounds to more than 600 pounds.

As for the vendors, they have, like their predecessors, chosen to live an alternative lifestyle—to not work in a walled-in office or adhere to a nine-to-five routine. Many are well-educated and could easily fit into mainstream America but simply choose not to. They're content with their less structured, less materialistic, and sometimes nomadic existence.

Recently, two members of our crew, "Big Tiny" and Steve Capps, came close to abandoning the less-beaten path for the more traditional route. They had been hawking dogs for several months when

"Big Tiny" sharing a laugh in the office.

they walked into my office and announced that they were heading to North Dakota. Their goal? To land a job in the northern oil fields.

Both have experience as heavy equipment operators, and both have the physical stamina to survive the rugged life. Tiny is 6 feet, 8 inches tall and weighs almost 400 pounds, and Capps is a solidly built 6 foot 10 and as strong as an ox. I wished them success and reminded them that our door would always be open.

Less than a month later, they called, broke and desperate. The only available jobs had been menial low-paying ones, and they wanted to return to New Orleans. They were praying that I would bankroll their trip. Of course, there was the obligatory promise to repay me as quickly as possible.

That was followed by a refreshing bit of honesty: they wanted me to know that they were hoping to find full-time employment as heavy machinery operators in the New Orleans area, but on their days off, they would work a cart. I didn't hesitate; I put their fares on my credit card, and by the weekend, they were back at the shop.

Tiny strolled into my office. After standing there for a second, he said, "I liked you before, but I really like you now. You didn't have to

Joe Bellomy in the shop.

do what you did. Is there anything that I can do for you? Anything? Do you need me to beat up anyone? Not a lot of people know this, but I was once an enforcer for a motorcycle gang."

"Tiny, I appreciate the offer, but at the moment, life's good. If anyone ever causes that to change, you'll be the first to know."

I wouldn't ever require his service, but I sure as hell didn't want the big guy to think I was ungrateful.

Joe Bellomy was another vendor who could make the move to corporate America if he put his mind to it. He is slightly over 6 feet tall with a medium build and is well-spoken, clean-cut, and very personable. His downfall, like the vendors of old, is that he enjoys partying to the point of excess.

Recently, Hudson called and was highly upset.

"We have to talk," he told me. "What Joe did last night wasn't right! I've never done anything to him!"

"What did he do?"

"No one's told you? I can't believe it! I can't believe that no one's told you!"

"Believe it."

"He came to my cart last night wearing nothing but a 60-gallon black trash bag."

"What did he have on under it?"

"Nothing!"

"Nothing?"

"He was wearing it like a big diaper, but it didn't always stay up. He was drunk and belligerent, and he kept hanging around annoying me and screaming at my customers. It was embarrassing! It cost me a lot of sales! What do you have to say about that?"

"At least he wasn't wearing a transparent one. I promise you I will look into it."

The following afternoon, Joe walked into the shop still hung over. All he could remember about the previous evening was that he had started off celebrating his birthday in one of the Quarter's bars. Another patron, a young woman, was also celebrating her birthday. Beyond that, everything was hazy.

The party's theme was come dressed in anything as long as it wasn't clothing. Joe chose to wear the trash bag diaper. The birthday girl, he recalled, made quite a fashion statement of her own, wearing a full-length dress of tied-together trash bags. One guest appeared wearing nothing but cereal boxes, while another was wearing only an outfit made of tied-together paper plates. There were other costumes that were even more creative. My only comment to him was, "It must have been one hell of a party."

Several weeks later, on Saturday, December 21, Tiny stopped by to give me a Christmas card. As he was leaving, he paused and said, "Remember, if you need me to do anything to anybody, all you have to do is ask. Merry Christmas."

"Merry Christmas, Tiny."

In a way, it reminded me of a warped version of the classic movie *A Christmas Carol*.

Later, on New Year's Eve, a Louisiana State Trooper stationed on the corner of Conti and Bourbon befriended Tiny. During the course of the evening, the two got to know one another. As the officer's shift was about to end, he turned to his new vendor friend and asked, "Have you ever considered becoming a policeman?"

"I thought about it once," Tiny responded, "but then I got arrested and did some time. That kinda killed that idea."

New Year's hadn't been over a week when Hudson informed me that he had already lined up his Mardi Gras help. He was ahead of the game.

"Who's going to work with you?" I asked.

"Conrad."

"Conrad?"

"I can trust him."

"He maced you."

"I know, but that's in the past. Besides, we work well together."

"As long as you two are happy, I'm thrilled."

As Conrad was returning to Lucky Dogs, so was Donald Plunkett. Earlier in the year, Plunkett had headed north to help his brother grow a crop of medical marijuana. Now, with Mardi Gras only weeks away, he was on his way back—hopefully minus the harvest.

A few other old-time vendors were also returning, but I was not see-ing any new recruits. Nationally, unemployment was high. We should have been turning people away, but seldom did anyone new come through our doors.

There were people standing on street corners with signs that read, "Will work for food," but they didn't really want to work. I know, because on several occasions, I stopped and offered them jobs. I admit that I was selective with whom I spoke, but I had to be; our vendors deal with the public, money, and food, and it's all done out in the open. Because of that, we have to be conscious of everything. What once might have been viewed as a humorous isolated street incident now has to be seen in a totally different light. Modern technology and the fact that things can go viral in a matter of minutes demand it. Thus, as management, we can no longer be quite as tolerant as in the past. We might be a low-tech company, but we're operating in a high-tech world.

On a more serious note, long-term vendor James Hudson was sud-denly fighting for his life. On March 21, 2014, he reported for work, but instead of coming into the shop, he stood across the street leaning against a freight zone pole. He appeared tired and beat. I walked over.

As I approached, he muttered, "My Lucky Dog days are over. My neck hurts, my back hurts, and the doctors want to operate again. It's time for me to give it up."

I understood and suggested that he go home and rest. Right after my suggestion, he did a complete 180 and insisted on working. I recommended that he at least have someone assist him. That way, he could work if he felt up to it, or he could just sit on his stool and supervise if he didn't.

Conrad had been working Hudson's cart during the day. If Hudson offered him additional compensation, I was confident he would stay with him for the remainder of the night. Hudson pondered the idea for a moment, then decided that it might not be a bad plan.

Two or three times during our conversation, he stressed that he had not been drinking and that he was simply tired and hurting. I gave him the benefit of the doubt.

At the end of the day when I left the shop, I walked over to Chuck's Sports Bar in search of George. I needed clarification on the number of hot dogs that had been issued to Conrad.

George wasn't there, but Hudson was sitting alone at a table with a glass in front of him. Again, he assured me that he wasn't drinking. He even requested that I smell his drink. I passed, but once again, I recommended that he take the night off.

At 9:30 p.m., Vincent, now the company's night manager, contacted me at home. Hudson was sitting on the sidewalk in front of the shop and appeared to be drunk. He wanted to know how to handle the situation.

I suggested that he try and convince James to take a cab home. Vincent tried, but Hudson refused. Instead, he wanted to sleep in the shop. Vincent was opposed to the idea; Hudson smoked, and if he lit up in the building and fell asleep while Vincent was out checking on the vendors, the shop could go up in flames. Vincent never called back, so I assumed that James finally agreed to go home.

The following morning, I discovered that was not the case. Hudson never left; he had stayed outside on Gravier Street all night. Vendors recalled seeing him sitting on the sidewalk in front of the shop and leaning against the building across the street. Initially, no one thought anything about it, because a few days earlier, Hudson had shown up at his cart to relieve Conrad but smelled of alcohol. On that occasion, Conrad had sent him home and worked the cart the rest of the night.

But, on this occasion, Hudson was not drunk. He was suffering the effects of a heart attack and stroke. Usually, when he drinks, he's antagonistic. This evening, he was mellow.

Earlier in the day, he had exhibited no signs of facial drooping. There were no slurred words and no confusion, and he even smiled and laughed as he, Jason, and I spoke. He was able to move both his arms. In fact, he had raised them slightly above shoulder level and then leaned on the back of a cart with both forearms.

His explanation of being tired and his back and neck hurting all seemed plausible. Years earlier, he had undergone spinal surgery, but the resulting relief had started to fade, and his doctor was recommending another operation.

In the meantime, there were days when Hudson would drink to mask the pain. Because of that, everyone misinterpreted his condition, but by early Saturday morning, the signs of a stroke had grown more pronounced. Doug Neve, a fellow vendor, recognized the severity of Hudson's condition and called 911. James was transported via ambulance to Tulane University Hospital, where he remained in intensive care for more than a week. That was followed by several more weeks in the hospital, then six weeks in a rehabilitation center. Hudson eventually recovered enough to be able to drive, but his dog days had finally come to an end.

William Palmer's days at Lucky Dogs were also coming to an end. Palmer had taken over the evening shift from George, who had assumed the position when Tammy headed for Tennessee. George had never wanted it on a permanent basis, so when Palmer agreed to replace him, George was thrilled.

Palmer had worked for more than a year as a vendor and had never come up short, had never been caught drinking, and had never been seen playing video poker or gambling at the casino. Tammy recommended him as her long-term replacement. Hudson, Bruce, Choya, George, Jason, and Burris all considered him to be the perfect candidate. I agreed.

For three weeks, I stayed at the shop each night, training him in all aspects of his new position. Additionally, I brought Tammy back to town to work with him during Halloween 2011, since it would be his first major holiday after taking over. She made the money runs with him, helped him check in vendors, and assisted him with the closing inventory.

The training was going well. Palmer was enthusiastic and seemed to have a good relationship with the vendors. Then the unexpected occurred. When I arrived at the shop the morning after Halloween, the previous night's 2 a.m. run money was not in the safe. The run total had been logged in on the night sheet, but the cash was not there. It turned out that Palmer, like Hager, had a gambling problem.

As I did with Hager, I deducted Palmer's payroll check from the amount stolen. That left him still owing $935. The loss of the money was disturbing, but just as frustrating was the amount of time that had been wasted training him, followed by the hours lost because of the lies that he told trying to cover up. If he had just manned up and confessed to what had truly taken place, we could have begun the process of correcting the wrong.

It was a given that he would never again hold a management position at Lucky Dogs, but as with Gene and Nick, we might have allowed him to work a cart and pay off his debt. However, unlike Gene and Nick, he simply could not admit to having, as they would say, "f—ked up."

Later, Palmer's wife confided that he was ashamed of what he had done and was too embarrassed to face his fellow vendors. Pride would not allow him to admit that he was no different and no better than the rest of the crew.

On paper, his record was clean, and that was one of the major reasons that charges were not filed. Unfortunately, Palmer proved to have inner demons. The freedom offered by the night shift and a pocket full of cash allowed those demons to resurface. No one had been physically harmed, but the company had sustained a financial loss—a loss he swore that he would make whole.

My gut feeling was that he was telling the truth, and at Lucky Dogs, gut feelings are important. Often, judgments have to be made as to what we believe is in a person's heart as compared to what is in their past. We're not always right, but we have one hell of a good batting average.

Because I believed him and because he had no previous history of coming up short in addition to no past criminal record, I typed out a promissory note and had him sign it. Instead of putting him behind bars, he was allowed to pursue employment elsewhere. Two years and four months later, on February 21, 2014, Palmer called. He wanted to come and pay off his debt. He owed $935; he insisted on giving the company $1,000.

As we spoke, I told him that we all make mistakes, but it's what we do after we make them that truly defines who we are. Before he left, I handed him the promissory note. From that moment on, the incident would be behind us. At some future time, he would probably return to hawking dogs on Bourbon Street. As far as rejoining the management team, the odds were overwhelmingly against that happening; if it did, it would be as the cart washer or day manager—positions not requiring the handling of cash.

Besides Palmer, another ex-management team member, Jim Campbell, was trying to overcome a personal tragedy. The last time I saw him was when he drifted through town after Katrina. Later, he returned to Alaska, where he and his wife, Carrita, had settled.

On March 19 at 3:22 a.m., he emailed, "Just wanted to let you know that Carrita passed away this evening about 9 p.m. I just wanted you to know. I don't know why, but just felt I should tell you. Hope I can keep it together, lots of people to help, will really need the help, I think. Hope things are well with you and you had a good Mardi Gras. We order a King Cake every year. I guess not next year."

Jim was hurting from a devastating loss, a loss that only time might possibly heal.

Meanwhile, Doug Talbot, the company's owner, was trying to overcome a loss of his own. Seven days a week for almost four decades, he had called me at 7:30 *every* morning to find out the previous night's gross sales. That no longer occurred. At seventy-seven years of age, his memory had started to fade.

He had beaten cancer five times during the past twenty-nine years, but multiple chemo treatments, several TIAs, and the natural aging process all had taken their toll. The sales figures, once so important to him, no longer had meaning.

Doug, unfortunately, was not the only person at Lucky Dogs suffering from memory loss. George called my office one morning requesting that I immediately come downstairs and handle a situation involving Smitty.

Smitty was now seventy years old and no longer worked his own cart. Instead, he worked with vendor Bruce Briant. Every morning, he would set up Briant's cart and have someone push it out to their corner. Several hours later, Briant would arrive and take over.

On this particular morning, Smitty reported as usual. He turned on the propane gas and was about to light the cart's burner when George called from the kitchen requesting that he come get his supplies. Smitty promptly complied.

However, in doing so, he failed to light his cart. Later, George in the kitchen and Puggini on the cart washing side of the building both smelled gas. The source was discovered and Smitty's propane tank was promptly shut off, but the shop reeked of gas. When I questioned Smitty about what happened, his response was, "George called me to come get my supplies."

"I know, but why didn't you first light the cart, or turn off the gas?"

"Because George wanted me to come get my supplies."

At that point, I realized that Smitty could not comprehend the seriousness of his mistake. Static electricity or someone entering the building smoking could have ignited the gas and turned the shop into a fireball.

Had he replied, "Oh, my God! I can't believe that I forgot to light the cart," or had he been the least bit remorseful, the situation could have been handled differently. Unfortunately, he was oblivious to the fact that there had even been a problem, and that he was the cause. His ability to reason had vanished.

I called Bruce and informed him of the situation. We agreed that Smitty would no longer be allowed to work alone. He could assist Briant, but that would be it.

Smitty would still have a reason to get up every morning—a purpose—but limited responsibility. Working the street was his life; I didn't want to take that away, but I could not allow him to endanger himself or others.

Besides Smitty, there was another vendor confronting a medical issue. On three recent occasions, Big Tiny had passed out and had to be taken via ambulance to the hospital. Twice it happened while he was in the shop, and the last time it occurred, he was working his corner. After spending several days undergoing tests at Tulane University Hospital, the doctors adjusted his medications and cleared him to work.

Not long after being released, he strolled into my office insisting that he needed to tell me something. Out of the blue, he blurted out, "If it wasn't for Lucky Dogs, I'd have probably died an ignorant racist."

"Would you mind clarifying that?" I asked.

He explained that while working a cart, he had gotten to know Gant, Raymond, Lindsey, and several other black vendors and discovered that he actually had a lot in common with them. Plus, while working outside of the Famous Door, he had become friends with one of the club's black bouncers.

This was all coming from a white man who, during his time in prison, had symbols representing the Aryan Nation tattooed on his arms—tattoos that he was now planning on having removed.

While Tiny was returning to work, Roy Gant was leaving. Unlike most vendors, Gant gave me notice. The street was starting to get to him, so he accepted a job offer from one of the clubs on Bourbon. Eventually, I knew, the club will would get to him and he would return to working a cart.

Going in the opposite direction, George decided to give up his position in the shop and go back to working the street. Dealing with the vendors was driving him crazy. Richard Anderson, another vendor, gave up working Jackson Square two days a week so that he could take over George's shifts. In the midst of all of this, Nick called to wish me a Happy Father's Day.

Through the decades, the vendors' names and faces have changed, but their stories, and in many cases, their offenses, have pretty much remained the same. A priest once told me that the most frustrating aspect of hearing confession was that it was always the same old sins over and over. Lucky Dogs has presented me with a similar set of repetitive problems.

However, in the not-too-distant future, those problems will no longer be my responsibility. After more than four decades as general manager, I, too, will finally join the Great Vendor Migration.

With my new freedom, I look forward to visiting the Scottish Highlands and the green rolling hills of Ireland. I want to drive from the eastern shores of Nova Scotia, across Canada's vast plains and northern Rockies, to the westernmost edge of Vancouver Island. I want to visit Denali National Park in Alaska, view the Northern Lights, visit Stonehenge, travel to Machu Picchu, and continue on to the Galapagos Islands. I want to make a beach landing in Normandy in Hughes Eliard's restored World War II Higgins-built LCVP landing craft, and then take a train east to Austria. I want to explore New Zealand and visit Israel. But most of all, I look forward to Jane and me spending time with our grandsons, Matthew and Jack. There are trails to hike and fish to catch; there are lightning bugs to chase and stars to gaze up at in the night sky.

Inevitably, I'll be drawn back to the shop, probably during a New Year's or Carnival season. I'll help out for a few days and then, like those I managed for so many years, I'll drift off again in search of some new adventure. Hopefully, down a road less traveled.

EPILOGUE

Suddenly, in late August 2013, after nineteen years, we were no longer operating in Harrah's New Orleans Casino. The gaming giant planned on expanding the bar bordering their poker room. To do so, they needed our floor space.

Eighteen months later we were back in; back in the same location. Their expansion project had been put on hold.

During this same period we added an additional kiosk at the Louis Armstrong New Orleans International Airport. We now had a presence on all three of the airport's concourses.

While the above was taking place Kirk, Mark, and I were also pursuing the possibility of retailing packs of Lucky Dogs. The result was Lucky Dogs were soon on the refrigerated shelves of Rouses' Supermarkets' forty-two locations across the Gulf Coast. In the future, we hope to have the packs available in additional local supermarket chains and national retail markets across the South and Southwest. Oscar Mayer, Hebrew National, and Nathan's have nothing to fear, but maybe, just maybe, we can capture a fraction of their market share.

As we worked on building a retail business, the New Orleans Saints called. The NFL team wanted to bring more of a local flavor to the Dome, thus, we were invited to sell Lucky Dogs inside the stadium. The decision was a no-brainer.

More good news followed. Home Girl and Nick tied the knot in a civil ceremony. The joyful nuptials were followed by an all-you-could-eat crawfish boil reception. They were a happy couple, at least for a while.

Also, word on the street has it that Becky found permanent work in a fast-food restaurant in the suburbs. I wish her luck.

Impressively, Matt left Beijing, returned to the States, entered a prestigious university, and earned an M.B.A. degree. He now works

Farewell, Doug.

for a highly respected investment company in New York. Daniel, his close friend, has also done well. He is now employed by a major international corporation and his territory includes India and the Far East.

On a more local note, Tim Danner spiraled downward. For weeks, he failed to show for work. We had no choice but to replace him. Thankfully, he now seems to be overcoming his inner demons. Before long I hope to have the old Tim back in the fold.

Rick Puggini has been working in the shop the past several years and for the most part has done an admirable job. During this the same period, Harold Vincent has been the night manager. He has run a tight, no-nonsense nightshift. However, after four years in the position, he's requesting to go back to working a cart in Jackson Square. It is the norm. Steve will move into Vincent's management position. The bus ticket from North Dakota is starting to paying dividends.

As for Joe Bellomy, it's been over a year since he introduced his fashionable trash-bag attire to the French Quarter. In his words, "With Hudson now gone, there's really no one that I want to harass." True to his word, garbage-bag diapers are no longer a part of his wardrobe.

Tiny still reminds me that he is ready and willing to kick anybody's ass that I want him to. The offer is really more a gesture of friendship than a statement of fact. I think.

Speaking of friendship, on August 29, 2013, Johnny Majoria, my longtime friend and the owner of Commerce Restaurant, died from cancer. His son, Brett, continues to open the restaurant daily as he helped his dad do for over twenty years. The coffee is still fresh, the atmosphere is still old-time New Orleans, and the tables remain full. Johnny would be proud.

Later, on December 7, 2014, Doug Talbot, my longtime boss, partner, and friend, lost his battle with cancer. We had been a team for forty-six years. That kind of longevity is less and less common in today's world of free-agency employment. Like with Brett, Mark and Kirk have taken their dad's place. It is the cycle of life.

As for me, I am still managing Lucky Dogs. Doug had been persistent and after several years, at his request, we finally signed a contract. Outside of work, I am continuing to help restore PT-305 at the National World War II Museum.

Speaking of the museum, I recently discovered that my name is on its original dedication plaque. It has been there for over sixteen years and until someone brought it to my attention recently, I never knew it. On the marker, under "Historical Advisors" only two names appeared: Stephen E. Ambrose and Jerry S. Strahan. Okay, they got my middle initial wrong, but that didn't matter. Seeing my name there under Steve's brought a feeling of satisfaction, even though my contribution had been incredibly miniscule.

As for the future, perhaps someday we'll meet out on the road. Until then, on behalf of all of the Lucky Dog vendors on Bourbon Street and everyone working in the hospitality industry in the French Quarter, I would like to leave you with a bit of wisdom that I recently read on a refrigerator magnet: "God knows if you don't tip."